The Great Acceleration ⁓

The Great Acceleration

An Environmental History of the Anthropocene since 1945

J. R. McNeill and Peter Engelke

The Belknap Press of Harvard University Press
CAMBRIDGE, MASSACHUSETTS
LONDON, ENGLAND

Originally published as Chapter 3 of *Global Interdependence: The World after 1945*, ed.
Akira Iriye (Cambridge, MA: Belknap Press of Harvard University Press, 2014), a
joint publication of Harvard University Press and C. H. Beck Verlag.
German language edition © 2013 by C. H. Beck Verlag.

Maps by Isabelle Lewis
Book design by Dean Bornstein

Library of Congress Cataloging-in-Publication Data

Names: McNeill, John Robert, author. | Engelke, Peter, author.
Title: The great acceleration : an environmental history of the anthropocene
    since 1945 / J. R. McNeill and Peter Engelke.
Description: Cambridge, Massachusetts : The Belknap Press of Harvard
    University Press, [2014] | Originally published as Chapter 3 of Global
    Interdependence : the world after 1945 / edited by Akira Iriye. Cambridge,
    MA : Belknap Press of Harvard University Press, 2014. | Includes
    bibliographical references and index.
Identifiers: LCCN 2015039497 | ISBN 9780674545038 (pbk. : alk. paper)
Subjects: LCSH: Nature—Effect of human beings on—History—20th century. |
    Nature—Effect of human beings on—History—21st century. | Human
    ecology—History—20th century. | Human ecology—History—21st century. |
    Global environmental change—History—20th century. | Global environmental
    change—History—21st century.
Classification: LCC GF75 .M39 2014 | DDC 304.2—dc23
LC record available at http://lccn.loc.gov/2015039497

Contents

The Great Acceleration ⌁

Introduction

> Whosoever is writing a modern History, shall follow truth
> too neare the heeles, it may haply strike out his teeth.
> —Sir Walter Ralegh, 1614

Since the nineteenth century, geologists, earth scientists, evolutionary biologists, and their colleagues have divided the history of the Earth into a series of eras, periods, and epochs. These are based, in a loose sense, on the environmental history of our planet, especially on the twists and turns in the evolution of life on Earth as revealed in the fossil record. We are (and have been for a long time) in the Cenozoic era and, within that, the Quaternary period. And within the Quaternary period, we are in the Holocene epoch, meaning the last 11,700 years or so. The Holocene is defined above all by its climate, an interglacial moment that has been agreeably stable so far compared to what came before. All of what is conventionally understood as human history, the entire history of agriculture and of civilization, has taken place in the Holocene. Or perhaps one should say it all *took* place in the Holocene.

This book takes the view that a new moment in the history of the Earth has begun, that the Holocene is over and something new has begun: the Anthropocene. Beginning in 2000, the idea of the Anthropocene was popularized by the Dutch atmospheric chemist Paul Crutzen, who won a Nobel Prize in 1995 for his work on depletion of the ozone layer in the stratosphere. The changing composition of the atmosphere, especially the well-documented increase in carbon dioxide, seemed to Crutzen so dramatic and so potentially consequential for life on Earth that he concluded that a new stage had begun in Earth's history, one in which humankind had emerged as the most powerful influence on global ecology. The crux of the Anthropocene concept is just that: a new period (whether epoch, period, or era in geologists' parlance) in which human actions overshadow the quiet persistence of microbes and the endless wobbles and eccentricities in the Earth's orbit, affecting the governing systems of the Earth, and therefore define the age.[1]

Crutzen argued that the Anthropocene began in the late eighteenth century, with the onset of the fossil fuel energy regime. By the 1780s, the use of coal was becoming integral to economic life in Britain and would thereafter play an ever-larger role in the world economy. New technologies and new energy demand led to the exploitation of other fossil fuels, oil and natural gas. By the 1890s, half of global energy use came in the form of fossil fuels, and by 2015 that share had climbed to nearly 80 percent. Modern history unfurled in the context of a fossil fuel energy regime and, as we shall see, of exponential growth in energy use.

Of less concern to Crutzen, modern history also played out amid runaway population growth. In 1780, about 800 million to 900 million humans walked the Earth. By 1930 there were some 2 billion, and by 2011, 7 billion. People at the time did not detect it, but in the middle of the eighteenth century a long-term surge in human numbers began. It started slowly and (as we shall see) built to a crescendo after 1950. No other primate, perhaps no other mammal, ever enjoyed such a frenzy of reproduction and survival in the history of life on Earth. There is nothing in the demographic history of our species anything like the modern rise of population—nor will there be again. Its chronology can support Crutzen's notion of an eighteenth-century origin for the Anthropocene. Both these twin surges, of energy use and population growth, started in the eighteenth century and continue today. How they will evolve in the future is anyone's guess—and from time to time in the pages that follow we will hazard a guess. In any case, since the late eighteenth century the human species has embarked on a bold new venture with no analogues anywhere in its history or biology.

An Indian coal miner carrying a basket-load of coal, ca. 1950. Coal and other fossil fuels, such as oil and natural gas, powered the world's economy after 1945 but entailed major public health and environmental costs associated with extraction and use. (Getty Images)

Since 2000 and Crutzen's first formulation of the concept, rival versions of the Anthropocene have sprung to life. Depending on the criteria one wishes to emphasize, one can find reasons to date the Anthropocene to 1610, 1492, some 7,000 years ago, 12,000 to 15,000 years ago, or back as far as the human control over fire, which might be as much as 1.8 million years ago.[2] Or one can find reasons, as this book does, to prefer a more recent date for the beginning of the Anthropocene. Those reasons, in brief, are, first, that since the mid-twentieth century human action (unintentionally) has become the most important factor governing crucial biogeochemical cycles, to wit, the carbon cycle, the sulfur cycle, and the nitrogen cycle. Those cycles form a large part of what is now called the "Earth system," a set of interlocking global-scale processes.[3] The second reason is that since the mid-twentieth century the human impact on the Earth and the biosphere, measured and judged in several different ways (some of which we will detail), has escalated.

The escalation since 1945 has been so fast that it sometimes goes by the name the Great Acceleration.[4] Within the last three human generations, three-quarters of the human-caused loading of the atmosphere with carbon dioxide took place. The number of motor vehicles on Earth increased from 40 million to 850 million. The number of people nearly tripled, and the number of city dwellers rose from about 700 million to 3.7 billion. In 1950 the world produced about 1 million tons of plastics but by 2015 that rose to nearly 300 million tons. In the same time span, the quantities of nitrogen synthesized (mainly for fertilizers) climbed from under 4 million tons to more than 85 million tons. Some trends of the Great Acceleration are still in high gear, but others—marine fish capture, large dam construction, stratospheric ozone loss—have now begun to slow down.[5]

This period since 1945 corresponds roughly to the average life expectancy of a human being. Only one in twelve persons now alive can remember anything before 1945. The entire life experience of almost everyone now living has taken place within the eccentric historical moment of the Great Acceleration, during what is certainly the most anomalous and unrepresentative period in the 200,000-year-long history of relations between our species and the biosphere. That should make us all skeptical of expectations that any particular current trends will last for long.

The Great Acceleration in its present form cannot last for long. There are not enough big rivers left to dam up, enough oil left to burn, enough forests left to fell, enough marine fish left to catch, enough groundwater left to pump up. Indeed, there are several indications that the accelerations are tapering off, and in a few cases reversing for one reason or another—as this book will explain. At root, it will probably come down above all to the character of the energy system and the size of the human population. If, as seems likely, we will craft an energy system in the decades to come in which fossil fuels play a much smaller role than they have recently, then our impact on Earth systems and the environment generally will abate sharply. And if the fertility declines among human populations around the world continue, as seems likely, then that will reinforce any future deceleration. One cannot say when the Great Acceleration will end, and one cannot say just how, but it is almost certainly a brief blip in human history, environmental history, and Earth history.

But the Anthropocene, barring catastrophe, is set to continue. Human beings will go on exercising influence over their environments and over global ecology far out of proportion to our numbers and far overshadowing that of other species. Our numbers are not likely to fall drastically. Nor are our appetites for energy and materials. Our powers to alter ecosystems will only increase, given the pace of change in biotechnology. Just how, and how long, humans will exert an outsized impact on the Earth and its systems in times to come is uncertain. But actions already taken, mainly between 1945 and now, assure a human imprint on the Earth, its climate, its biota, the acidity of its oceans, and much else that will linger for many millennia yet to come.

Before venturing any further into the temptations of futurology, it is well to remember the words of Sir Walter Ralegh quoted in the epigraph. Only some of the future is already determined (there *will* be lots of plastic and concrete lying around and buried under sediments). Much of it will be the result of choices and accidents yet to come. So it is best to return to the firmer ground of the past, to try to see how the present came to be what it is, how the Great Acceleration jump-started the Anthropocene. That will not allow us to know the future—nothing will, not even the most sophisticated modeling exercises—but it may help us to imagine the range of possibilities or, as Saint Paul put it, to see through a glass, darkly.

CHAPTER ONE

Energy and Population

Energy is a vexingly abstract concept. The word is derived from a term apparently invented by Aristotle to signify movement or work. Modern physicists have gotten only a bit further than the venerable Greek. They believe that energy exists in finite quantity in the Universe but in several different forms. Energy can be neither created nor destroyed, but it can be converted from one form to another. For instance, when you eat an apple, you convert chemical energy (the apple) into bodily heat, into muscular motion, and into other forms of chemical energy (your bones and tissues).[1]

The Earth is awash in energy. Almost all comes from the Sun. For human purposes, the main forms of energy are heat, light, motion, and chemical energy. The Sun's payload comes chiefly in the form of heat and light. A third of this is instantly reflected back into space, but most lingers for a while, warming land, sea, and air. A little of the light is absorbed by plants and converted into chemical energy through photosynthesis.

Every energy conversion results in some loss of useful energy. Plants on average manage to capture less than 1 percent of the energy delivered by the Sun. The rest is dissipated, mainly as heat. But what plants absorb is enough to grow, each year, about 110 billion tons of biomass in the sea and another 120 billion tons on land. Animals eat a small proportion of that, converting it into body heat, motion, and new tissues. And a small share of those new animal tissues is eaten by carnivores. At each of these trophic levels, well under 10 percent of available energy is successfully harvested. So the great majority of incoming energy is lost to no earthly purpose. But the Sun is so generous, there is still plenty to go around.

Until the harnessing of fire, our ancestors took part in this web of energy and life without being able to change it. The only energy available to them was what they could find to eat. Once armed with fire, probably more than 1.5 million years ago, our hominin ancestors could harvest more energy, both in the form of otherwise indigestible foods that cooking now rendered edible, and in the form of heat. Fire also helped them scavenge and hunt more efficiently, enhancing their access to chemical energy in the form of meat. This low-energy economy remained in place, with some modest changes, until agriculture began about ten thousand years ago.

Growing crops and raising animals allowed ancient farmers to harvest considerably more energy than their forebears could. Grain crops are the seeds of grasses such as rice, wheat, or maize, and are packed with energy (and protein). So, with farming, a given patch of land provided far more usable energy for human bodies than it could without farming, perhaps ten to one hundred times more. Big domesticated animals, although they needed huge quantities of feed, could convert the otherwise nearly useless vegetation of steppe, savanna, or swampland into usable energy, helpful for pulling plows (oxen, water buffalo) or for transport (horses, camels). Farming slowly became widespread, although never universal.

Eventually, watermills and windmills added a little more to the sum of energy available for human purposes. Watermills might be two thousand years old and windmills one thousand. In suitable locations, where water flowed reliably or reasonably steady winds blew, these devices could do the work of several people. But in most places, wind and flowing water were either too rare or too erratic. So the energy regime remained organic, based on human and animal muscle for mechanical power, and on wood and other biomass for heat. The organic energy regime lasted until the eighteenth century.

Then in late eighteenth-century England the harnessing of coal exploded the constraints of the organic energy regime. With fossil fuels, humankind gained access to eons of frozen sunshine—maybe 500 million years' worth of prior photosynthesis. Early efforts to exploit this subsidy from the deep past were inefficient. Early steam engines, in converting chemical energy into heat and then into motion, wasted 99 percent of the energy fed into them. But incremental improvements led to machines that by the 1950s wasted far less energy than did photosynthesis or carnivory. In this sense, culture had improved upon nature.

The enormous expansion of energy use in recent decades beggars the imagination. By about 1870 we used more fossil fuel energy each year than the annual global production from all photosynthesis. Our species has probably used more energy since 1920 than in all of prior human history. In the half century before 1950, global energy use slightly more than doubled. Then in the next half century, it quintupled from the 1950s level. The energy crisis of the 1970s—two sharp oil price hikes in 1973 and 1979—slowed but did not stop this dizzying climb in the use of fossil sunshine. Since 1950 we have burned around 50 million to 150 million years' worth of it.

The fossil fuel energy regime contained several phases. Coal outstripped biomass to become the world's primary fuel by about 1890. King coal reigned for about seventy-five years, before ceding the throne to oil in about 1965. Lately natural gas has grown in importance, so that in 2013 the world's energy mix looked as shown in Table 1.

These data do not include biomass, for which figures are sketchy. But the best guess is that it accounts for perhaps 15 percent of the grand total, fossil fuels for about 75 percent, and hydroelectricity and nuclear power together for about 10 percent. King oil's reign, now fifty years in duration, will likely prove as brief as coal's, but that remains to be seen. We have used about one trillion barrels of oil since commercial production began around 1860, and now use about 32 billion barrels yearly.[2]

The global totals belie tremendous variation in energy use around the world. In the early twenty-first century, the average North

TABLE I

Global commercial energy mix, 2013

Type of energy	%
Oil	33%
Coal	30%
Natural gas	24%
Hydroelectric	7%
Nuclear	4%

Data source: BP Statistical Review of World Energy, June 2014.

American used about seventy times as much energy as the average Mozambican. The figures since 1965, in Table 2, speak volumes about the rise of China and India, and about the distribution of wealth within the world.

In 1960, most of the world outside of Europe and North America still used little energy. The energy-intensive way of life extended to perhaps one-fifth of the world's population. But late in the twentieth century that pattern, in place since 1880 or so, changed quickly. In the fifty years after 1965, China increased its energy use by 16 times, India by 11, Egypt by 10 or 11. Meanwhile US energy use rose by about 40 percent. The United States accounted for a third of the world's energy consumption in 1965, but only a fifth in 2009; China accounted for only 5 percent in 1965, but a fifth in 2009, and in 2010 surpassed the United States to become the world's largest energy user.

In sum, the burgeoning rate of energy use in modern history makes our time wildly different from anything in the human past. The fact that for about a century after 1850 high energy use was confined to Europe and North America, and to a lesser extent to Japan, is the single most important reason behind the political and economic dominance these regions enjoyed in the international system. Since 1965 the total use of energy has continued to climb at only slightly diminished rates,

TABLE 2

Annual energy consumption, 1965–2013
(in millions of tons of oil equivalent)

Year	World	China	India	USA	Japan	Egypt
1965	3,813	182	53	1,284	149	8
1975	5,762	337	82	1,698	329	10
1985	7,150	533	133	1,763	368	28
1995	8,545	917	236	2,117	489	38
2005	10,565	1,429	362	2,342	520	62
2010	11,978	2,403	521	2,278	503	81
2013	12,730	2,852	595	2,266	474	87

Data source: BP *Statistical Review of World Energy,* June 2010, June 2012, 2014.
Note: Amounts are for commercial energy only, not biomass, which might add 10 to 15 percent.

but the great majority of the expansion has taken place outside of Europe and America, mainly in East Asia.

Fossil Fuel Energy and the Environment

The creation and spread of fossil fuel society was the most environmentally consequential development of modern times. Part of the reason for that lies in the direct effects of the extraction, transport, and combustion of coal, oil, and (to a much lesser extent) natural gas. These were (and are) mainly a matter of air, water, and soil pollution. The other part resides in the indirect effects of cheap and abundant energy: it enabled many activities that otherwise would have been uneconomic and would not have happened, or perhaps would have happened but only much more slowly.

Extracting fossil energy from the crust of the Earth has always been a messy business. Coal, mined commercially in over seventy countries since 1945, had the most widespread impacts. Deep mining brought changes to land, air, and water. Carving galleries out from beneath the surface honeycombed the Earth in coal districts such as South Wales, the Ruhr, eastern Kentucky, the Donetsk Basin, and Shaanxi Province. Occasionally underground mines collapsed, as in the Saarland (Germany) in 2008, producing a small earthquake. In China, as of 2005, subsidence due to coal mines affected an area the size of Switzerland. Mine tailings and slag heaps disfigured the landscape around coal mines. In China (by 2005) coal mine slag covered an area the size of New Jersey or Israel. Everywhere tailings and slag leached sulfuric acid into local waters. In some Pennsylvania and Ohio waterways, acidic liquids from mine drainage had killed off aquatic life by the 1960s, although in some spots life has since returned. Deep mining also often put extra methane in the atmosphere, adding perhaps 3 to 6 percent on top of the natural releases of this potent greenhouse gas.

Deep mining has always put people in dangerous environments. In China, for example, where roughly one hundred thousand small mines opened up during the Great Leap Forward (1958–1961), mining accidents killed about six thousand men annually at that time, and at least that many yearly in the 1990s. In the United Kingdom in 1961, about forty-two hundred men died in mine accidents. In the United States, the most dangerous year for coal miners was 1907, when more than three thousand died; since 1990, annual deaths have ranged from 18 to 66. Early in the twenty-first century, accidents killed a few thousand miners each year in China, several times the figure for Russia or India. Black lung disease, a consequence of years spent underground inhaling coal dust, killed far more wherever coal was mined.[3]

Surface mining, often called strip mining in the United States, was far safer for miners. It began with simple tools centuries ago, but steam technology made it more practical in the early twentieth century. After 1945, new excavation equipment and cheap oil ushered in a golden age of strip mining. Today it accounts for about 40 percent of coal mining worldwide, and outside of China is usually much more common than deep mining. In surface mining, which is practical to depths of nearly 50 meters, big machines claw away earth and rock above coal seams, destroying vegetation and soils. In the United States it aroused fervent opposition in many communities, which provoked federal regulation after 1977. Since that time, mining companies have been legally obliged to fund landscape restoration.

One particularly unpopular variant of strip mining was "mountaintop removal," practiced especially in those parts of Kentucky and West Virginia that had low-sulfur coal. High energy prices in the 1970s made these procedures lucrative as never before. Tighter air pollution laws in the 1990s, which made using high-sulfur coal more difficult, added to the economic logic of mountaintop removal. Blasting the tops off the Appalachians had many environmental consequences, none so important as the filling in of streams and valleys with waste rock ("overburden"), which buried forests and streams and led to accelerated erosion and occasional landslides.

Mountaintop removal, and surface mining generally, aroused spirited opposition from the 1930s onward and made environmentalists out of ordinary rural people throughout Appalachia. Their farms, fishing streams, and hunting grounds were sacrificed for coal production. In the 1960s and 1970s, opposition to strip mining reached its height in Appalachia, proving divisive in communities where mining companies offered most of the few jobs around. But the practice of mountaintop removal remained economic, and lasted into the twenty-first century.[4]

Drilling for oil brought different environmental issues but no less discord. In the early twentieth century, oil drilling occurred in many heavily populated places, including East Texas, southern California, central Romania, the city of Baku, and the then-Austrian province of Galicia. Gushers, spills, and fires menaced hearth and home. But by midcentury the technologies of drilling and storage had improved, so that oil fields were no longer necessarily the oleaginous equivalent of the Augean stables. And production increasingly shifted to places where people were few, such as Saudi Arabia and Siberia, so the consequences of oil pollution became less costly—at least in economic and political terms.

But the hike in energy prices of the 1970s inspired oil drilling in new and often challenging environments, including the seafloor, tropical forests, and the Arctic. Leaks, accidents, and blowouts became more common, thanks to Arctic cold and deep-sea pressures. Crude oil except in small concentrations is toxic to most forms of life and is extremely hard to clean up. By 2005 the world had some forty thousand oil fields, none of them free from pollution. Routine drilling involved building new infrastructure, moving heavy equipment sometimes weighing thousands of tons, and splashing vast quantities of oil and contaminated water into the surrounding environment. In the decades after 1980, about 30 million tons (or 220 million barrels) of oil dripped and squirted into the environment every year, about two-fifths of it in Russia.[5]

Offshore drilling, pioneered in California waters in the 1890s, remained confined to shallow waters for many decades. In the 1920s the practice spread to Lake Maracaibo in Venezuela, and to the Caspian Sea—both enduringly polluted as a result—and in the 1930s to the Gulf of Mexico. Technological advances, and the huge pools of investment capital available to oil companies from the 1940s on, opened new offshore frontiers in deeper waters. By the 1990s deepwater platforms dotted the North Sea, the Gulf of Mexico, and the coasts of Brazil, Nigeria, Angola, Indonesia, and Russia, among others. Big platforms stood over 600 meters above water, rivaling the tallest skyscrapers.

Offshore drilling operations were inherently risky. When hit by tropical storms or errant tankers, rigs splashed oil into the surrounding seas. The worst accidents occurred in the Gulf of Mexico. In 1979 a rig operated by the Mexican state oil company suffered a blowout and spewed oil for more than nine months before it was successfully capped. Some 3.3 million barrels escaped (equivalent to about six hours' worth of US oil use in 1979). It resulted in a surface oil slick roughly the size of Lebanon or Connecticut that ruined some Mexican fisheries and damaged Texan ones.[6]

In April 2010 the *Deepwater Horizon,* an oil platform leased by BP, exploded and sank, killing eleven workers and springing a leak some 1,500 meters below the waves on the seafloor off the Louisiana coast. It defied all containment efforts for more than three months. Some five million barrels in all spewed into the Gulf, the largest accidental oil spill in world history. The coastal wetlands ecosystems and what in previous years had been tourist-filled beaches of the Gulf Coast sopped up some of the wandering oil. Tar balls and oil washed up on the coasts of Louisiana, Mississippi, Alabama, and Florida. Fisheries ceased operations, and dead and damaged birds began to pile up. One of the victims was the Louisiana brown pelican, once brought to the edge of extinction by DDT in the 1950s and 1960s. Conservation work had given the brown pelican second life to the point where in 2009 it migrated off the federal endangered species list. In the first two months of the BP spill, 40 percent of the known population of brown pelicans died oily deaths. Some forty-eight thousand temporary workers and an armada of vessels not seen since D-Day tried to limit the ecological damage. Oceanographers and marine biologists will be assessing the spill's impacts for years, and lawyers will be kept busy for decades ascertaining who will be held responsible and just how tens of billions of dollars will change hands.[7] In the Gulf of Mexico, small spills occurred daily, huge ones every few years, but nothing yet matches the *Deepwater Horizon* disaster.

Drilling for oil in the forests of Ecuador presented different challenges from offshore environments. In the remote upper reaches of the Amazon watershed, in northeastern Ecuador, a Texaco-Gulf consortium struck oil in 1967. Over the next half century, the region yielded over two billion barrels of crude oil, most of it sent by pipeline over the Andes, making Ecuador the second largest oil exporter of South

America and keeping its government solvent. To operate in the rainforest, the consortium, and Ecuador's national oil company, which took over all operations by 1992, had to build new infrastructure of roads, pipelines, pumping stations, and so forth. Almost unencumbered by regulation, drilling in Ecuador took an especially casual course. Vast quantities of toxic liquids were dumped (or leaked) into the streams and rivers, creating the unhappy irony that in one of the most water-rich provinces on Earth, many people have no potable water. Inevitably, accidents happened. In 1989 enough oil spilled into the Rio Napo, which is about 1 kilometer wide, to turn it black for a week.[8]

Part of the local indigenous population, mobile forager-hunters called Huaorani, tried to fight off the oil invasion. Armed only with spears, the Huaorani failed and were relocated by the government. Other indigenous groups in Ecuador have struggled, usually unsuccessfully, to keep oil production at bay. According to some epidemiologists, the populations living near the oil fields have shown elevated rates of diseases, notably cancer.

Oil revenues proved so tempting to the Ecuadorian state that it scheduled two-thirds of its Amazonian territory for oil and gas exploration. By 2005 it had leased most of that, including blocks within the Yasuni National Park. In conventional calculations, it made sense for Ecuador (and for oil companies) to make money from oil drilling in Oriente (as Ecuadorians call it), because the indigenous peoples whose lives it disrupted contributed next to nothing to the state. Likewise the ecosystems of western Amazonia, among the world's most biologically rich and diverse, produced little that the state valued. Identical logic prevailed in Peru, although its government did not permit drilling in national parks. In 2010, Ecuador and the UN Development Program (UNDP) cut a deal whereby a trust fund would pay Ecuador $3.6 billion not to produce oil in one of the Yasuni National Park blocks, where nearly a billion barrels of oil lay, preserving (for the time

An exploratory oil-drilling site in the Ecuadorian rainforest. Pollution from oil extraction in Ecuador and other oil-producing regions led to fierce environmental struggles between foreign companies and local populations. (© G. Bowater/Corbis)

being) broad swaths of rainforest. Nigerian authorities showed instant interest in this novel arrangement, and with good reason.[9]

The Niger Delta region of southeast Nigeria, a patchy rainforest area, and one of the world's biggest wetlands, is a maze of creeks, marshes, and lagoons with once-rich fisheries. As in Oriente, the population of the Niger Delta is divided among several ethnic groups, notably the Ijaw, Igbo, and Ogoni. Unlike Oriente, it is densely populated, home to several million people. Shell and BP began oil operations here in the 1950s, happy to find a low-sulfur crude that is easy to refine into gasoline. Other companies followed, creating some 160 oil fields and 7,000 kilometers of pipelines. For decades, tankers filled up on crude where centuries before wooden ships had loaded slaves.

The Nigerian government, in what could well be an understatement, recorded about seven thousand oil spills between 1976 and 2005 in the Delta, involving some three million barrels of crude.[10] Some of the spills resulted from routine accidents, normal in the industry but especially frequent in the Delta due to poor maintenance and challenging conditions, both geographic and political. Others were acts of sabotage undertaken by locals, some of whom were seeking revenge for something, others of whom sought extortion or compensation payments from oil companies. The Niger Delta was, and remains, one of the poorest parts of Nigeria despite the several billions of dollars' worth of oil pumped out. For most residents, oil production made life harder. Dredging canals for oil exploration eliminated much of the mangrove swamp in which fish spawned, which together with oil pollution undercut a long-standing source of sustenance in the Delta. Air pollution and acid rain, largely from gas flares at oil wells, damaged crops. In the early 1990s the United Nations declared the Niger Delta the world's most ecologically endangered delta. Locals felt (and feel) that their natural wealth has been either destroyed or stolen by foreign companies and the Nigerian state, whose leadership has shown remarkable persistence in skimming off oil wealth. Resulting frustrations fed both liberation movements of local minorities and criminal syndicates. Lately Nigeria and its multinational partners have emphasized drilling offshore, where there is no local population to consider.[11]

The quest for oil led to new drilling in the chilly latitudes of Siberia and Alaska as well as in rainforests. The Soviet Union developed the huge oil and gas fields of western Siberia beginning in the 1960s (the

Soviets used nuclear explosions to help in seismic explorations between 1978 and 1985, so some Siberian oil is slightly radioactive).[12] The much more modest fields of northern Alaska opened up in the 1970s. Both regions, but especially Siberia, had their normal accidents and intentional releases of oil, "produced water," and other toxic substances. In high-latitude wetlands, taiga, and tundra, where biological processes move slowly, the ill effects of spills as a rule lingered longer than in the tropics, as we shall see.

Oriente and the Niger Delta are extreme examples of sacrifice zones, where the cost of energy extraction included pervasive ecological degradation. Among local species, only oil-eating bacteria benefited from the fouling of the soils and waters of these regions. But people far away also benefited, in the form of cheap oil for consumers, tidy profit for the companies involved, and luxurious revenue streams for state officials. The world enjoyed great benefits thanks to oil extraction, but specific places paid a high price. People living near strip mines would likely say the same of the history of coal extraction.

Coal and Oil Transport

While extraction of coal and oil exacted an environmental price upon a fixed archipelago of mining districts and oil fields, the transport of fossil fuels had a scattered impact. Coal transport took place mainly in rail cars and barges. Very few accidents occurred, and when they did what coal toppled out onto land or into canals and rivers led to minimal consequences.

Oil was a different matter. Part of the appeal of oil over coal is the ease of transport. As a liquid, oil (except for the heaviest varieties) can ooze through pipelines. Even more glided over the seas in tankers. After 1950 oil increasingly was drilled in one country and burned in another, a reflection of the emergence of the Persian Gulf giant fields. So tankers plied the high seas in ever greater numbers. Today oil makes up half the tonnage of maritime cargoes, and there are more miles of pipeline than of railroad in the world.[13]

Pipelines and tankers proved remarkably susceptible to accident. One reason tankers had so many accidents is that they became too big to stop. In 1945 a big tanker held 20,000 tons of oil, in the 1970s about half a million, and today 1 million tons. Supertankers are 300 meters in length and the least nimble vessels on the seas. They need several kilometers in which to slow to a stop.

Fortunately, in the same decades tankers became harder to puncture. In the 1970s most new tankers had double hulls, which sharply reduced the likelihood of spills resulting from collisions with rocks, icebergs, and other ships. But when spills occurred, they could be large, and they always happened near shore where oil could foul rich ecosystems and valuable property.

Though small tanker spills happened almost every day, most of the escaped oil came in a few big accidents. The English Channel witnessed two giant tanker spills, in 1967 and 1978. The biggest spill of all occurred off of Cape Town in 1983, leaking more than six times as much oil as did the famous *Exxon Valdez* in 1989. Tanker spills could happen almost anywhere, but they were most numerous in the Gulf of Mexico, in Europe's Atlantic waters, in the Mediterranean Sea, and in the Persian Gulf.[14] The most recent big tanker spill, in 2002, occurred when a single-hulled vessel broke up in a storm off the northwest coast of Spain.

Pipelines carried a smaller, but growing, share of the world's oil after 1945. Their builders intend them to last fifteen to twenty years, but many, perhaps most, pipelines are asked to serve beyond that span. They corrode and crack, especially when subject to extreme ranges of climate. By and large, pipeline design improved over time, but accidents increased because the world's network of pipelines grew so quickly.[15]

The most affected landscapes were in Russia. The most serious single pipeline leak occurred near Usinsk, in Komi Republic, Russia, about 1,500 kilometers northeast of Moscow in 1994. Outsiders estimate the leak at six hundred thousand to one million barrels. Officials initially denied any leaks, a position they soon had to abandon.[16] Another large one occurred in 2006. Altogether, about 7 to 20 percent of Russian oil production leaked out of faulty pipelines in the 1990s, a reflection of oil's low price, a business culture that put scant value on routine maintenance, especially in an economically disastrous decade, and the challenges of both remoteness and climate. Thousands of leaks and spills, large and small, happened every year in the 1990s. The sub-zero winter cold of regions such as the oilfields of Komi Republic—most of which lie north of the Arctic Circle—was hard on pipelines and other components of oil infrastructure.[17] Some indigenous Siberians, not surprisingly, tried to organize themselves against oil and gas development. Pipeline leaks imperiled their hunting, fishing, and reindeer herding. On at least one occasion some attempted armed resistance, which succeeded no better than the efforts of Ecuador's Huaorani.[18]

In human terms, the worst oil pipeline accident occurred in the Niger Delta in 1998 when a line maintained by Shell and the Nigerian state oil company sprang a leak. As villagers gathered to help themselves to free oil, an explosion and a fireball incinerated more than a thousand people. Two villages burned to cinders. In 2006 two additional oil pipeline fires elsewhere in Nigeria killed about six hundred people. As a means of ferrying energy from point of extraction to point of use, oil tankers and pipelines were both more economical and more hazardous than coal transport.[19]

Fossil Fuel Combustion and Air Pollution

Coal mine accidents and oil pipeline explosions took many thousands of lives in the decades after 1945, but nowhere near as many as the routine, peaceable combustion of fossil fuels. Air pollution, mainly from coal and oil burning, killed tens of millions of people.

To get an idea of the air pollution resulting from coal combustion, consider the annual pollution output of an average coal-fired American power plant about 2010, after decades of regulation and technical improvements. The average plant annually released millions of tons of carbon dioxide, the main greenhouse gas, and thousands of tons of sulfur dioxide, the main ingredient in acid rain. It put a few dozen kilograms of lead, mercury, and arsenic into the air as well. This was part of the price of turning coal into electricity, and forty years ago the price was much higher because coal combustion was much dirtier. And this does not include ash and soot.

Urban air pollution has a long history. In the twelfth century, Maimonides—no doubt justly—complained about air quality in Cairo, a dung- and straw-burning city. A century later London enacted the first recorded ordinances aimed against air pollution. The adoption of coal as a basic fuel made matters much worse, never more so than in London in the second week of December 1952.

When a cold air mass settled over the Thames valley in early December, bringing temperatures below freezing, Londoners added more coal to their hearths. Each day their million chimneys spewed out a thousand tons of coal soot and nearly 400 tons of sulfur dioxide. People could not see to cross the street at noon. Natives who knew the city like the back of their hand got lost on daily errands. A few walked into the Thames and drowned. During December 5–9, some forty-seven hundred people died, about three thousand more than normal. Over the next three months mortality remained well above normal for London winters, so that epidemiologists now attribute twelve thousand deaths to pollution during the December episode.[20] In the winter of 1952–1953, coal smoke, soot, and sulfur dioxide killed Londoners at roughly twice the rate the Luftwaffe managed during the blitz of 1940–1941. Undertakers ran out of caskets.[21]

The public and press raised a hue and cry, prompting one cabinet minister, Harold Macmillan, to write in a memo he wisely kept secret during his lifetime: "For some reason or another 'smog' has captured the imagination of the press and people. . . . Ridiculous as it appears, I suggest we form a committee. We cannot do very much, but we can be seen to be very busy."[22] Macmillan, whose insouciance about air pollution and its effects was characteristic of his time, went on to have a distinguished political career, including a stint as prime minister from 1957 to 1963. Pea-soupers, as Londoners called their densest fogs, persisted in London for a few more years. But between 1956 and the mid-1960s, mainly on Macmillan's watch, air pollution laws and fuel switching (to oil and natural gas) made London's killer fogs a thing of the past.[23]

Oil burned cleaner than coal. Combustion of oil and its derivatives, such as gasoline, releases lead, carbon monoxide, sulfur dioxide, nitrogen oxides, and volatile organic compounds (VOCs). VOCs together with sunshine help brew photochemical smog. Oil made its main contribution to urban air pollution through tailpipes rather than chimneys. Vehicle exhausts provided the raw material for photochemical smog, which was first observed in Los Angeles during World War II. Photochemical smog developed where motorization took hold and where the Sun shone brightly. Cities at lower latitudes, especially those with nearby mountains that keep pollution from drifting off with the winds, were especially affected: Los Angeles, Santiago, Athens, Tehran, and the world champion, Mexico City.

Mexico City had one hundred thousand cars in 1950, when it was still renowned for its clear vistas of distant volcanoes. By 1990, by which time it was enveloped in a near-permanent haze, four million cars clogged its streets. Trucks, buses, and cars accounted for 85 percent of Mexico City's air pollution, which by 1985 was occasionally so acute that birds fell from the sky in midflight over the central square (the Zócalo). After careful monitoring began in 1986, it emerged that Mexico City exceeded legal limits for one or more major pollutants more than 90 percent of the time. In the 1990s, estimates suggested some six thousand to twelve thousand annual deaths were attributable to air pollution in the city, four to eight times the annual number of murders. Various efforts to curb air pollution since the 1980s have produced mixed results, but the death rate seems to have declined slightly since the early 1990s.

Both coal and oil turned out to be mass killers in the world's cities. In Western Europe around 2000, vehicle exhausts killed people at roughly the same rate as vehicle accidents.[24] Meanwhile, in China air pollution from all sources killed about five hundred thousand Chinese annually and, due to pollutants wafting eastward with the winds, another eleven thousand in Japan and Korea together.[25] In the 1990s, estimates had put the global annual death toll attributable to air pollution at about half a million. One study from 2002 put it at eight hundred thousand per year.[26] From 1950 to 2015, air pollution probably killed about thirty to forty million people, lately most of them Chinese, roughly equal to the death toll from all wars around the world since 1950.[27] Many millions more suffered intensified asthma and other ailments as a result of the pollution they inhaled. Fossil fuel combustion accounted for the lion's share of these deaths and illnesses.

In addition to these unhappy effects upon human health, fossil fuels, especially coal, were responsible for widespread acidification. Volcanoes and forest fires released quantities of sulfur to the atmosphere, but by the 1970s coal combustion emitted about ten times more. Sulfur dioxide in contact with cloud droplets forms sulfuric acid, which returns to Earth with rain, snow, or fog (commonly called acid rain). Acid rain often contains nitrogen oxides too, from coal or oil combustion. High-sulfur coal of the sort found in the Midwest of the United States, in China, in Bengal, and elsewhere, acidified ecosystems far and wide. Mountain forests and freshwater ecosystems showed the most acute effects, and some sensitive species (brook trout, sugar maple) disappeared altogether in high-acid environments. Broadly speaking, by the end of the twentieth century the world had three acidification hot spots:

northern and central Europe, eastern North America, and eastern, especially southeastern, China.

Acid rain became a policy issue by the end of the 1960s. For local communities the easiest solution was to require tall smokestacks that lofted the offending gases farther afield. In the 1970s acid rain became an international issue, as Canadians objected to the acidification of their lakes by (mainly) American power plant emissions, and Scandinavians discovered damage to their waterways attributable to British and German coal combustion. Poland and its neighbors, which used coal that was especially high in sulfur, splashed one another's landscapes with acid rain that occasionally reached the pH level of vinegar. Railway trains had to observe low speed limits in parts of Poland because the iron of the train tracks had weakened from acid corrosion. With the dramatic rise of coal use in China after 1980, transboundary acidification became a source of contention in East Asia too, as Koreans, Japanese, and Taiwanese felt the consequences of Chinese power plants and factories.

Beyond sensitive ecosystems, acid emissions also had modest effects on human health and major ones on buildings made of limestone or marble. Greek authorities found it advisable to put the most precious statuary of the Acropolis indoors to save it from corrosion by acid rain. In the Indian city of Agra, pollution from a nearby oil refinery, among other sources, threatened the marble of the Taj Mahal.[28]

Acidification, happily enough, turned out to be one of the easiest of environmental problems to address. In Europe and the United States, after some delay occasioned by the objections of coal utilities and their political allies, cap-and-trade schemes were devised that allowed polluters to choose their means of reducing emissions and to buy and sell permits to pollute. Beginning around 1990 this reduced sulfur emissions by 40 to 70 percent in short order, at a cost that turned out to be a small fraction of that anticipated. It takes a while for ecosystems to rebound from acidification, but in northern Europe and eastern North

America, by 2000 the recovery had begun to show. China, awash in acid rain, tried to address its sulfur emissions, but its heavy reliance on coal hamstrung the effort until 2006, after which date some reductions in sulfur emissions occurred. In northern China the consequences of acid rain were checked by the prevalence of alkaline dust (neutralizing acid), but in the south, soils and ecosystems proved as vulnerable as those of northern Europe and eastern North America.[29]

By and large, the rich world after 1970 achieved healthy reductions in its emissions of sulfur dioxide as well as other coal-based pollutants. Copenhagen, for example, reduced its SO_2 concentrations by 90 percent between 1970 and 2005.[30] London lowered its smoke and soot levels by 98 percent between the 1920s and 2005.[31] In 1950 the residents of Glasgow, Scotland, each inhaled about 1 kilogram of soot each year; by 2005 their lungs received almost none. In Japan, a polluter's paradise until the mid-1960s, even hotbeds of sulfur emissions such as the industrial city of Osaka managed to clear the air by 1990.[32] These remarkable changes in urban air pollution came about because of fuel switching (less coal, more oil and gas), deindustrialization, and new technologies made economically practical mainly by new regulations. In most cases, citizen agitation lay behind the new regulations. Germany shows the importance of citizen activism: In West Germany air pollution levels declined markedly from the 1960s onward; in East Germany, where the secret police provided citizens with good reason to keep their views to themselves, air pollution remained unchecked through to the end of the communist regime in 1989.

Fossil fuel combustion played a central role in another modification of the atmosphere, the relentless buildup of carbon dioxide. Here, in contrast to the story with sulfur dioxide, public policy to date has been ineffective. High-level international efforts, such as the negotiations at Kyoto (1997) and Copenhagen (2009), led to no significant reductions in carbon emissions. China's emissions alone after 1990 swamped what minor reductions could be achieved here and there around the world. The spectacular climb in fossil fuel use since 1950 is the main reason behind the parallel rise in atmospheric carbon.

The Strange Career of Nuclear Power

Unlike other forms of energy use, nuclear power has a birthday: December 2, 1942. On that day the Italian émigré physicist Enrico Fermi oversaw the first controlled nuclear reaction, in a repurposed squash court under the stands of a football stadium at the University of Chicago. The power of the bonds within atoms dwarfs that of other energy sources available to humankind. A fistful of uranium can generate more energy than a truckload of coal. This astonishing power was first used in bombs, thousands of which were built, and two of which were used, both by the United States and against Japan in August 1945, bringing the Second World War to a close.

Peaceful uses of atomic power soon followed. By 1954 the first reactor providing electricity for a grid, a tiny one near Moscow, opened. Much bigger ones started up in the United Kingdom and the United States in 1956–1957. In the middle of the 1950s the prospects for nuclear power seemed bright and endless. Scientists foresaw nuclear-powered visits to Mars. One American official predicted that electricity would soon be "too cheap to meter." In both the United States and the Soviet Union, visionaries imagined vast engineering uses for nuclear explosions, such as opening a new Panama Canal or smashing apart menacing hurricanes.[33] Nuclear technology enjoyed tremendous subsidies in many countries—not least a law in the United States that fixed a low maximum for lawsuits against nuclear utilities, allowing them to buy insurance, which otherwise no one would sell them. Between 1965 and 1980, the share of the world's electricity generated in nuclear power plants rose from less than 1 percent to 10 percent. By 2013 that figure approached 13 percent.

Countries with scientific and engineering resources but minimal fossil fuels converted most fully to nuclear power. By 2010 France, Lithuania, and Belgium relied on it for more than half their electricity; Japan and South Korea for about a quarter of theirs; and the United States for a fifth.

The rosy expectations for a nuclear future withered in the 1970s and 1980s due to well-publicized accidents. Civilian reactors had suffered dozens of accidents large and small in the 1950s and 1960s, the worst of them in the USSR. But they were kept as secret as possible. The 1979 accident at Three Mile Island in Pennsylvania attracted public scrutiny. It turned out to be minor, as nuclear accidents go, but came close to being much worse and was not hidden from view. It served to turn US public opinion away from nuclear power.[34] In the rest of the world the public at large took less notice, although the mishap invigorated antinuclear movements and watchdog groups in every country that had a nuclear industry. Their concerns about nuclear safety led to reforms, more stringent controls, and higher construction and operation costs. In March 1986 the British highbrow magazine *The Economist* opined, "The nuclear power industry remains as safe as a chocolate factory."[35]

Four weeks later, at Chernobyl in Ukraine (then in the USSR), a three-year-old reactor vessel exploded. The ensuing fire released a plume of radioactivity hundreds of times greater than those over Hiroshima and Nagasaki in Japan some forty-one years earlier. For days the Soviet government, led by Mikhail Gorbachev, tried to keep it secret and declined to warn local populations of the risks of venturing outdoors or drinking milk (one of the pathways of radioactivity goes from grass to cattle to milk). Radioactivity spread with the winds over Europe and eventually in small amounts over everyone in the Northern Hemisphere. Some 830,000 soldiers and workers ("Chernobyl liquidators") were dragooned into the cleanup effort; radiation poisoning quickly killed 28, another few dozen soon after, and in the course of time, many thousands more of these unfortunate liquidators died than actuarial tables would predict. Some 130,000 people were permanently resettled due to contamination of their homes, leaving a ghost zone that will host unsafe levels of radioactivity for at least two hundred more years. A few brave and stubborn souls still live there.

The Chernobyl Exclusion Zone has since become a de facto wildlife reserve teeming with wild boar, moose, deer, wolves, storks, and eagles, among other creatures. They roam in areas with radioactivity levels deemed unsafe for humans—because of the risks of predation and starvation, few wild animals live long enough to develop cancers. But from beetles to boars, all species show unusual rates of tumors, accelerated aging, and genetic mutations. Plant life in "the zone"—as locals call it—also shows high mutation rates. So do the tiny proportion of soil microorganisms so far studied. Because the average human body contains about 3 kilograms of bacteria, viruses, and microfungi, their modification by Chernobyl may prove to have interesting effects upon human beings. The zone became a curious biological contradiction in the wake of the catastrophe of 1986: abundant wildlife and resurgent vegetation, far more prolific than in surrounding precincts because free from quotidian human actions such as mowing, weeding, paving, and hunting—but at the same time less healthy than wildlife and vegetation elsewhere precisely because of the accident.[36]

The human health consequences of Chernobyl remain controversial. Cancer rates spiked in years after the disaster, especially thyroid cancers among children, leading to perhaps four thousand excess cases up to 2004. The toll could have been much lower without the government attempt to hush up the accident. This much is widely accepted. The full extent of Chernobyl's health consequences is much disputed.

Epidemiologists, often extrapolating from the experience of survivors of Hiroshima and Nagasaki, ventured many estimates of the likely mortality from Chernobyl. A conglomerate of UN bodies called the

Chernobyl Forum in 2006 estimated nine thousand deaths and two hundred thousand illnesses related to Chernobyl, totals its spokesmen found reassuring. These figures are at the low end of the spectrum of expert opinion. More recently, researchers from the Russian Academy of Sciences and Belarus Laboratory of Radiation Safety reported a welter of insidious effects. For example, they noted early aging and signs of senility among irradiated people, and spikes in the rates of Down syndrome, low-birthweight babies, and infant mortality all over Europe in the months after Chernobyl. In Ukraine by 1994 more than 90 percent of the Chernobyl liquidators were sick, as were 80 percent of the evacuees and 76 percent of the children of irradiated parents. So many people suffered weakened immune systems that health workers spoke of "Chernobyl AIDS." The most affected populations were those who received high doses of radiation because they lived near Chernobyl; the Chernobyl liquidators; and babies born in the months following April 1986—*in utero* was a very dangerous place to be that spring. Based on the elevated mortality rates in irradiated parts of the former Soviet Union, these researchers calculated that by 2004 Chernobyl had already killed some 212,000 people in Russia, Ukraine, and Belarus, and, they estimated, caused nearly one million deaths worldwide. These figures are toward the high end of the spectrum. But thanks to inherent difficulties in assessing causes of death and deliberate Soviet falsification of health records among Chernobyl liquidators, no one will ever know the true human cost of Chernobyl.[37]

Chernobyl came at the same time as a collapse in world oil prices. The ecological and economic logic of building nuclear power plants suddenly seemed less persuasive. The share of the world's electricity derived from nuclear power, which had been rising fast, leveled off for the next twenty years.

The chilling effect of Chernobyl on the nuclear industry lasted for decades, but not forever. In 1987 Italy had passed a referendum against nuclear power; in 2009 it revoked it. The ever-growing demand for electricity, especially in China, led authorities to build more nuclear power plants. As of 2010 about 440 were in operation around the world (in forty-four countries) and about 50 more were in the works, 20 of them in China, 10 in Russia, 5 in India. The fact that nuclear power contributes very little in the way of greenhouse gases made it popular with many people who took global warming seriously, despite concerns over safety, the dependence on government subsidies, and the as-yet unresolved problem of what to do with dangerous nuclear wastes. By 2010 the United States had accumulated about 62,000 tons of spent nuclear fuel and had nowhere to put it.[38] According to the US Environmental Protection Agency, after ten thousand years the problem would solve itself because the fuel would no longer pose a threat to human health. Despite arousing environmental anxieties and requiring subsidies to compete in the marketplace, nuclear power rose from the ashes of Chernobyl to become politically viable almost everywhere in the world by 2010.

Then came Fukushima.[39] In March 2011 a powerful earthquake, 9.0 on the Richter scale, launched a tsunami toward the northeastern coast of Japan. Towering waves—about 14 meters high—crashed ashore, killing about twenty thousand people and wreaking destruction on a scale likely to make it the most expensive natural disaster in world history.

The Fukushima Daiichi nuclear power plant, one of the world's biggest, had opened in 1971. It survived a 1978 earthquake. It was operated by the Tokyo Electric Power Company, known as TEPCO. But in 2011 the waves easily topped retaining walls built to withstand a tsunami less than half the height of this one. The six working reactors shut down, generators and batteries failed, and the plant lost all electric power, and thus the capacity to pump cold water over fuel rods—which generate heat even when a reactor is not functioning, due to the continuing decay of fission products. Fires and explosions followed. Three reactors melted down. TEPCO workers drowned the fuel rods in seawater, hoping to forestall the worst. The quantities of radiation leaked into the environment in the first month after the tsunami were about 10 percent of those from Chernobyl. Dozens of workers at Fukushima Daiichi absorbed heavy doses of radiation.

The government, which had initially sharply underestimated the severity of the disaster, eventually created an exclusion zone extending 20 kilometers from the plant. Some 350,000 people departed for safer ground. Just where that was initially seemed hard to specify. The government also officially determined that the water supply in Tokyo, some 200 kilometers south, was unsafe for infants due to radiation. Both TEPCO and the government came in for withering criticism in Japan for their unpreparedness and dishonesty.[40]

Small amounts of radiation floated around the Northern Hemisphere, tainting milk in North America and arousing anxieties everywhere. The German government announced a shutdown of some of its elderly reactors, and several countries announced reviews of their nuclear safety procedures. China, although closer to the catastrophe than most, kept up its record pace of nuclear power plant construction.

In Japan itself, sentiment surged away from support of nuclear power, and all fifty-four of the country's reactors were gathering dust within fourteen months after the disaster, although two have since returned to duty. Few local communities wished to host an active nuclear power plant. To make up for the resulting shortfall of electricity, Japan increased its fossil fuel imports by half, substantially raising its energy costs. Whether or not the tsunami at Fukushima's power plant will dampen enthusiasm for nuclear power for long remains to be seen.

The Contentious Career of Hydropower

In terms of output, hydroelectric power matched nuclear. In terms of controversy and tragedy, it trailed not far behind. People had used water power from ancient times for grinding grain, and for powering factories from the eighteenth century, but it was not until 1878 that water sent through turbines produced electricity. In Europe and North America, hundreds of small-scale hydroelectricity stations were built between 1890 and 1930. The United States—quickly followed by the USSR—pioneered giant hydroelectric stations in the 1930s. These behemoths became, like nuclear power plants, symbols of technological virtuosity and modernity. Jawaharlal Nehru, India's prime minister from 1947 to 1964, often called hydroelectric dams "the temples of modern India." The world went on a dam-building spree after 1945, peaking in the 1960s and 1970s, by which time most of the good sites in rich countries had been taken.

Hydropower offered great attractions. For the engineers, it held the advantage that it could deliver power at any time (except in the event of big droughts that starved reservoirs). The potential power, captive water, stayed put and available at no cost (except where evaporation rates were high, as in the case of Egypt's Aswan Dam reservoir, Lake Nasser). Moreover, reservoirs could serve multiple purposes, as sources of irrigation water, sites for recreation, or fisheries. For environmentalists, who often found big dams objectionable on many grounds, hydropower held the charm of releasing no greenhouse gases in operation. Dam construction was another matter, but even taking all phases into account, hydroelectricity was probably the best form of electricity generation from the climate-change point of view, and certainly far, far better than using fossil fuels.

Its drawbacks, however, were legion. Big dams could bring big accidents, as at the Banqiao Dam in China's Henan Province in 1975. During a typhoon the dam broke, unleashing a wave—an inland tsunami—that drowned tens of thousands. Subsequent starvation and waterborne epidemics killed another 145,000. Hundreds of other dams failed less catastrophically. More prosaically, dam reservoirs silted up, so that the useful life of a hydroelectric plant might be as little as ten or twenty years in some poorly designed cases, most of which were in China. Reservoirs also sometimes desecrated cherished landscapes, as when Brazil inundated a national park to cooperate with Paraguay on the Itaipu Dam, opened in 1982 on the Paraná River. Its power station is the world's second largest. Archeological treasures were obliterated by some reservoirs, notably the Aswan Dam in Egypt and Turkey's several dams on the Tigris and Euphrates in eastern Anatolia. "Salvage archeology" usually could rescue only a fraction of what disappeared beneath the rising waters.[41]

The most politically volatile aspect of dam building was the displacement of people. Reservoirs took up a lot of space—about twice the area of Italy in total. Some of the big ones, in Ghana or in Russia, are the size of Cyprus or Connecticut. Globally, some forty to eighty million people—twenty million in India alone—had to get out of the way for reservoirs, in rare cases fleeing for their lives without any advance warning.[42] In many cases ethnic minorities living in hilly districts with swift rivers were the ones relocated in the interests of electric power wanted elsewhere in their countries.[43]

In India, where dam building (for irrigation as well as electricity) formed a major part of the state's development plans after independence in 1947, peasant resistance to dams became a widespread movement by the 1980s. Resistance rarely deflected the state's ambitions, but in the case of dams along the Narmada River in western India, it led to huge protests, political tumult, and lengthy lawsuits. The Narmada scheme involved thousands of dams, large and small, on which construction began in 1978. Local resistance, occasioned mainly by displacements, grew more and more organized throughout the 1980s, and successfully reached out to international environmental organizations for support. In 1993–1994 the World Bank, a longtime proponent of dam building in India, withdrew its support. Foreign criticism stoked the fires of Indian nationalism. Indian novelists and actors got involved, both for and against additional dams. But India's Supreme Court stood by the government and the engineers, the work con-

Members of the Save Narmada Movement demonstrate against the US utility company Ogden Energy Group near the American Embassy in New Delhi, April 4, 2000. Hydroelectricity generated little pollution but typically required the construction of reservoirs that uprooted local people, as in the case of a string of dams on India's Narmada River. (Getty Images)

tinued, and so another hundred thousand or so Indians—"oustees" as they are known in India—moved to accommodate the Narmada's reservoirs.[44]

While Europe and North America had exhausted their best sites for hydroelectric development by 1980, the rest of the world continued to build dams apace. Half of the big dams built in the world after 1950 are in China. Between 1991 and 2009, China built what is by far the world's largest hydropower installation, the Three Gorges Dam on the Yangzi. Like the Narmada project, it too attracted environmental controversy, as roughly 1.3 million people had to make way for its reservoir. As the dam trapped most of the enormous silt load behind it, the downstream Yangzi delta began to erode while the reservoir slowly filled. The reduction in organic matter delivered to the East China Sea imperiled China's richest fishery.[45] Moreover, the potential for instant disaster should the dam break—it is built on a seismic fault—is beyond imagination. But the Three Gorges Dam illustrates the environmental tradeoffs of hydropower: without it China would burn tens of millions more tons of coal annually.

As of 2015, enormous possibilities for hydropower remained in Africa and South America, unexploited because of the weak markets for electricity. But the growing concerns over climate change raised the odds that the remaining opportunities for the development of hydropower would not go begging, population displacement and other problems notwithstanding.

The (Tentative) Emergence of Alternative Energies

The manifest environmental drawbacks of fossil fuels, nuclear power, and hydropower made people long for healthy and "green" energy sources. Long-standing anxieties about exhaustion of fossil fuel supplies added to the urge to find alternatives. In 1917 the Scottish American inventor Alexander Graham Bell championed the cause of ethanol, a fuel made from crop residues, on the grounds that coal and oil would one day run out. Falling prices for fossil fuels and the optimism of the early years of nuclear power, however, discouraged work on energy alternatives until the 1970s. Then the oil price hikes of 1973 and 1979, and the disillusionment with nuclear power that climaxed with Chernobyl in 1986, sparked a surge of interest in solar and wind power, as well as tidal, geothermal, and a few other as yet less important possibilities. Ethanol, for its part, became a major fuel in Brazil beginning in the 1970s. Sugarcane stalks supply the basic energy for an automobile fleet that burns a blended fuel that is about 75 percent gasoline and 25 percent ethanol.

Nothing is more renewable than the wind. Windmills for grinding grain originated in Iran or Afghanistan. Fantail windmills for pumping up aquifer water became common more than a century ago, especially on the Great Plains of North America. Wind power as the basis for electricity became practical in 1979 with the work of Danish engineers who built modern wind turbines. Technical improvements followed quickly, so that with the help of government subsidies, by 2010 wind power supplied about a fifth of all electricity in Denmark. In Spain and Portugal, the figure came to around 15 percent. In the United States, less than 2 percent of electricity came from wind power, but the figure was rising fast, as it was in China. After 2008 more new capacity was installed globally each year for wind power than for hydroelectricity.

Everywhere, the attraction of wind power was chiefly environmental. Although big wind farms aroused minor controversies here and there because they changed the look of landscapes and in some cases killed birds and bats, by and large wind power had negligible environmental consequences. For green citizens and governments it seemed to promise a way out of the climate change morass. More precisely, it seemed to offer a partial solution, because wind power requires wind, and even in Denmark and Portugal the wind does not always blow when electricity is needed. It is hard to store power for those times when the winds are calm.

The same limitations applied to solar power, the other darling of green citizens. Clouds and night interfered with the steady delivery of solar energy. But the potential of solar power was hard to resist. The Sun donates more energy to the Earth in an hour than humankind uses in a year. And a year's worth of the Sun's bounty is more energy than all that contained in all the fossil fuels and uranium in the Earth's crust. More than any other energy source available, solar power promised an infinitude of energy.

The technologies of photovoltaic cells emerged in the late nineteenth century but languished for decades. Like wind power, in the

1970s solar appealed to many people due to the high oil prices. For remote places not connected to a power grid, solar panels proved very practical. After several slow years, resulting mainly from the oil price collapse of 1985–1986, investment in solar power surged ahead again after 2000. European countries that provided subsidies played a large role, notably Germany. The biggest single solar energy projects under construction in 2015, however, were in China, where western regions such as Xinjiang and Tibet have plenty of sunshine but are a long way from China's coal.[46]

Worldwide, wind and solar power together in 2015 accounted for less than 4 percent of electricity consumption, despite their recent exponential growth. Unlike fossil fuels, they are hard to store. They may be the best hope for cutting greenhouse gas emissions, but they have a very long way to go to challenge fossil fuels—especially in the transport sector, where oil's advantages are strong.

Indirect Effects of Abundant Energy

The fossil fuel energy path brought profound consequences for the world's air, water, and soil, as well as for human health. Beyond all that, the mere fact of cheap energy (cheap by the standards of the past) led to all manner of environmental change. Cheap energy, and the machines that used it, remade timber cutting and farming, among other industries. By and large, cheap energy expanded the scope of what was economically rewarding, thereby extending the scale or intensity of these energy-guzzling activities.

Consider timber harvesting. The surge of deforestation around the world since 1960, especially in moist tropical forests, is one of the great environmental transformations of modern history. Cheap oil enabled it. Had loggers used axes and handsaws, had they transported logs only by animal muscle and via waterways, they would have deforested far less than they did. Loggers with gasoline-powered chain saws became one hundred to one thousand times as efficient at cutting trees than men with axes and crosscut saws. From the 1990s, huge diesel-powered machines that look like "insects from another planet" snipped off tree trunks at the base, allowing timber cutting with no human feet on the forest floor.[47]

Oil transformed agriculture even more fundamentally. In the 1980s one person with a big tractor and a full tank of fuel in the North American prairies could plow 110 acres (50 hectares) in a day, doing the work that seventy years before had required 55 men and 110 horses. Mechanization of this sort emptied the farmlands of North America and Europe of horses and people. In 1920 the United States had devoted nearly a quarter of its sown acreage to oats for horses; in 1990, almost none. Tractors transformed agriculture in parts of Asia too, where there are now more than five million tractors (Africa has perhaps two hundred thousand).[48]

Mechanization is only the most obvious change cheap energy brought in agriculture. The enormous use of nitrogenous fertilizers also depended on cheap energy. About 5 percent of the world's natural gas is devoted to fertilizer production. Many pesticides used oil as their chemical feedstock. Irrigation, too, especially when it involved pumping water up from aquifers, relied on cheap energy. All these practices of modern farming had profound ecological effects, and all of them needed cheap energy.

Cheap energy transformed the scale, intensity, and environmental implications of several other arenas of human interaction with nature, including mining, fishing, urban design, and tourism. Without cheap energy, it would not be practical for machines to grind through tons of Australian hillscapes in search of a few grams of gold. Nor would trawlers be able to scrape the seafloor with nets several miles across. Nor would cities such as Toronto and Sydney have sprawled over landscapes to the extent they have, gobbling up forests and farmland. Nor would millions of North Americans routinely fly to places such as Cozumel, or

Europeans to the Seychelles, or Japanese to Saipan or Guam—all of which in the past forty years were transformed, environmentally as well as economically and socially, by mass tourism. In these and dozens of other cases, the cheap energy involved usually came from fossil fuels, but had it come cheaply from any source, the outcome for mountains, fish, forests, farmland, and beachfronts would have been much the same. The indirect effects of energy upon the environment resulted from the massive deployment of energy, from its abundance and low cost, not from any specific attributes of the energy source.[49]

Although one cannot hope to disentangle all the forces and processes that shaped the Anthropocene, from almost any viewpoint energy seems to be at the heart of the new epoch. The quantities of energy in use after 1945 became so vast, they dwarfed all that went before. The specific qualities of fossil fuels, of nuclear energy, and of hydroelectricity etched themselves into the biosphere through pollution, radiation, reservoirs, and so forth. Cheap energy gave people new leverage with which to accomplish things, move fast and far, make money, and, if inadvertently and often unknowingly, alter the environment. Almost everyone who could take advantage of cheap energy did so.

The Population Bomb

The demographic history of humankind in the years after 1945 was unlike anything that came before. The increase in human numbers impressed contemporary observers from the late 1940s onward. Most of those who paid attention to the question decried population growth—sometimes, but by no means always, on environmental grounds. Perhaps the classic statement of population anxiety came from Paul Ehrlich, a Stanford University biologist who popularized the term *population bomb* in a book of that title published in 1968. Ehrlich was wrong in many of his predictions, but he was right that the human animal was then in the middle of a population explosion, by far the biggest in its long history.

The Second World War brought early death to about sixty million people. During the war, the world contained well over two billion people, and each year some sixty to seventy million babies were born. In China, Japan, the USSR, Poland, Germany, Yugoslavia, and a few other countries, wartime mortality, and suppressed fertility, did leave a sharp imprint on demography. But in global terms all this death was swamped by a rising tide of births.

Still, the war had some delayed demographic effects. Its end triggered baby booms in several parts of the world. More importantly, medical and public health techniques and procedures, learned or refined during the war, helped launch a boom in survival, especially among infants and children. War's exigencies had legitimated massive public health interventions and taught administrators and health professionals how to deliver vaccines, antibiotics, and sanitation to the masses at modest cost, even in difficult conditions. So after 1945 human demography entered upon the most distinctive period in its two-hundred-thousand-year history. In the span of one human lifetime, 1945 to 2015, global population tripled from about 2.3 billion to 7.2 billion. This bizarre interlude, with sustained population growth of more than 1 percent per annum, is of course what almost everyone on Earth now regards as normal. It is anything but normal.

The first billion was the hardest. It took our species many thousands of years, including a brush or two with extinction, to become one billion strong. That came around 1800 or 1820. By 1930 the human population had doubled to two billion. It took only another thirty years, until 1960, to add the third billion. Then the crescendo came. The fourth billion arrived in 1975, joined by another by 1987, and then another by 1999. By 2011 or 2012 the world counted seven billion people, and had been adding a billion every twelve to fifteen years for two human generations. Between 1945 and 2015, some two-thirds of the population growth in the history of our species took place within one human lifetime. Nothing like this had ever happened before in the history of humankind.

TABLE 3

Global population increase per year, 1950–2015 (in millions)

Period	Population increase per year
1950–1955	47
1955–1960	53
1960–1965	61
1965–1970	72
1970–1975	76
1975–1980	76
1980–1985	83
1985–1990	91
1990–1995	84
1995–2000	77
2000–2005	77
2005–2010	80
2010–2015	82

Data source: UN Population Division.

One way to look at this extraordinary burst of population growth is to consider the absolute increase in the number of people per year, the annual increment or the net of births minus deaths. From 1920 to 1945 the globe had added, on average, a little over twenty million people every year. By 1950 the annual increment approached fifty million, after which it surged to about seventy-five million by the early 1970s, stabilized briefly, then in the late 1980s reached what is likely to be its all-time maximum at about eighty-nine million per year—equivalent to adding a new Germany or Vietnam (at their 2010 populations) every twelve months. Table 3 summarizes this record from 1950 to 2015.

A further way to look at the great surge in population is to focus on growth rates. For most of human history, growth rates were infinitesimal. By one careful estimate, for the seventeen centuries before 1650, annual growth came to about 0.05 percent per annum. In the

TABLE 4

Global population growth rate, 1950–2015

Period	Population growth rate (%)
1950–1955	1.79
1955–1960	1.83
1960–1965	1.91
1965–1970	2.07
1970–1975	1.96
1975–1980	1.78
1980–1985	1.78
1985–1990	1.80
1990–1995	1.52
1995–2000	1.30
2000–2005	1.22
2005–2010	1.20
2010–2015	1.15

Data source: UN Population Division.

nineteenth century, growth attained a rate of about 0.5 percent per annum, and in the first half of the twentieth, about 0.6 percent.[50] A great spike followed the Second World War (summarized in Table 4). Growth reached its apex about 1970, at some 2 percent per year. Then the rate of growth declined again, very fast after 1990, so that by 2015 it came to 1.15 percent per year. What the future holds is anyone's guess, but UN demographers project that the growth rate by 2050 will slacken to 0.34 percent, slower than in 1800. In any case, the era from 1950 to 1990, when global growth exceeded 1.75 percent per year, amounted to a burst of reproduction and survival, never before approached and never to be repeated in the history of our species. If we did somehow keep it up for another few centuries, the Earth would soon be hidden inside a giant ball of human flesh expanding outward at a radial velocity approaching the speed of light—an unlikely prospect.[51]

So we are in the waning stages of the most anomalous episode in human demographic history. The main reason (there are several others) for the steep fall in fertility is essentially environmental: urbanization. City people almost always prefer to have fewer children than their country cousins. As the world has urbanized at a dizzying pace, our fertility rates have slipped.

Nonetheless, our recent biological success is remarkable. As of 2015 we outnumbered any other large mammal on Earth by a large margin. Indeed, our total biomass (about 100 million tons) outweighed that of any mammalian rival except cattle, of which there were about 1.3 billion, weighing in at 156 million tons. Humans (whose average body size increased by half between 1800 and 2000)[52] now account for perhaps 5 percent of terrestrial animal biomass, half as much as all domestic animals combined. Ants, however, easily outweigh us.

Why did this bizarre episode in our demographic history happen? On the most basic level, it happened because the global death rate fell rapidly, from about 30 to 35 per thousand per year in 1800 to about 20 per thousand in 1945, before plummeting to 10 by the early 1980s. It now stands at 8.1. The birth rate fell also, but more gradually. Globally the crude birth rate slid from 37 per thousand in 1950 to 20 per thousand in 2015, a notable fall, but less so than the precipitous decline in the death rate.

On a less elementary level, what happened was that techniques of death control temporarily outstripped techniques of birth control. In the course of the eighteenth century in some parts of the world, notably China and Western Europe, better farming techniques, improved government response to food shortage, combined with gradual buildup of disease resistance, slowed death rates. In the nineteenth century, these processes continued and were joined by revolutionary changes in urban sanitation, mainly the provision of clean drinking water, and in the early twentieth century by vaccinations and antibiotics as well. States (and colonial administrations) created public

health agencies that sought to impose vaccination and sanitation regimes wherever they could. Medical research also identified several
disease vectors—lice, ticks, and mosquitoes, for instance—and in some
cases proceeded to find ways to keep vectors and people apart. Successful
mosquito control sharply curtailed the domain of diseases such as yellow
fever and malaria. Moreover, food scientists in the 1920s and 1930s figured out the role of specific vitamins and minerals in checking malnu-
trition diseases, and agronomists figured out how to help farmers
double and triple crop yields per acre.[53]

After 1945 all of these developments came together to lower death
tolls very quickly in most parts of the world—hence, a tremendous
surge in life expectancy, derived mainly from the survival of billions of
children who in earlier times would have died very young. In the
second half of the twentieth century, even poor people lived far longer
(on average, about twenty years longer) than their forebears had a
century previously. The gaps between rich and poor in life expectancy
narrowed almost to nothing.[54]

This rollback of death was a signal achievement of the human species and one of the greatest social changes of modern times. The end of
the twentieth century brought two exceptions that proved the rule.
First, in Russia, Ukraine, and some of their smaller neighbors, life expectancy (which in the Soviet Union had lengthened rapidly between
1946 and 1965) declined after 1975, at least for males. This departure
from the prevailing trend is usually attributed to alcoholism. Second,
after 1990 in the most AIDS-ravaged parts of Africa, a parallel reverse
of lengthening life expectancy occurred. These two exceptions had
only a slender effect on the overall pattern of longer life and faster population growth. It was a pattern that provoked considerable worry,
partly on environmental grounds.

Attempts to Curb Population

Even long ago some people worried about overpopulation. Around 500 BCE, the Chinese sage Han Feizi fretted, "Nowadays no one regards five sons as a large number, and these five sons in turn have five sons each, so that before the grandfather has died, he has twenty-five grandchildren. Hence the number of people increases, goods grow scarce, and men have to struggle and slave for a meager living."[55] The Latin author Tertullian (a North African and early Christian apologist) wrote around 200 CE: "The earth itself is currently more cultivated and developed than in early times.... Everywhere there is a dwelling, everywhere a multitude.... The greatest evidence of the large numbers of people: we are burdensome to the world, the resources are scarcely adequate to us . . . already nature does not sustain us."[56] For many centuries occasional voices repeated these concerns, and in 1798 Hong Liangji and Thomas Malthus each published essays giving a plausible theoretical underpinning to notions of overpopulation.[57]

Modern versions of these ancient anxieties gained currency in the 1940s, giving rise to sustained efforts to check population growth. For most of human history, when rulers concerned themselves with population in their domains, their aim was to maximize the number of their subjects in the interests of military strength. With the rise of social Darwinism after the 1870s, some thinkers developed doctrines of eugenics, in essence arguments that other (and "lesser") people should reproduce less. But after World War II, a chorus of voices arose warning of excess population, of impending mass starvation, of violent social unrest, and in some cases of environmental degradation—and their views attracted interest in the corridors of power.

These voices, the most prominent of which came from Europe and America, urged population limitation mainly upon the rest of the world, above all upon Asia. The motives involved were decidedly mixed,

TABLE 5

Crude birth rates (number of births per 1,000 people per year),
India and China

Year(s)	India	China
1950–1955	43	44
1970–1975	37	29
1990–1995	31	19
2010–2015	21	13

Data source: UN Population Division (http://esa.un.org/unpp/p2kodata.asp).

but in any case, in several Asian countries the same goal made sense to people coming into power as colonial rule gave way.

India, for example, an independent nation after 1947, by 1952 undertook to limit its own population. In the 1970s India even put a birth rate target in its economic five-year plan and tried to mandate sterilization for people who already had three children. This last measure encountered robust resistance, provoking violent incidents and contributing to the downfall of Indira Gandhi's government in 1977. Fertility reduction in India (see Table 5) happened much more slowly than its backers wished.[58]

In China, sterner measures brought stronger results. The People's Republic of China, born in revolution and civil war in 1949, traveled a meandering road to birth control. For millennia Chinese emperors had favored high fertility, and later Chinese nationalists such as Sun Yat-sen and Chiang Kai-shek were equally pro-natalist. At the time of the revolution, Mao Zedong agreed, feeling, as most Marxists did, that birth control would be unnecessary in communist society because communes would unleash productive forces hitherto constrained by capitalism, yielding a cornucopia of food. Soon after, he also judged that World War III was imminent and reasoned that China would need all the people it could get. In 1958 the Communist Party's second in command, Liu Shaoqi, looked forward to the day when China might have six billion people, but allowed that in this rosy future everyone would have to share beds. Others among Mao's lieutenants saw matters differently, thinking that further growth of China's huge population imperiled the economy, and after the horrendous famine of the Great Leap Forward of 1959–1961 their views acquired greater weight. But the Cultural Revolution (1966–1976), a violent political movement that plunged China into administrative and economic chaos, prevented any effective policy. In 1970 China began to encourage birth control by distributing free contraceptives. In the course of the 1970s, engineers trained in cybernetics (rocket guidance systems in particular), influenced by dour ecological forecasts of the Club of Rome, worked out the scientific rationale for drastic reductions in fertility. Through personal connections with party leaders, their views gradually prevailed, first in a series of carrots and sticks devised to encourage small families, and in 1979 in the "one-child policy." This gave party cadres great power to determine who would be allowed to have children in any given year, and imposed stiff penalties (loss of job, loss of apartment, loss of educational opportunities) on couples who did not follow instructions. Urban couples by and large fell into line; villagers sometimes did not and eventually were permitted greater leeway. The policy made exceptions for ethnic minorities, who likely would have resisted it strenuously. In China, extended families and heads of lineages had long exercised influence over when couples might have a child. This tradition made the concept of state-regulated fertility easier for Chinese to accept than it was for Indians. With these measures, among the most forceful efforts at social engineering anywhere in modern history, China reduced its annual population growth from about 2.6 percent in the late 1960s to 0.4 percent by 2015. The success of its population policy assisted China's economic miracle.[59]

A billboard promoting China's "One Child Policy," Chengdu, 1985. Implemented in 1979 by Chinese leaders fearful about overpopulation, China's program is the largest-scale effort in world history to restrict demographic growth. The policy has had many critics, but without it the world would have several hundred million more human inhabitants. (LightRocket/Getty Images)

Other East and Southeast Asian societies, notably South Korea, Singapore, and Malaysia, introduced less-draconian population limitation policies in the 1970s and 1980s, and also saw their demographic growth rates decline precipitously. This has probably helped them become much richer on a per capita basis than they otherwise would be, a matter of some consequence for their environmental history. They were swimming with the tide: Fertility declines happened almost everywhere in the post-1970 world, with or without state policies. They happened fastest in East Asia, and fastest of all in China, where unquestionably state policy played a large role.

By the 1980s the great majority of countries around the world had some sort of population policy. In Europe it usually consisted of ineffective measures to raise fertility. In most of the rest of the world, it consisted of measures, sometimes in vain, sometimes powerful, to defuse the population bomb by lowering fertility. Without these policies the world would likely have several hundred million more people, many of them Chinese.

Population and Environment

At first glance it stands to reason that population growth, especially at the rampant pace of 1945–2015, is disruptive to the environment. This has been an axiom in most strands of modern environmentalism. Its logic is straightforward: more people mean more human activity, and human activity disturbs the biosphere. As a first approximation this is true. But it turns out that it is not true always and everywhere. When and where it is true, the degree to which it is true is extremely variable. The main reason for this is that the notion of "environment" is capacious, so what may be true for soil erosion may not hold for air pollution. For example, population growth probably had a great deal to do with the clearing of West African forests since 1950 but almost nothing at all to do with nuclear contamination at the Soviet atomic weapons sites.

Population growth played its strongest role in the environment through processes connected to food production. The threefold growth in human population (1945–2010) required a proportionate expansion in food production. But even here the matter is not straightforward. Soils provide a fine example. Without a doubt, population growth pushed upward the demand for food, and also the demand for agricultural land. In China, for example, growing population and food requirements helped inspire a state-sponsored push onto the grasslands of the north, converting steppe pasture into grain fields. Frontier expansion had a long tradition in Chinese history, but rarely did it proceed at the pace achieved in the decades after 1950.[60] As is often the case when year-round grass is replaced by annual crops, the Chinese surge onto the steppe led to heightened rates of soil erosion, desertification, and downwind dust storms. Population pressure also helped push farmers onto semi-arid lands in the West and Central African Sahel (the southern fringe of the Sahara), a strategy that worked well enough in the 1960s, when rains in the region were plentiful, but turned disastrous in the 1970s when rains failed.

Population pressures also played a role in driving people to cut and burn tropical forest in search of new farmland. In Guatemala, Côte d'Ivoire, Papua New Guinea, and a hundred places in between, frontier farming edged into old forests. The effects on soils were often profound and enduring. Wherever the farmers cleared sloping land, they invited spates of soil erosion, not via the wind as on the world's grasslands, but via running water. Moreover, in many settings soils with high concentrations of iron oxides quickly turned to laterite, a brickhard surface, when exposed directly to strong sunshine. Tropical deforestation, with its attendant effects upon soils, was not always mainly a matter of population pressure. Indeed, in Latin America and Southeast Asia, quests for ranch land and timber played a larger role. But everywhere, especially in Africa, population was part of the equation.

In a few places matters worked out very differently, because population growth actually helped to stabilize landscapes. Where farmers had carved new fields out of sloping lands, they put soils at high risk to erosion. But where there was enough labor, farmers could secure their soils by cutting terraces into the hillsides. In the Machakos Hills district of Kenya's highlands, for example, rapid population growth provided the labor power for the Akamba people to build and maintain terraces and thereby reduce erosion from their fields and plots. (The soil conservation service of Kenya helped out too.) Agricultural terraces, ancient and modern, are widespread around the world, especially in the Andes, the Mediterranean hills, the Himalayas, and East and Southeast Asia. In these settings, high population densities could keep terraces and soils in place. Where population thinned, as in southern European hill districts after 1960, soil erosion often spurted.[61]

Population, Water, and Fish

Population growth was also a major factor behind the rapid climb in the use of fresh water. As Table 6 shows, between 1950 and 2010, when population tripled, water use did as well. Most of the additional water, perhaps as much as 90 percent, went to irrigation. Most irrigation water nourished food crops, although a fair bit went to cotton and other fiber crops. The world's irrigated area also tripled (1945–2010), led by India, China, and Pakistan. But in some places, including the United States, after 1980 water use leveled off (due to improved efficiency) while populations and economies continued to grow. Nonetheless, it seems a reasonable conclusion that the main reason behind the tripling of water use was the tripling of population, because irrigation for food production took the lion's share.[62]

In the seas, a similar story played out. Between 1950 and 1960, the global marine fish catch doubled, and then doubled again by 1970. It stagnated in the 1970s, grew by a quarter in the 1980s, and ever since has remained fairly steady—because all the world's major fisheries by then were fished at or above their capacity. Most famously, the historically abundant cod fisheries of the North Atlantic, from Cape Cod to Newfoundland, crashed and never recovered.[63] But the fastest expansion in marine fishing took place in Asian waters, in part because those were closest to the region of fastest-growing food demand. Indonesia, for example, which in 1950 landed less than half a million tons of fish, by 2004 brought in over four million tons. Fishermen almost everywhere had incentives to catch as much as they could as fast as they could, lest someone else get the fish first. Management regimes for fisheries that would conserve fish for another day proved especially hard to implement and enforce.[64]

TABLE 6

Global freshwater use, 1900–2011

Year	Use (km³)
1900	580
1950	1,366
1980	3,214
2011	3,900

Data sources: Peter H. Gleick, "Water Use," *Annual Review of Environment and Resources* 28, no. 1(2003): 275–314; World Bank, http://data.worldbank.org/indicator/ER.H2O.FWTL.K3/countries ?display=graph.

Again, as with the changes to forests and soils, population was only part of the story with fisheries. The global marine fish catch quintupled between 1950 and 2008, while population growth nearly tripled. As a rough estimate, one can say that 60 percent of the expansion of the marine fish catch derived from population growth.[65] But this arithmetic remains rough, and in any case does not capture cases in which tremendous expansions of fishing took place because of new technologies that lowered costs. The humble menhaden of the western North Atlantic, fished for centuries, after 1945 became the target of intensified industrial fishing efforts, abetted by airplane spotters that made it easy for fishing boats to follow the schools. Population growth had little, if anything, to do with the rapid exhaustion of menhaden fisheries.[66]

Population and the Atmosphere

Some environmental changes had no direct relationship with food production. In these cases the role of population pressure is harder to specify. Consider, for example, the accumulation of carbon dioxide, the most important greenhouse gas, in the atmosphere. Over the past two hundred years, carbon emissions have come from two main sources, fossil fuel use (about three-quarters) and the burning of forests (one-quarter). Population growth no doubt increased demand for fossil fuels and helped drive the encroachment on the world's forests. So to some degree, population growth has led to growth in carbon emissions. But how much?

As we will see later in more detail, carbon dioxide concentrations in the atmosphere climbed after the Industrial Revolution. By 1945 they stood at about 310 parts per million, and in 2014 surpassed 400. In that span, carbon emissions (not concentrations) increased about eightfold. So at a first approximation, given the tripling of population in the same time period, one might suppose that population growth is responsible for about three-eighths, or 37.5 percent, of the accumulation of carbon dioxide.

But that can stand only as a first approximation. Afghanistan, which showed high population growth, emitted very little carbon, less than 2 percent of the United Kingdom's total. The carbon consequences of population growth depended heavily on where it happened. Not only did an additional person in the UK lead to more carbon emissions than the addition of a person in Afghanistan, but there was a difference between an Afghan in Kabul (more likely to use more fossil fuel) and one in a remote village. And when population growth happened mattered too. In the rich countries after 1980, programs of energy efficiency, fuel switching away from carbon-rich coal, deindustrialization, and other developments meant that the impact of each additional person was less than it had been in the 1950s. For the years 1975–1996, one mathematically inclined scholar found that population growth was a major force behind carbon emissions, but, interestingly, least so in both the very poor and the very rich countries. The sad truth is that there is no reliable way to calculate the impact of population growth upon carbon emissions over time.[67]

Sometimes Population Did Not Matter at All

While the important case of carbon emissions is an elusive one, it is easy to find examples of environmental change in which one can confidently say population growth scarcely mattered at all. Whaling, which in the years after 1945 brought several whales—blue, grey, humpback, for example—to the brink of extinction, bore only the smallest relationship to population. The great whaling nations—Norway, Iceland, Japan, the USSR—had slow population growth rates, and their whalers were responding to long-standing cultural preferences for whale meat rather than seeking more food due to population growth.

The corrosion of the stratospheric ozone layer, which occurred almost entirely after 1945, also had virtually nothing to do with population growth. The chemical releases that destroyed stratospheric ozone, mainly chlorofluorocarbons (CFCs), were used chiefly as insulation, refrigerants, aerosol propellants, and solvents. Very little in the way of CFC releases occurred where population growth was high. The only ozone-destroying substance used in agriculture, a pesticide called methyl bromide, was used mainly in places such as California for high-end crops such as strawberries and almonds, demand for which had everything to do with elevated tastes and improved shipping capabilities and almost nothing to do with population growth.

To take a final example, environmental disasters, frequent enough in the decades after 1945, had no discernible relationship to population growth. The great industrial accident near Seveso in 1976, which splattered dioxin over the countryside north of Milan, occurred in a region of extremely low population growth. In the worst industrial accident in history, in 1984, a Union Carbide chemical plant spewed 40 tons of lethal methyl isocyanate onto Bhopal, a city of one million in central India, killing several thousand people and sickening many more. It too had nothing to do with population growth.[68] The Chernobyl catastrophe occurred in 1986. The reactor existed to provide electricity; the accident occurred because of design flaws and human error. In the 1980s population growth in Ukraine was negligible.

Migration and Environment

Like population growth, migration had variable impacts upon the environment. The largest migration after 1945 was the stampede of villagers to cities, with myriad environmental effects. Migration from one city to another had much smaller effects, except in cases where new cities bloomed in formerly sparsely inhabited places. Migration from one rural area to another, however, often triggered profound environmental changes.

The decades after 1945 were an age of migration. Tens of millions moved from one country to another.[69] Even more moved within their countries, although often to very new environments. Millions of Americans moved from the "Rust Belt" to the "Sun Belt," to Florida, Texas, and California in particular. San Antonio, which had a quarter million inhabitants in 1940, by 2010 had nearly 1.5 million and had become the seventh largest city in the United States.[70] Cities such as Phoenix and Las Vegas grew from almost nothing into major metropolises, sprawling into surrounding deserts and siphoning off all available water for many miles around. Residents air-conditioned their homes and workplaces for most months of the year, leading electricity-intensive lives that encouraged additional fossil fuel use and the building of more hydroelectric dams, especially on the already overdrawn Colorado River.

A smaller, Chinese sunbelt migration took place into the even drier regions of Xinjiang and Tibet after 1950. Government policy had more to do with it than air conditioning. Millions of Chinese went to Xinjiang in northwest China, an autonomous region consisting of a string of oases thinly populated with ethnic minorities. Many of the migrants were compelled to go, especially during the Cultural Revolution

(1966–1976). In Xinjiang, ethnic Chinese are now probably a majority, despite having a much lower birth rate than the Uighurs and other local populations. These migrations led to cultural and ethnic frictions, but also to new environmental stresses such as water and fuelwood shortages and desertification. Increased water demand, partly due to the influx of migrants, has reduced Xinjiang's lake area by half since 1950.[71]

In Mao's time, few Chinese moved to Tibet, the elevated plateau region bordering on the Himalayas that was incorporated into China in the 1950s. But in the 1980s and 1990s several hundred thousand went, often as laborers on road and railway projects. Since the 1980s the government has encouraged Chinese migration. According to the official census, ethnic Chinese made up 6 percent of Tibet's population in 1953 and slightly more by 2000. But unofficial estimates suggest Han Chinese now outnumber Tibetans in Tibet—if one counts their actual rather than official residence. Unlike in Xinjiang, the migrants flocked mainly to the cities of Tibet, but also to mining enclaves and labor camps around construction projects. The delicate high-altitude ecosystems of Tibet are easily disrupted, and wetlands, grasslands, wildlife, and air quality all suffered from the population expansion and development projects. In recent years the government has tried to check the environmental disturbance caused by railroads, by, for example, building overpasses for migratory wildlife. It has also tried to settle Tibetan nomadic herders into villages in the name of ecological stability, on the grounds that Tibetans and their herds were degrading grasslands.[72]

Migrants altered rainforests in Brazil and Indonesia at least as much as they did arid lands in the United States and China. Again, state policies played crucial roles. Many states, including Brazil and Indonesia, often encouraged and subsidized migration. Moreover, states obliged or encouraged migrants to engage in certain activities that just so happened to carry powerful environmental consequences.

For centuries, outsiders had seen in Amazonia—nine times the size of Texas and nearly twice the area of India—a sprawling storehouse of riches and resources, awaiting development. A rubber boom (ca. 1880–1913) gave tantalizing evidence of the wealth one might tap. But even businessmen with the savvy and resources of Henry Ford failed in their quests to convert Amazonian nature into money. Ford tried to build an empire of rubber plantations, called Fordlandia, beginning in the mid-1920s, but fell afoul of his own delusions and uncooperative local conditions, especially a rubber-tree fungus. When Ford's grandson sold off the ruins of Fordlandia in 1945, Amazonia had only about thirty thousand people in it.[73]

In the 1950s and early 1960s, the Brazilian government undertook another development scheme for the two-thirds of Amazonia that falls within Brazil. It was, as the saying went, a land without men for men without land. The government—a military regime from 1964 to 1985—intended to relieve poverty (and deflate the recurrent pressures for land reform) in the dry northeast of Brazil. It also wished to populate the country's border regions with loyal Brazilians, and to mobilize the presumed natural wealth of the world's largest moist tropical forest. Thousands of miles of highways soon pierced the forest, and millions of migrants flowed into the region. They cut and burned patches of forest, mainly in order to run cattle on the newly cleared land. Parts of Amazonia increasingly became a land without trees for men with cattle. Soils in most of the region are low in nutrients, so ranchers usually found that after a few years they needed to move on, to cut and burn more forest to keep their cattle in pasture. Soybean farmers, increasingly prominent since the 1990s, found the same conditions. By 2010 about 15 to 20 percent of the forest area of 1970 had been cleared for grass or crops, but the rate of forest clearance had dropped sharply. The issue of Amazonian deforestation had become a perennial one in Brazilian politics and in global environmental politics as well.[74]

A section of rainforest in the Amazon Basin, Brazil, clear-cut for transformation into farmland, 2009. Forested area in Amazonia shrank by about 15–20 percent from 1965 to 2012. (© Ton Koene/Visuals Unlimited/Corbis)

Indonesia became an independent, if rickety, country in 1949. Most of the population, and all of the leadership, lived on the fertile volcanic island of Java. Most of the other islands had poorer soils and scant population, usually of minorities with no love for Javanese rule. Building on a small program pursued by their former colonial masters, the Dutch, the rulers of independent Indonesia launched the so-called transmigration scheme in 1949. Military men (like their counterparts in Brazil), they hoped that some fifty million politically reliable Javanese would resettle on the other islands, notably Borneo and Sumatra. The plan was to relieve population pressure and poverty on Java, harvest the natural resources of the outer islands, and swamp the local populations with durably loyal Javanese.

By 1990, when the transmigration program had wound down, something under five million Javanese migrants had taken the lure of free land on the outer islands. They found their rice-farming skills did not yield encouraging results on the poor soils of Sumatra and Borneo, and until 1984 the government decreed that they should raise only rice. Like ranchers in Amazonia, they had to move to new land frequently, burning as they went, in order to gain access to the nutrients stored in the ash of former forests. Coming from a thoroughly deforested island, the Javanese often found it comforting to eliminate what felt like an alien habitat. Their efforts added to the pace of deforestation in Indonesia, which from 1970 to 2000 was one of the world's most active frontiers of forest destruction.[75]

These great migrations, and others like them, led to environmental changes of considerable magnitude. The changes were mainly local and regional in scope, although deforestation anywhere added appreciably to the carbon dioxide loading of the entire atmosphere. Despite their limited scope, the environmental changes provoked by migration were often thorough and of much more consequence, where they occurred, than greenhouse gas accumulation or climate change—at least up to the present.

Migration also contributed to heating up the global greenhouse through the relocation of people to places where they could lead much more energy-intensive lives. Tens of millions left Central America or the Caribbean for the United States and Canada, or North Africa for Western Europe, or South Asia for the Persian Gulf. To the extent that they succeeded in adopting the lifestyles of their new homes— driving cars, heating and cooling their dwellings with fossil fuels— their migration added to global energy consumption and thereby to greenhouse gas accumulation and the warming of the planet.

The period 1945–2015 witnessed a great crescendo in the human population history of the world. No period of similar duration—one human lifetime—was anywhere near as peculiar as this one. If population growth ever mattered for environmental change, it surely should have done so in these decades.

And it did matter. But not always and everywhere, and not necessarily in clear and obvious ways. For some forms of environmental change, such as West African deforestation, population growth played a leading role. For others, such as whaling, it played only a small role at most. As is normal in human affairs, population growth was never the sole cause of anything, but always operated in concert with other factors.

The same was true of migration. The decades after 1945 saw an upturn in rates of long-distance migration. This too brought environmental consequences, especially in those cases where people went from one sort of environment to a very different and unfamiliar one. Their accustomed ways of doing things, whether growing rice or raising cattle, often carried unforeseen and dramatic environmental consequences in their new homes.

For more than fifty years now, environmentalists have anxiously pointed to population growth as a major cause behind environmental change. That claim has often been justified, but it falls well short of a universal truth. By unpacking the concept of "environment" into specific biomes and processes, one can get a little further than this blanket proposition. In fifty more years, if the demographers are right and population growth has slowed to zero or close to it, we shall have a firmer idea of its significance for environmental change, both in general and for the exuberant age of 1945–2015. Let us hope that no gigantic ecological catastrophe intervenes to complicate the analysis.

CHAPTER TWO

Climate and Biological Diversity

The Earth's climate is enormously complex, involving subtle and imperfectly understood relationships between the Sun, atmosphere, oceans, lithosphere (Earth's crust), pedosphere (soils), and terrestrial biosphere (forests, mostly). But over the course of the twentieth century, in particular from the late 1950s onward, knowledge of the Earth's climate advanced very quickly. By the late twentieth century, scientific research had reached near-consensus on the accuracy of a long-advanced and troubling forecast for the Earth's climate. This, of course, was the idea that human activities since the beginning of the Industrial Revolution had altered climate and begun heating the Earth. Variously labeled the "enhanced greenhouse effect," "global warming," or "anthropogenic climate change," the problem centered mostly on human interference in the planet's carbon cycle. By burning fossil fuels and emitting carbon dioxide (CO_2) and other gases, humans were increasing the concentrations of powerful heat-trapping gases in the atmosphere. Scientists feared potentially catastrophic consequences for the world's climate if these trends were left unchecked. Spurred by the increasing volume and quality of research on the subject, as well as by new technologies that enabled improved monitoring of the Earth's climate, these predictions became increasingly dire. Yet there was an enormous gap between what scientists thought needed to happen to avoid catastrophe and the reality of global climate-change politics. By 2015 there was increasingly strong evidence that the Earth's climate and the operation of its many ecosystems had already begun to change in response to higher CO_2 levels.

Climate and the Industrial Revolution

The Earth's atmosphere is the reason the planet is neither freezing cold nor burning hot. In highly simplified terms, almost one-third of solar radiation is instantly reflected back into space. A bit more than two-thirds of the incoming solar radiation that strikes the Earth is absorbed and converted into infrared energy (heat) by the Earth's surface, oceans, or atmosphere, and re-radiated in all directions. Greenhouse gases (GHGs), of which there are several types, absorb most of this infrared (or long-wave) energy. Naturally occurring greenhouse gases include water vapor, methane, carbon dioxide, and nitrous oxide. There are also several that do not occur in nature but that have been created by humans. The most important of these are CFCs, first invented in the laboratory in the 1920s. Each gas captures energy at different wavelengths, and each has different characteristics, such as absorptive power and duration in the atmosphere. Each, moreover, exists in the atmosphere at different concentrations, and the concentration of each gas has varied substantially over geological time. Very recently, at the onset of the Industrial Revolution, the naturally occurring concentrations were about 0.7 parts per million (ppm) for methane, 280 ppm for CO_2, and 288 parts per billion (ppb) for nitrous oxide. The concentration of every one of these has risen since.[1]

Atmospheric gas concentrations are not the only determinants of climate. Other factors influence the amount of solar radiation that reaches the Earth's surface and the amount absorbed or reflected. Developments that occur in and on the Earth itself also have an influence on climate. These, in turn, can interact in complicated fashion with GHG concentrations. The output of the Sun itself can vary, which influences the amount of solar radiation reaching the Earth. Slight oscillations of the Earth's axial rotation and orbit about the Sun are other factors affecting climate. These oscillations, known as Milanković cycles, occur over many thousands of years and help shape the timing of the Earth's ice ages. The amount of solar radiation that reaches the Earth's surface is also influenced by aerosols, which are airborne particles that block incoming radiation. Volcanic eruptions can influence global temperatures. The ash and soot emitted by volcanoes can reach the stratosphere and encircle the globe, increasing the amount of aerosols. If large enough, a single volcano's eruption can be sufficient to reduce global temperatures, albeit temporarily (a few years), until rain washes the particles out of the atmosphere. The largest recorded eruptions in world history have had significant short-term temperature effects in just this manner, as occurred after the Laki eruption of 1783 (in Iceland) and the Tambora eruption of 1815 and the Krakatau eruption of 1883 (both in Indonesia).

Although more stable than what occurred before, the Holocene climate (which began roughly twelve thousand years ago) has had marked fluctuations. Temperatures in the early Holocene were as much as 5 degrees Celsius warmer than during the trough of the previous ice age. During the Holocene, the peak occurred between eight thousand and five thousand years ago, when temperatures ranged up to 3 degrees Celsius warmer at the highest (most northerly) latitudes than the average for the Holocene. Natural temperature variation has occurred in more recent history as well. Between 1100 and 1300 CE, Europe experienced a warm spell called the medieval climate anomaly, followed by the Little Ice Age, which lasted from roughly 1350 to 1850 and had temperatures almost a degree Celsius colder on average than currently.

The concern about anthropogenic climate change centers primarily on human interference in the natural cycling of carbon during the industrial era. The world's store of carbon is cycled between the lithosphere, pedosphere, biosphere, atmosphere, and oceans. However, human activities since the Industrial Revolution have altered the distribution of carbon across these spheres. In essence, the climate change problem arises from the fact that humans have removed carbon from the Earth and placed it in the atmosphere at rates much faster than occurs naturally. Humans have also increased the concentration of other carbon-containing greenhouse gases. Methane (CH_4), also known as natural gas, when burned is transformed into CO_2 and water. The main problem with methane, however, stems from direct release into the atmosphere. On a per-molecule basis, methane is far more powerful than carbon dioxide at trapping heat.[2]

There are two basic ways humans have added carbon to the atmosphere. First, carbon is released through deforestation, via burnt or decaying wood and from newly exposed, carbon-rich soils. Deforestation is an ancient phenomenon, but the greatest acceleration of deforestation on a global level has occurred since 1945. Conversely, growing forests absorb carbon from the atmosphere. Hence, the amount of carbon added to the atmosphere through deforestation is always a net figure, in effect deforestation minus afforestation. Net deforestation and other land-use changes currently add about 15 percent of total anthropogenic carbon into the atmosphere (as of 2015).[3]

Second, and more importantly, carbon is released through the burning of fossil fuels. Humans have shifted carbon stored in the lithosphere (in the form of coal, oil, and natural gas) to the atmosphere and thereby to the oceans. Consider the amount of carbon released into the atmosphere from fossil fuel burning. In 1750, before the Industrial Revolution began, humankind released perhaps 3 million metric tons of carbon into the atmosphere in this manner annually. A century later, in 1850, the figure was around 50 million tons. Another century later, at the end of World War II, it had increased more than twenty-fold, to about 1,200 million tons. Then after 1945 humankind embarked upon a fiesta of fossil fuel combustion. Within fifteen years after the war ended, humans were putting around 2,500 million tons of carbon into the atmosphere each year. In 1970 this figure increased to over 4,000 million tons, in 1990 to over 6,000, and in 2015 to some 9,500 million tons—about 3,200 times more than in the year 1750 and eight times the total in 1945. By the turn of the twenty-first century, fossil fuels had become responsible for around 85 percent of anthropogenic carbon added to the atmosphere.[4]

Increased anthropogenic carbon emissions translated into increased atmospheric CO_2 concentrations. Carbon dioxide concentrations are now around 400 ppm, compared with the 280 ppm preindustrial baseline. This concentration is the highest CO_2 level reached in the last several hundred thousand years and possibly the last twenty million years. In 1958, when the first reliable, direct, and continuous measurement of atmospheric CO_2 began, concentration levels stood at 315 ppm. Since then the measured concentration has increased every year. It is unlikely that at any other time in the long history of the atmosphere CO_2 concentrations have jumped by one-fourth within fifty years.

Recent emission trends have been especially noteworthy. The rate of increase in carbon dioxide emissions during the 2000s was more than twice that of the 1990s (3.3 percent versus 1.3 percent global annual growth). The continuing if uneven growth of the global economy provided only part of the explanation. More troublesome was the carbon intensity of the global economy (CO_2 emissions per unit of economic activity). The global economy had been decarbonizing since about 1970, yet after 2000 the process went into reverse. Economic growth became more, rather than less, dependent on carbon-heavy fuels, in particular coal burned in China.[5]

By the last decades of the twentieth century, it appeared as if the world's climate was indeed shifting as a result of increased atmospheric carbon dioxide, methane, and other GHGs. Temperature data showed a mean surface atmospheric warming of about 0.8 degrees Celsius over the average of the twentieth century. The rate of change was greatest at the end of the century. Roughly three-quarters of the increase occurred after the mid-1970s, the remainder before 1940. Since the 1970s, each successive decade has been warmer than all previous recorded ones; in 2010 the National Aeronautics and Space Administration (NASA) in the United States announced that the decade of the 2000s was the warmest on record. Temperature increases were greatest at the highest latitudes in the Northern Hemisphere, consistent with climate models that forecast the greatest warming at the poles and the least in the tropics.[6]

Increased carbon dioxide in the atmosphere also had important consequences for the world's oceans. As with the atmosphere, measurements showed that the oceans had warmed during the second half of the twentieth century. The upper 300 meters of the oceans warmed a bit less than 0.2 degrees Celsius after 1950, while the upper 3,000 meters warmed just shy of 0.04 degrees. This may not sound like much, but given the density of water and the immense volume of the oceans, these small increases represented an enormous amount of thermal energy. Since 1950 the upper 3,000 meters of ocean had absorbed more than fourteen times the amount of energy absorbed by the continents.

Increasing oceanic temperatures began to have real effects, especially on sea levels and sea ice. Sea levels rose slightly over the twentieth century—about 15 centimeters, roughly half of which was from the thermal expansion of water and the other half from melting ice sheets in places such as Greenland. Arctic sea ice also began melting. Spring and summer sea ice cover in the Arctic Ocean retreated perhaps 10 to 15 percent over the second half of the twentieth century. As with atmospheric temperatures, the rate of change was greatest toward the end of the twentieth century and the beginning of the twenty-first. Trends for the sea ice surrounding the Antarctic were less clear. A disconcerting event occurred in 2009, when a part of the enormous Wilkins Ice Shelf collapsed; but while some areas around the continent were losing ice, others appeared to be gaining. The total amount of Antarctic sea ice may even have increased since 1970.[7]

Increasing temperature was not the only consequence for the world's oceans. Part of the atmosphere's CO_2 is absorbed by the world's "sinks," meaning soils, forests, oceans, and rocks. The precise functioning of sinks is still debated, but roughly half the CO_2 emitted through burning fossil fuels winds up in various sinks. Oceans are responsible for about half of this figure. Without this service provided by the oceans, atmospheric concentrations of CO_2 would be far higher. Unfortunately, this service is not without consequences. By the turn of the twenty-first century, there was good evidence that the cumulative, additional CO_2 taken up by the oceans had begun to alter their chemistry. Increasing carbon dioxide levels acidify the oceans, which makes it more difficult for some organisms to manufacture their skeletons and shells. A few of these imperiled creatures are critical food for whales and fish. Even more ominously, there is some evidence that oceans and other sinks such as forests may be having an increasingly difficult time absorbing atmospheric carbon dioxide. It is possible that some sinks could switch to net producers rather than absorbers of CO_2, as might occur if tropical forests dry out due to higher temperatures.[8]

The potential risks of climate change are numerous, few more threatening than the alteration to the world's water supply. Increased atmospheric temperatures likely will alter a great many of the world's ecosystems, change regional precipitation patterns, cause more frequent and extreme weather events, raise sea levels and erode coastlines, harm the world's biological diversity, enhance the spread of infectious diseases, and cause more heat-related human fatalities, among many other effects. By the onset of the twenty-first century, most scientists believed that increasing atmospheric temperatures had already begun to have such impacts. Glacial melt was one example. During the twentieth century there was increasing evidence that the world's glaciers were retreating, with the rate of decline much quicker at the end of the century than at the beginning. Glaciers in the European Alps, for instance, melted at the rate of 1 percent per year between 1975 and 2000, and at a rate of 2 to 3 percent after 2000. This was a global trend. Scientific tracking of thirty "reference" glaciers scattered around the globe revealed that melting after 1996 was four times as great as between 1976 and 1985.[9]

Concerns about glacial retreat might seem esoteric. Glaciers are far away in both mind and geography. The great majority of the world's ice is locked up at the poles, within the glaciers covering Greenland and Antarctica. Nearly everyone has heard of the risks of sea-level rise from the melting of these polar glaciers, but this particular problem seems to be a concern for the distant future. As for the world's glaciers that are not at the poles, what does it matter if they melt? How important is it to most Americans, for instance, that the glaciers in their soon-to-be-inaccurately-named Glacier National Park (in Montana) are almost gone? Not much, perhaps, outside of some aesthetic lament. Yet in many parts of the world, the spring and summer melt from glaciers is a matter of life and death. A critical illustration of this is provided by the Himalayas and nearby Central Asian mountain ranges, which hold the largest amount of ice outside the polar regions. These ranges are the source of Asia's most important rivers, including the Indus, Yangzi, Mekong, Ganges, Yellow, Brahmaputra, and Irrawaddy, which collectively sustain more than two billion people. Higher temperatures in the Himalayas, in particular at high elevations, has meant increased glacial melt over the past several decades. The fear is that decreased glacier sizes and snowpack will alter both the amount and the seasonal timing of river water, with dramatic and negative effects for downstream communities that depend on these rivers for irrigation agriculture, for drinking water, and for much else. Indeed, the ecosystems that support these two billion people are likely to undergo major changes.[10]

While the melting of glaciers that people have come to depend on has filled some observers with foreboding for the future, millions of people unconcerned with climate change likely have felt its indirect effects. One indirect effect of a warmer atmosphere is the increased capacity of air to hold water vapor. This, paradoxically, has improved the odds of both droughts and downpours. In dry parts of the world, warmer air can hold more moisture and so less falls as rain. In places already

An empty chasm left behind by the retreat of the South Annapurna glacier in the Nepalese Himalayas, 2012. Since the end of the nineteenth century, many glaciers around the world have retreated due to rising average temperatures. Rapid glacier retreat in the Himalayas since 1980 threatens to create water shortages in South, Southeast, and East Asia. (© Ashley Cooper/Corbis)

given to heavy rain, warmer air allows still greater rainfalls, because there is more moisture to be squeezed out of the clouds. Thus, areas such as the American Southwest have become more subject to drought, while drenching monsoon rains have brought more drastic floods to the Himalayan foothills.[11] Meanwhile, warmer sea surface temperatures have probably spawned more tropical cyclones. Even though one cannot attribute any specific weather event, whether Hurricane Katrina in 2005 or the Pakistan megaflood of 2010, to climate change, over time such events became more likely as a result of warmer temperatures. Trotsky is credited (probably wrongly) with saying, "You may not be interested in war, but war will be interested in you." So it has been with climate change and the world's vulnerable populations, whether in the low-lying wards of New Orleans or along the Indus River: they may not be interested in climate change, but climate change will be interested in them.

History of Climate Science

Given the complexity of the Earth's climate, it should come as no surprise that advanced scientific understanding of climate is very recent. Scientific understanding has required a high degree of interdisciplinary cooperation involving geophysicists, oceanographers, meteorologists, biologists, physicists, geologists, mathematicians, and specialists from a host of other disciplines. As a global phenomenon, climate change has provoked scientific collaboration across international boundaries. The history of climate science thus has been marked by both of these forms of cooperation. Although there is much yet to learn about how the climate changes, the past half century has seen enormous scientific progress. Concern about rising CO_2 levels has motivated a good part of the increased scientific attention to the problem. Technological instruments, such as satellites that became available only after the onset of the Cold War, helped translate that attention into information and understanding. These instruments have been fundamental to gathering and assessing the data needed to map the history of the Earth's climate, to model its workings, and—within sharp limits—to predict its future.

The first attempts to explain why the Earth has a habitable atmosphere occurred during the nineteenth century. The French natural philosopher Jean-Baptiste Joseph Fourier, writing in the 1820s, argued that the atmosphere traps a portion of incoming solar radiation, thereby raising its temperature far above what would otherwise be the case. He likened the atmosphere's influence on temperature to the glass covering a greenhouse, an imperfect analogy that nonetheless stuck. Over the course of the nineteenth century, scientists in other parts of

Europe wrestled with basic questions about how the Earth's climate functioned. They were provoked in large part by the Swiss polymath Louis Agassiz, who wrote in 1840 that the Earth had experienced past ice ages. Hence, much of the subsequent scientific work centered on understanding how the climate could change so dramatically over time. Among these curious scientists was John Tyndall, a British physicist who in the 1850s discovered the infrared absorptive capacity of CO_2. Even more important was the work of the Swedish scientist Svante Arrhenius, who published a groundbreaking paper in 1896 that outlined the basic relationship between CO_2 and climate. Arrhenius calculated the global temperature changes that might result if levels of the gas were to increase or decrease. He estimated a temperature increase of 5.7 degrees Celsius if CO_2 levels were to double, but dismissed the possibility that humans could emit so much carbon into the atmosphere.[12]

Arrhenius's paper sparked considerable debate, but its impact was limited by a lack of basic scientific understanding of various Earth systems, poor data, and a conceptual lens that refused to consider that humans had the power to alter the Earth's climate. For instance, Arrhenius could only estimate the concentration of atmospheric CO_2, as no one had yet been able to measure it reliably. But the early decades of the twentieth century nonetheless were marked by scientific progress in other areas relevant to the study of climate. In interwar Europe, the Serbian mathematician Milutin Milanković refined the theory that the Earth's oscillations and solar orbit were responsible for the ice ages. His painstaking calculations resulted in an understanding of the cycles that bear his name. At about the same time in the Soviet Union, the geochemist Vladimir Vernadsky was working on the natural carbon cycle. He argued that living organisms in the biosphere were responsible for the chemical content of the atmosphere, adding much of its nitrogen, oxygen, and CO_2. Hence, plants and other living organisms were foundational to the Earth's climatic history.[13]

The basic understanding of Earth systems developed in the nineteenth and early twentieth centuries, but one big breakthrough in climate science occurred after 1945. As the Cold War spurred increases in public funding of the hard sciences, it was not surprising that American scientists became important figures. In the 1950s a group of scientists at Scripps Institution of Oceanography, near San Diego, funneled small amounts of defense-related funding toward their studies of CO_2 in the atmosphere and oceans. Two of them, Charles Keeling and Roger Revelle, created the first reliable atmospheric carbon dioxide monitoring station. They placed newly developed, sophisticated equipment atop Hawaii's Mauna Loa volcano, chosen because the air circulating about the remote location was not contaminated by emissions from local power plants or factories. The Mauna Loa station gave scientists their first true and reliable measurements of atmospheric CO_2 concentrations. Within a couple of years, the station established that concentrations were indeed rising. The Mauna Loa time series has produced data continuously since 1958; in the process, its sawtooth upward curve has become one of the most widely known visuals of anthropogenic climate change.[14] The sawtooth pattern represents the seasonal changes in CO_2 in the Northern Hemisphere: in the summer months when the leaves are out, more carbon is in trees and bushes and less in the atmosphere. In the winter the atmosphere has a little more CO_2.

The Mauna Loa initiative occurred within the context of the International Geophysical Year (IGY), a collaborative global research effort that highlighted both US and Soviet technical and scientific capabilities. But the IGY also spoke to scientists' desire to develop geophysical monitoring and assessment systems using the powerful new tools that had recently become available to them. Between the 1950s and 1970s, scientists could take advantage of the first satellites to study the Earth and the first mainframe computers to develop and run crude models of the Earth's climate. Cold War–driven exploration of the polar regions

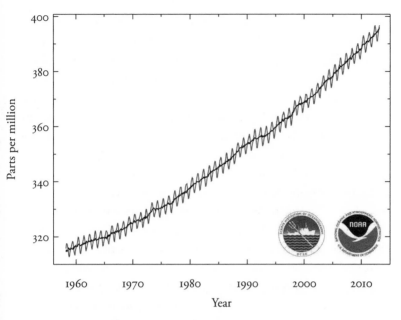

Atmospheric CO_2 at the Mauna Loa Observatory, Hawaii.

generated the first ice core drilling programs. These enabled scientists to analyze air bubbles buried in the polar ice caps that were hundreds of thousands of years old, thereby discovering information about past climates. The Americans drilled the first ice core in the late 1950s, for purely military reasons, at Camp Century in Greenland; it gave scientists useful data anyway. The Soviets had their own program at Vostok Station in the Antarctic. Starting in the 1970s, their drilling eventually produced cores extending back more than four hundred thousand years, giving scientists access to air pockets over several glacial periods.[15]

Cold War–related research overlapped with increasing scientific effort in other international contexts. The scale of the research problem, the resources needed to tackle it, and a desire to share expertise meant not only increasing scientific cooperation but also greater support from international institutions such as the World Meteorological Organization (WMO) and, later, the United Nations Environment Programme (UNEP). By the 1960s a number of prominent scientists had begun to address the possibility that anthropogenic climate change was possible. Research was sufficiently advanced to place the issue on the agenda of the UN-sponsored 1972 Stockholm environmental conference. Scientific advances continued through the 1970s, prodded by continuing technical and methodological improvements, better data, and more sophisticated research networks. American scientists continued to be leaders in the field, owing in part to support provided by organizations such as the National Academy of Sciences. The 1970s closed with the first international conference dedicated exclusively to climate change, held in Geneva in 1979 and organized by the WMO and UNEP.[16] Climatology, hitherto a domain of specialists trained in the precise sciences, would soon enter the messy arena of politics.

Climate Science Meets Climate Politics

Until the 1980s, discussion of anthropogenic climate change had been confined largely to the scientific community. There had been some political awareness and media coverage during the 1970s, but the issue was too new and abstract to receive much of a hearing. Moreover, the scientific consensus about warming was relatively weak. But the 1980s were a watershed decade, as scientific agreement about anthropogenic warming strengthened and the issue became political for the first time.

Partly this change stemmed from heightened awareness of atmospheric environmental problems. Acid rain became an important political issue regionally, in Europe and eastern North America, from the late 1970s. Political concern about the thinning of the ozone layer suddenly emerged during the 1980s, but, in contrast to acid rain, on a global level. The 1986 discovery of an ozone "hole" over the Antarctic stimulated public interest and gave a major boost to negotiation of the Montreal Protocol in 1987. This agreement, which committed signatories to reduce their emissions of CFCs, brought scientists into global atmospheric politics. Public awareness of the ozone hole was still fresh in 1988, when record-breaking heat and drought in North America helped stimulate public and governmental interest in institutionalizing climate change politics at the global level. That year the WMO and UNEP helped to create the Intergovernmental Panel on Climate Change (IPCC), a scientific body charged with arriving at a consensus position on anthropogenic warming. Since then the IPCC has produced four large assessment reports, in 1990, 1995, 2001, 2007, and most recently in 2014. All were based on comprehensive reviews of the scientific evidence surrounding climate change. These became increasingly assertive in linking climate change to human activities and in warning of the urgent need for a global political response. The 2014 report was blunt: "Human influence on the climate system is clear, and recent anthropogenic emissions of greenhouse gases are the highest in history. Recent climate changes have had widespread impacts on human and natural systems." The IPCC leadership had to defend each report, in particular from a small but vocal and well-placed group of climate skeptics who attacked the IPCC's approach, evidence, motives, or legitimacy.[17]

The IPCC's work occurred in parallel to global political negotiations aimed at lowering anthropogenic CO_2 emissions. The process began in earnest in 1988, when the UN General Assembly labeled climate change a "common concern of mankind." In a startlingly short period, diplomats hammered out a Framework Convention on Climate Change, signed at the Rio Earth Summit in 1992. Although its provisions were nonbinding, the treaty put into motion regular diplomatic negotiations aimed at creating a more substantive agreement. Follow-up meetings over the next few years set the stage for negotiation of the Kyoto Protocol in 1997, a binding agreement that mandated small emissions cuts (compared with the baseline year established in the Protocol, 1990) by the world's rich countries.

But trouble appeared immediately as rifts among the world's biggest greenhouse gas emitters threatened to undermine the Kyoto agreement. These divisions cast a pall over subsequent diplomacy, which for twenty years achieved nothing of substance. (In those twenty years, 1995–2015, the total tonnage of global carbon emissions from the energy sector nearly equaled that of all human history prior to 1995.)[18] The two largest polluters, the United States and China, resisted binding agreements on emissions. In general, both China and the United States took self-serving positions in climate diplomacy, content to let the perfect become the enemy of the good.

In the American case, domestic political resistance made it exceptionally difficult for even the most willing presidential administration to commit the United States to deep emissions cuts. A sizable chunk of the American public did not accept the consensus of climate change science, and interested industries both encouraged that skepticism and lobbied Congress to prevent emissions agreements. US per capita emissions remained among the highest in the world even after the US total was eclipsed by China's in 2006. Nonetheless, the US diplomatic position emphasized the need for the largest developing countries, in particular China, India, and Brazil—all of which had much lower per capita emissions—to be party to any mandatory greenhouse gas emission cuts framework.

China, on the other hand, argued that the industrialized countries should make commitments first, on the grounds that their cumulative emissions over the centuries were highest and that they had already benefited economically from heavy use of fossil fuels in ways that China had not. China also pointed to the per capita emissions rates as a key measure of responsibility and a reason the United States should move first to restrain its emissions. Chinese diplomats championed the Kyoto

Protocol, which exempted China from any constraints on its carbon emissions.

Other large developing countries took positions similar to China's. India, for instance, which in 2009 overtook Russia to become the third-largest CO_2 emitter, argued that the world's richest countries had a moral duty to make emissions cuts. New Delhi's diplomats, like Beijing's, maintained that poorer countries had the right to continued high emissions in the interest of their own economic development. Together with several other developing countries, India lobbied hard for the transfer of mitigation technologies and expertise from the rich to the poor world, and for a sliver (0.7 percent) of rich-world GDP to help poorer countries limit their emissions.

Domestic pressures, unsurprisingly, shaped diplomatic positions on climate politics in Russia as well. In 2004 the Russian parliament cheerfully ratified the Kyoto Protocol. Russia's economic collapse of the 1990s had resulted in emissions levels well beneath those required by Kyoto, and Russia stood to benefit from any emissions trading scheme. Subsequently, however, as Russia's economy recovered and as its oil and gas industry boomed, Russia's leaders lost their enthusiasm for international climate agreements. Many Russians, most notably Vladimir Putin, maintained that a warmer future would bring them more benefit than harm, a record heat wave in 2010 notwithstanding. In any case, few Russian politicians saw merit in policies that might restrict their oil and gas revenues.

Other countries also altered their positions as domestic political and economic conditions shifted. A 2007 election in Australia, for instance, brought to power a government eager to reduce greenhouse gas emissions. The new prime minister often named climate change the great moral challenge of his generation, and for several years climate policy was an urgent political issue in Australia. Subsequent prime ministers, however, did not share the same ardor. Australia enacted a carbon tax on some emitters in 2012 but scrapped it in 2014. Canada, on the other hand, ratified Kyoto in 2002 but failed to meet its targets. In 2006 Canadians elected a prime minister hostile to restriction on emissions, and withdrew from the Protocol in 2012. Most Candians felt uneasy about that stance, and in 2015 another election brought a new climate policy, one committed to carbon pricing and emissions targets.

The countries keenest on Kyoto and subsequent proposals to limit emissions were those of the European Union together with some small island nations. Kiribati, the Maldives, and several other countries that are low-lying atolls expected to be swamped by rising sea levels, giving them an urgent stake in emissions reductions. Most EU countries favored emissions agreements too. Their per capita emissions stood well below those of the United States, Canada, or Australia, and fuel shifts late in the twentieth century, toward nuclear power (1960s–1986) and toward Russian natural gas (post-1970s), put them in a favorable position with respect to most proposed emissions reduction schemes. But their flexibility could not overcome the reluctance of the United States, China, India, and others to embrace meaningful control of greenhouse gases.

The prospects for diplomatic breakthroughs on a scale corresponding to the urgency of the issue seemed very remote through 2013. Climate politics kept running into the same roadblocks. First, for politicians focused on staying in office, addressing climate change seriously held little charm: the costs of inaction would be felt only after they had retired from the political stage, whereas any emissions reductions that entailed economic sacrifice would cost them popular support instantly—as Australian politicians discovered. Thus climate change was one of those political problems that seemed to elected officials to reward procrastination. Second, climate stabilization was (and is) a public good, meaning that all parties can benefit from it regardless of who sacrifices to achieve it—so negotiators were tempted to "free ride," hoping to induce others to make sacrifices from which all would benefit.

Then in 2014 the United States and China surprised the world with a joint promise to reduce carbon emissions, or in China's case to cap their growth, over the next ten to fifteen years. The following year, prodded by German chancellor Angela Merkel, the G-7 countries vowed to phase out fossil fuels altogether by the end of the century. Whether the promises can be kept and whether they will inspire imitation from other countries around the world is unclear. These hopeful outcomes would require an end to the twenty-year-old pattern in which expedience in domestic politics trumps other considerations in climate politics. Pope Francis sought to raise the odds of political breakthrough in an encyclical in 2015 framing climate change as a great and urgent moral challenge, putting the moral weight of the Vatican firmly on the side of climate stabilization.

Optimists found reason to hope that renewable energy would make emissions targets attainable. By 2015 solar power had become competitive in price with fossil fuels as a way to generate electricity. Other renewables, as noted in Chapter 1, showed promise as well. The International Monetary Fund estimated that government subsidies to fossil fuels around the world amounted to $5.3 trillion annually, between 6 and 7 percent of the size of the world economy, and had accounted for more than a third of all global carbon emissions since 1980. Phasing out these subsidies, optimists believed, would go a long way toward reducing reliance on fossil fuels and therefore toward carbon emissions reductions.[19] Even if politics might not permit slashing subsidies for fossil fuels, the long-term trend of falling prices for kilowatts produced via solar power augured poorly for the future of fossil fuels, at least coal and oil if not natural gas, in electricity generation. In that sector, at least, a large part of the future appeared (in 2015) to belong to renewable energy.

Others, less optimistic about emissions reductions, figured that the best hope for avoiding unwelcome climate change lay in geo-engineering schemes. These ranged from the prosaic, such as sequestering carbon underground in abandoned salt mines, to the heroic, such as installing arrays of mirrors in space to reflect incoming sunshine away from Earth. The most popular suggestions, among scientists and engineers, were seeding the oceans with iron filings to stimulate the growth of carbon-absorbing plankton and spattering the stratosphere with sulfate aerosols to reflect sunlight into space. Whether or not international climate politics, new energy technologies, or geo-engineering will offer a way out of the climate quandary is perhaps the greatest question of the twenty-first century.

The environmental history and politics of the recent past will exert influence over the distant future. Carbon emissions of the industrial era will affect climate long after no one can remember Kyoto, Chancellor Merkel, or for that matter China and the United States. Some proportion, perhaps as much as a quarter, of the roughly 300 billion tons of carbon released to the atmosphere between 1945 and 2015 will remain aloft for a few hundred thousand years.

Biological Diversity

Scientific, philosophical, and occasional public concern about certain vanishing species can be traced back centuries, but until recently few people worried that humankind was capable of systematically decreasing the Earth's living heritage. This began to change only in the postwar era, when a small number of scientists started to ponder cumulative human impacts on the world's biomes. These concerns, first articulated sporadically by a few in the 1950s and 1960s, took roughly two additional decades of observation and argumentation to ripen into a critical mass. The terms *biological diversity* and the shorthand *biodiversity* were largely unknown within the scientific community until the 1970s and 1980s. But the scientific and popular use of both exploded during the 1980s, especially after a 1986 conference on the topic orga-

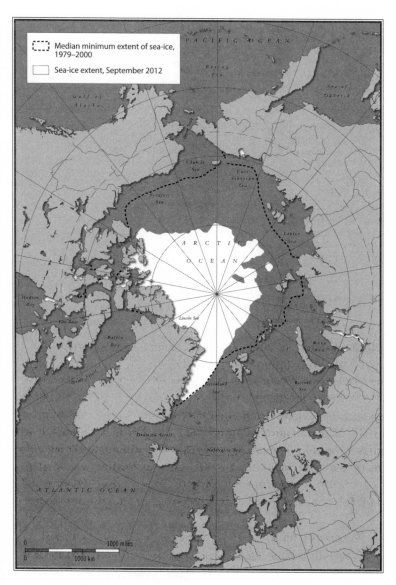

Sea-ice cover at the Arctic Circle, 1979–2012.

nized in Washington, DC, by the eminent biologist E. O. Wilson. The conference proceedings, published as a book under the apt title *Biodiversity*, sounded an alarm. The volume, Wilson wrote, "carries the urgent warning that we are rapidly altering and destroying the environments that have fostered the diversity of life forms for more than a billion years." This message, picked up and broadcast by the world's press, fed on increasing popular and scientific fears about global environmental conditions, from tropical deforestation to ozone depletion. Within a remarkably short time, concern about global extinctions had become a key feature of environmental politics and the word *biodiversity* had become a part of the world's popular lexicon.[20]

Biodiversity had great appeal, but in scientific practice it proved a difficult and blunt instrument. What, exactly, did it mean? What would be measured and how? Did biodiversity mean, for instance, genetic diversity, species diversity, or "population" diversity (meaning geographically distinct populations of animals or plants within a species)? Even if a measure was agreed upon, how did it matter? It would be far better, many scientists claimed, to focus on measuring and maintaining ecosystem functioning and healthy biotic landscapes rather than to obsess over the number of species or quantity of genetic matter. These issues are still hotly debated, but scientists acknowledge that species diversity is a simple, readily understandable measure that has powerful popular resonance. Even if flawed, so the argument goes, species extinction is still the most tangible way to measure global biotic decline.[21]

Attempts to identify and catalog the world's species go back several decades, but despite intense and sustained attempts to do so, biologists can only guess at the total number of extant species. Estimates vary widely, ranging from a few million to one hundred million species or more. Biologists have tended to settle toward the lower end of this spectrum, but they freely admit that their figures are rough estimates. Part of the variation is due to what is included in the count—for instance, whether to include microorganisms such as bacteria—but the problem arises from the simple fact that most species remain unknown to science. Fewer than two million species have been identified and "described" by scientists, and only a small percentage of these have been thoroughly assessed. Of the described species, invertebrates dominate (about 75 percent of all species), followed by plants (18 percent) and vertebrates (less than 4 percent).[22]

There is more agreement about where most life forms are located. Tropical forests in South America, Africa, and Southeast Asia contain the bulk of the world's species. Just 10 percent of the Earth's terrestrial surface is thought to hold between one-half and two-thirds of its species. The broadleaf rainforests have the most. By far the greatest number of described species of mammals, birds, and amphibians are found there. Rainforests are also richest in plant species, although there is wide plant biodiversity in other regions and biomes, such as the Mediterranean basin and South Africa's Cape Province. Stadium-size plots of Ecuador's lowland rainforest, for example, contain more than one thousand species of plants, shrubs, and trees. Ecuador alone (a small country roughly the size of Great Britain) is thought to have 40 percent more plant species than all of Europe. At the low end of the plant biodiversity scale are the world's deserts (although, counterintuitively, a very few deserts are relatively rich in plant biodiversity) and landscapes at very high (northern) latitudes.[23]

Terrestrial species form only a portion of the world's biodiversity. The rest exists in the world's oceans and seas and, to a lesser extent, in its freshwater. Some scientists have estimated that perhaps 15 percent of the world's species live in the oceans, but this is admittedly guesswork. Although freshwater systems represent only a fraction of the world's total surface area and water, they too contain a relatively high number of species, by some estimates as much as 7 percent of all described species. The problems with estimating species numbers and abundance are compounded by the nature of underwater environments: the oceans and seas are vast, and marine environments can be exceptionally difficult to reach and study. As a result, knowledge of marine species diversity and abundance lagged far behind that of terrestrial species through the twentieth century. Only recently has this begun to change.[24]

Oceans and lakes seem to show some similarities with terrestrial ecosystems. For instance, aquatic life is not uniformly distributed across the globe's waters. As with tropical rainforests, some aquatic ecosystems are incredibly rich in species. The continental shelves, coral reef systems, and those parts of the oceans exposed to nutrient-rich currents (such as Newfoundland's Grand Banks) possess enormous species abundance and/or diversity. (One attempt to count all the mollusk species at a single site in tropical waters off New Caledonia, for instance, uncovered 2,738 different species.) Otherwise, much of the ocean is relatively barren, akin to the world's land deserts. Further, as is the case with terrestrial species, a great many aquatic species are not highly mobile. Certain species, in particular the largest pelagics (some species of whales, dolphins, sharks, and fish that are found in deep water), do migrate over very long distances. This is not the case, however, for a great number of others. Many species can exist only in specific habitats and are therefore found in only a few places. Thus, as in terrestrial systems, endemism is an important feature of both freshwater and saltwater ecosystems. Grouper, for example, is a fish that survives in tropical and subtropical waters, with individual species of grouper found only in certain locations.[25]

Concern about species decline has been the primary motive behind attempts to estimate the number of species globally. Over the last three decades in particular, scientific concern increasingly has focused on whether humankind has begun the "sixth extinction," meaning a mass extinction of species that would rival in scale the five known such events in planetary history, the last of which occurred sixty-five million years ago. Scientific worry about mass extinctions emerged coincidentally with heightened concern about tropical deforestation and its effects during the 1970s and 1980s. Biologists began to speculate that human activities were forcing large numbers of species into extinction, far faster than the normal or "background" rate. Again E. O. Wilson was one biologist at the forefront in mainstreaming the idea, calculating in 1986 that extinctions in the world's rainforests were one thousand to ten thousand times greater than normal due to human activities. Many other biologists since have arrived at different estimates of the true extinction rate, with discrepancies once more explained by a combination of unknown species numbers and inexact assessments of human impact. All, however, concede that current rates are many times higher than background. Moreover, they generally agree that increased human interference in the planet's ecosystems was the reason for rapidly increasing extinction rates during the last half of the twentieth century. By 2000, some scientists estimated that perhaps as many as a quarter of a million species had gone extinct during the twentieth century, and feared that ten to twenty times as many might vanish in the twenty-first. Because most species disappeared before they could be described by scientists, the great majority of extinctions in the twentieth century were of creatures unknown to biology.[26]

Though the idea of listing the world's threatened species had been floated as early as the 1920s, it was not until 1949 that European conservationists produced the first tentative list, which contained fourteen mammals and thirteen birds. That same year these conservationists, including the first UNESCO director, Julian Huxley (brother of the writer Aldous Huxley), created the International Union for the Protection of Nature (IUPN). Headquartered in Switzerland, the organization charged itself with preserving "the entire world biotic community." During the 1950s the IUCN (in 1956 "Conservation" replaced "Protection" in the organization's title) began producing lists of threatened species, and in the 1960s it began publishing them. Now known as the Red List of Threatened Species, these are the most highly respected global assessments, compiled by thousands of scientists.

Nonetheless even the prodigious efforts made to produce the Red List could yield insights into the status of only a small fraction of all species. The list issued in 2012 contained nearly sixty-four thousand species, of which about twenty thousand (32 percent) were categorized as threatened. The list contained a heavy bias toward terrestrial species, with much more known about birds, mammals, amphibians, and some categories of plants than about aquatic species.[27]

Changes in Terrestrial Biodiversity

As with so many areas of environmental change during the last decades of the twentieth century, population growth, economic development, and technological capabilities combined to drive the decline of biodiversity. On land, the leading cause was habitat destruction. During the twentieth century the area devoted to cropland and pastures on Earth more than doubled, with roughly half of that occurring after 1950. This increase occurred at the direct expense of the world's forests and grasslands. This was the greatest threat to terrestrial species, because heterogeneous landscapes containing great plant and animal diversity were replaced by highly simplified ones managed by human beings for their own purposes. Such landscapes could and did continue to support some indigenous species, but a great many other species could not prosper in these modified landscapes. Replacing native habitat with other land uses systematically reduced the spaces for wildlife. Cropland and pastures, for instance, host only a fraction of the birds counted in the world's remaining intact grasslands and forests. Landscapes already long ago biologically simplified by conversion to farm or pasture grew still more simplified after 1945. Farmland almost everywhere was increasingly subjected to mechanization, intensive monocropping, and chemical pest control. After land-use changes, the next biggest threat to biodiversity came from exploitation due to hunting, harvesting, and poaching for subsistence or trade. In addition, invasive species were a major problem for biodiversity. Invasives preyed upon or crowded out indigenous species, created "novel" niche habitats for themselves and other exotic intruders, and altered or disrupted ecosystem dynamics in general. Finally, by the end of the century some scientists reported instances of species beginning to suffer from the adverse consequences of climate change.[28]

Global deforestation was the most important type of land-use change after 1945, especially in the tropics where the bulk of the world's species lived. The clearing of tropical rainforests spurred scientists to put biodiversity on the international agenda during the 1980s. Yet the exact amount of tropical forest lost in the postwar decades remained unknown. Analysts arrived at different figures for tropical deforestation, as they did with species estimates, because they used diverse methodologies and data sets. While deforestation remains a subject of intense debate and disagreement, the consensus is that it has proceeded rapidly. One estimate, for instance, put the total loss of tropical forest at 555 million hectares, an area a bit more than half the size of China, in the half century after 1950.

In contrast, over the same period temperate forests (largely in the Northern Hemisphere) were roughly in balance, losing only a bit more from clearing than they gained in regrowth. This difference represented an abrupt shift in relative fortune. In the eighteenth and nineteenth centuries, deforestation had been much faster in the Northern Hemisphere than in the tropics. This imbalance remained even into the early twentieth century, as North American forests became the world's largest suppliers of wood and forest products. By then, however, a shift from temperate to tropical forests was under way. The specter of wood shortages had induced reforms in the United States and elsewhere, which meant that large tracts of forest acquired protected status and aggressive afforestation measures began. The European empires also had taken advantage of rapidly decreasing transportation costs to increase logging for export in their colonial possessions in tropical Africa and Southeast Asia, for example, and to relieve pressure on their own forests.[29]

By World War II the global deforestation shift from temperate to tropical forests was largely complete. After the war, economic expansion further increased pressure on forests, especially those in tropical regions. Newly independent governments in equatorial regions were happy to supply timber to North America, Europe, and Japan; converting forests into lumber for export was a quick and simple means of gaining much-needed foreign currency. Rapidly growing human population in the tropics was also an important driver of deforestation, leading to greater migration into tropical forests. Governments often encouraged such migration, preferring that landless workers claim new cropland and pastures rather than enacting politically contentious land reforms. Finally, technological changes after the war made it much easier to deforest the tropics. The spread of trucks, roads, and chain saws allowed even the smallest operators to work with greater efficiency. All of these factors worked in combination. By the late 1970s and early 1980s, much scientific concern about the tropics centered on the clearing of the Amazon rainforest. Although Southeast Asian forests also had been cleared at a prodigious rate, the deforestation of the Amazon became the focus of global attention, due to its enormous size, perceived pristine state, and symbolic importance.[30]

Island ecosystems were as severely affected as tropical forests, if in different ways. Islands are home to isolated ecosystems containing many endemic species of plants, mammals, birds, and amphibians. Island species have no place to escape to when humans hunt them, alter their habitat, or introduce invasive species. Island nations therefore routinely appear at the top of the IUCN Red List of Threatened Species for having the highest percentage (but not the highest absolute numbers) of threatened species. Madagascar, for instance, contains thousands of endemic species of plants and animals. After 1896, when the French annexed the island, its forests were systematically logged. Deforestation and habitat alteration continued through independence in 1960, much of which owed to the country's high rate of population growth and consequent pressure to clear more land for farming. The result was that by century's end, more than 80 percent of the island's native vegetation had been removed, placing its endemic species under relentless pressure. Isolation also makes islands highly susceptible to invasive species. Islands have been home to the majority of the world's known bird extinctions, from the great auk to the dodo. On Guam, the brown tree snake, introduced by accident around 1950, found the Micronesian island to its liking and reproduced prolifically. In the following decades, snakes consumed a good portion of the island's endemic bird species and a few of its mammal species to boot. Efforts to eradicate the snake on Guam have failed, and biologists remain concerned that it will be inadvertently exported to other vulnerable Pacific islands. Small and remote islands, of which the Pacific has its full share, were the most vulnerable to biodiversity loss in general and through invasive species in particular.[31]

Changes in Aquatic Biodiversity

The decades after 1945 witnessed dramatic alterations to freshwater and marine ecosystems. After World War II humans accelerated their campaign of taming the world's rivers, to the point where few big ones anywhere were left in their original states. Engineers built tens of thousands of dams, reservoirs, levees, and dikes. The Nile's Aswan High Dam, installed during the 1960s, symbolized the world's infatuation with colossal dams. Engineers dredged streambeds and river bottoms and rerouted entire rivers, changing water flow patterns and temperature levels. Pollutants from cities and industry added chemicals of many different types and toxicities. Agricultural runoff increased the load of organic nutrients in streams and rivers. This led to the eutrophication of downstream water bodies and the creation of oxygen-deprived "dead zones," as in parts of the Gulf of Mexico, the Baltic, and the Yellow Sea. Increased siltation from mining, agriculture, and deforestation also reshaped stream, river, bay, and estuarine habitats. Finally, the world's marshes and wetlands, home to rich collections of unique fish, birds, amphibians, mammals, plants, and insects, shrank dramatically. This occurred nearly everywhere, although rates varied substantially. Marshes and wetlands were converted into other types of uses, filled in to make land for agriculture or cities. River diversions, especially in arid regions where freshwater for irrigation was precious, starved marshes and wetlands of water. Water diversions in some rivers, like South Africa's Orange or America's Colorado, reduced flow to the point of seasonal dryness, endangering species-rich wetlands at the river mouths.[32]

As on islands, invasive species in freshwater ecosystems proved increasingly disruptive after 1945. While invasives were nothing new, the accidental or deliberate introduction of such species became a commonplace thereafter. The Nile Perch, introduced from other parts of Africa into Lake Victoria sometime during the 1950s, was a dramatic example of what could occur when exotics encountered endemic species. By the 1970s this large predator reproduced exuberantly in Lake Victoria. It fed on the lake's endemic fish species, including many of its tiny and beautiful species of cichlid, and put the entirety of the lake's ecosystem in jeopardy. Biologists debate the perch's exact role in changing Lake Victoria, but they are in agreement that the fish was a major contributor to biodiversity decline in Africa's largest lake.[33]

Invasive species may have had their greatest effects on the world's estuaries, which are transition zones between freshwater and saltwater ecosystems. Estuaries are also natural harbors and provide the global economy with many of its ports. During the twentieth century estuaries felt the destructive effects of several combined forces. Changes made to upstream river systems altered sedimentation and temperature levels, among other things. Agricultural runoff changed nutrient balances. Urban and industrial centers added pollutants. Wetland conversion reduced animal habitat in estuaries. With estuaries so disturbed, exotic species, often introduced via ships' bilge tanks, easily colonized these habitats. San Francisco Bay provides a good illustration. By the end of the twentieth century, the bay had been subject to more than a hundred years' worth of urban growth, agricultural runoff, and re-plumbing of its rivers and wetlands. The ports of Oakland and San Francisco, moreover, were among the most important on the American West Coast, which meant that thousands of oceangoing vessels traversed the bay every year, each one a potential carrier of invasive species. As a result, San Francisco Bay is now home to over two hundred exotic species, including some that have become dominant in their new ecological niches.[34]

After 1945 the human impact on oceanic biodiversity intensified, just as it did in the world's freshwater and estuarine environments. Humans began interfering in the ecology of the deep ocean, which until then had felt little or no human presence of any kind. Commercial fishing was by far the most important activity. Humans had fished the oceans and seas for millennia, but the postwar era saw unprecedented increases in the scale, location, and impact of oceanic fishing. Global demand for fish increased rapidly along with rising wealth and growing world population. Supply increased in large part because postwar technologies allowed fishers to catch ever-larger quantities of fish in ever-deeper waters. Much of this technology had been developed initially for military purposes. Sonar, for instance, had been refined during World War II to track and hunt submarines, but after the war it was also used to locate schools of fish. Over the subsequent decades, improved Cold War–era sonar systems eventually enabled fishers to map the seafloor, giving them the ability to place trawls and nets in the most lucrative locations. When married to other postwar technologies such as shipboard computers, global positioning systems, and monofilament nets, fishing vessels became highly lethal machines.

Moreover, states subsidized the construction of oceangoing vessels that were capable of not only catching greater amounts of deepwater fish but also processing and freezing the fish on board. These "factory" ships could stay at sea for long stretches, giving their prey no rest. By the 1980s and 1990s, fleets of massive vessels equipped with these technologies were plying the seven seas, fishing the deep waters of the Indian, Pacific, and Atlantic Oceans and venturing into polar waters as well.[35]

At the outset of the postwar era, almost everyone believed that oceanic fisheries had a near-infinite capacity to replenish themselves. Pushed by the United States in the 1940s and 1950s, fishery managers around the world adopted a model known as maximum sustainable yield (MSY) that reflected this faith in oceanic abundance. MSY elaborated the view that fish were resilient creatures capable of replacing their numbers easily, at least up to a point (the maximum yield), before they declined. By taking older and larger fish, so the argument went, commercial fishing opened up more space for younger fish to find food, grow to maturity faster, and reproduce quicker. Proponents of MSY thus placed the emphasis upon harvesting, essentially mandating that a species show signs of decline before conservation policies were considered. The MSY approach presumed that scientists could estimate fish populations, assign appropriate quotas, and thereby manage fisheries sustainably. This confidence ignored the fact that marine ecosystems were very poorly understood and always in flux, and that fish are impossible to count.[36]

Increased fishing effort substantially increased the global catch after 1945, but it also had major consequences for the oceans. Deepwater fishing, made ever more efficient by the new methods, severely reduced the number of top predators such as bluefin tuna. Pelagic net fishing took huge numbers of unwanted and unlucky species, euphemistically termed the "bycatch," including seabirds, dolphins, turtles, and sharks. Trawling reached increasingly deeper areas of the seafloor, scouring and removing everything. These benthic environments contained rich marine life that was hauled to the surface, the unmarketable portion of which would be thrown overboard. By the 1980s and 1990s, the world's major fisheries were showing signs of stress, with most going into decline and a few into collapse. The fishing industry was able to keep up with demand by using ever more sophisticated technologies to chase ever fewer fish in ever deeper waters and by investing in aquaculture, which by 2000 accounted for 27 percent of the fish, crustaceans, and mollusks eaten worldwide.[37]

The whaling industry did much the same thing. During the late nineteenth and early twentieth centuries, inventive whalers (many of whom were Norwegian) began to use a range of new technologies, including the cannon-fired harpoon, steam-driven chase boats, and huge factory ships that allowed whale carcasses to be quickly hauled aboard for processing. Together these technologies enabled whalers to expand their efforts into remoter waters and to target species that had heretofore been too fast to catch. Norwegian, Soviet, and Japanese whalers (among others) now targeted blue, fin, and minke whales in addition to the species such as sperm and right whales that had been hunted with abandon during the nineteenth century. Driven by the profits from selling whale oil, meat, bone, and other products, hunters took more than a million whales worldwide during the twentieth century. The industry was entirely unregulated until 1946, when a conference of the main whaling nations resulted in the founding of the International Whaling Commission (IWC). Ostensibly dedicated to assessing and managing the world's stock of whales, the IWC proved to be more interested in coordinating the industry's effort than anything else, a team of foxes guarding the henhouse. This only began changing after whaling economics worsened, forcing many nations out of the industry (by 1969, for instance, only Japan and the Soviet Union continued hunting in the most lucrative waters around Antarctica). Just as critically, after 1970, pressure from environmentalists and the wider

A green sea turtle (*Chelonia mydas*) and several species of butterfly fish swim along the Great Barrier Reef, off Queensland, Australia, 2008. In the late twentieth century, ocean acidification had begun to damage the world's coral reefs, which are home to an enormous diversity of marine life. (Jeff Hunter/Getty Images)

public forced the IWC to adopt ever-stricter quotas. Ultimately the IWC agreed to a complete hunting moratorium (passed in 1982, implemented in 1986). But the issue never went away entirely. A very small number of nations with populations having strong tastes for whale meat campaigned to get the IWC to partially lift the moratorium. Japan, Iceland, and Norway continued hunting a few species of whales in small numbers under Article VIII of the IWC's 1946 convention, which allowed hunting for "scientific" research purposes. Japan took about three hundred minke whales annually in Antarctic waters between 1987 and 2014, and remained in defiance of the IWC in its commitment to "lethal sampling" for purposes it alone regards as scientific. The net effect of whaling and its modern regulation was to keep all marketable whales near the edge of extinction without (so far) tipping any over that edge.[38] In *Moby-Dick* (1851) Herman Melville, a keen student of whaling, opined that whales were numerous enough to withstand human hunting. So far he remains right, but just barely.

Beyond the challenges to life in the deep oceans, human activity menaced shallow-water environments such as coral reefs. Among the planet's most biologically diverse habitats, coral reefs were built over the ages by the accumulation of skeletons of tiny creatures called coral polyps. Relatively untouched in 1900, reefs over the next century came under heavy pressure. They were fished more intensively for food and for the aquarium trade, because many of the fish that lurk around reefs are brightly colored and popular among collectors. In many locales, accelerating erosion sent river-borne sediments onto nearby reefs, suffocating the coral polyps. In the Caribbean and the Red Sea, tourist resort pollution damaged still more reefs, as did the skin-diving tourists themselves who enjoyed them. The gradual acidification of the oceans (a result of pumping extra carbon into the atmosphere) also proved hard on coral reefs. In the early 1980s scientists who studied reefs began to notice general damage patterns, resulting in the first conferences on reef protection. By the 1990s the worries included coral-killing diseases and predators as well as coral "bleaching" (signifying reef stress), especially from higher ocean temperatures. A 1998 global bleaching outbreak was particularly worrisome, destroying an estimated 16 percent of the world's coral reefs, mainly in the Indian and Pacific Oceans. In 2005 a severe coral bleaching killed many reefs in the Caribbean. Worldwide, about 70 percent of coral reefs showed signs of ill effects by 2010. Although reefs sometimes showed remarkable resilience, the weight of evidence showed that climate change and other forces damaged reef habitats and thereby diminished the oceans' biodiversity.[39]

Biodiversity Conservation

Given the pressures on the world's species during the twentieth and early twenty-first centuries, it is tempting to adopt a gloomy narrative. Yet the period also witnessed intense activity aimed at conserving species and habitat. Wildlife-themed television programming became popular in North America and Europe from the 1950s. New conservation organizations emerged, such as the World Wildlife Fund, spun off by the IUCN in 1961. Within another decade the mass environmental movement had succeeded in placing species conservation on the popular agenda in some parts of the world. In 1973 the United States passed the landmark Endangered Species Act (ESA). The ESA has been controversial, but it has succeeded in reintroducing some species, such as wolves, to some of their former habitats. Similarly, in 1973 India launched the Project Tiger program, designed to save the country's remaining wild tigers; unlike the ESA, Project Tiger focused its primary effort on setting aside large tracts of land (reserves) as protected tiger habitat. During the 1970s organizations such as Greenpeace spearheaded global campaigns to ban whaling, leading to the global moratorium in 1986.

Diplomatic activity matched these national efforts. Major international agreements and initiatives focused on biodiversity conservation, beginning when UNESCO hosted a 1968 biosphere conference. Others included the 1971 Ramsar Convention on wetlands, the 1973 Convention on International Trade in Endangered Species (CITES), the 1979 Bonn Convention on migratory species, and the Convention on Biological Diversity (CBD), negotiated at the 1992 Rio Earth Summit. Since the 1970s, biodiversity concerns have increasingly garnered political attention, both domestically and internationally.[40]

Nature reserves and national parks were the most common conservation tools. A legacy of the nineteenth century, reserves and parks were created the world over during the twentieth and twenty-first centuries. Game reserves in Africa, for instance, had been established in Great Britain's colonies starting around 1900 in order to protect species favored by aristocratic white hunters. While these sportsmen correctly surmised that hunting had reduced or eliminated some species, they tended to blame African and nouveau-riche and plebian white hunters for undisciplined slaughter of wildlife. Gradually the idea of turning thinly protected reserves into national parks along American lines took hold. Several such parks were created between the 1920s and 1940s, including South Africa's Kruger and Tanganyika's (now Tanzania's) Serengeti. After independence, new African governments supported the parks, and in fact created several new ones, seeing them as sources of national pride and identity as well as of tourist income. In 2002 Gabon created thirteen national parks covering 10 percent of its territory, much of it lush rainforest. Gabon thereby hoped to emulate Costa Rica as an ecotourism destination, but thus far success has proven elusive.[41]

Toward the end of the twentieth century the reserve idea was also applied to the oceans. The concept of marine reserves had been formulated in 1912 and largely forgotten until the 1970s, when biologists began conducting small-scale trials. These showed that marine reserves, areas where nearly all fishing was banned, might regenerate degraded ecosystems. Because there were few signs that commercial fishing could be regulated sufficiently to protect oceanic biodiversity, by the 1980s and 1990s biologists began pushing for large reserves. By the early twenty-first century many such reserves existed. Moreover, a few governments created several reserves of enormous size, including a large chunk of Australia's Great Barrier Reef and immense areas around the Pacific's Marianas and Hawaiian Islands and the Indian Ocean's Chagos Archipelago.[42]

Science informed the campaign to create marine reserves for fish, and it also contributed to debates about preserving whales. New research showed that the world's oceans might have been far richer before modern commercial whaling. This was more than an academic exercise, as it threw a wrench into whaling management. In 2010, for example, a dispute erupted at the International Whaling Commission (IWC) over plans to lift the 1986 whaling moratorium. The longtime whaling nations Japan, Iceland, and Norway backed IWC models showing that whale populations had rebounded enough to resume hunting. Critics, however, pointed to genetics-based evidence suggesting that historical whale populations might have been much higher than the IWC models showed, implying that whale populations were nowhere near robust enough to resume hunting.[43]

Biodiversity conservation has become a global norm in a very short period of time, in reaction to mounting evidence of biodiversity decline. Despite real conservation successes, human activities since 1945 greatly intensified the number and severity of threats facing the world's living organisms. Human beings increasingly order the world. We have selected a handful of preferred plant and animal species, living in managed and simplified landscapes, and have unconsciously selected another handful of species that adapt well to these landscapes (rats, deer, squirrels, pigeons, and such). In so doing we have greatly reduced or eliminated the number of other plants, birds, mammals, insects, and amphibians that lived in and on these landscapes just a short time ago. In this regard the ethical question is much the same as ever: Are we content with a world containing billions of humans, cows, chickens, and pigs but only a few thousand tigers, rhinoceroses, polar bears—or none at all?[44]

The twenty-first century portends still greater pressure on biodiversity than did the twentieth. Rising affluence, at least for some, plus three to five billion additional people, will menace the world's forests, wetlands, oceans, seas, rivers, and grasslands. But climate change likely will set the twenty-first century apart. Scientists fear that even modest temperature rises will have serious negative effects on all types of ecosystems. Some have estimated that a 2-degree Celsius increase might send one-fifth to one-third of the world's species into extinction. Such studies, it should be noted, often optimistically assume that species will have perfect "dispersal capabilities," meaning the ability to retreat to adjacent cooler environments. But perfect dispersal is usually no longer possible. There are now so many human-dominated landscapes— farms, roads, fences, cities, dams, reservoirs, and so on—that many species attempting to flee a warming climate will have no migratory option whatsoever. Protectors of biodiversity in the twenty-first century have their work cut out for them.[45]

CHAPTER THREE

Cities and the Economy

We live on an urban planet. In 2008 demographers at the United Nations announced that more than 50 percent of humans were living in cities. This symbolized a profound change in human history. Never before had a majority of the world's population lived in urban areas. The world today has five hundred cities with populations of at least a million people, seventy-four with at least five million, and twelve with at least twenty million. The largest city in the world, Tokyo, has over thirty-seven million people if one includes attached areas.[1] The full effects of so many cities and of so many people living in cities are as yet unknown. What is known is that cities have always depended upon and shaped their natural surroundings.

Cities concentrate people to levels far higher than the immediate environment can support. As they cannot exist in isolation from their surroundings, cities require access to natural resources and to waste sinks beyond their borders. Natural resource inputs consist of materials and energy. Materials range from food, clean water, ores, and basic construction materials (stone, wood) to an enormous range of manufactured goods. Energy resources are contained in some of the raw materials shipped into the city, in water that may flow through a city and that is captured by a mill or turbine, or electricity that is transmitted by wire from outside the city's borders. Before the onset of the Industrial Revolution, energy from raw materials entering the city took the form of wood and coal and of food for human or animal consumption. After the Industrial Revolution, cities required far greater amounts of energy, initially for factories and later for the technical innovations that have since become synonymous with urban living (electric lighting, trolleys and subways, automobiles, and such). Fossil fuels have provided the bulk of this energy. During the nineteenth century, coal became the dominant energy source used in the rapidly industrializing cities of Europe and North America. Petroleum became an increasingly important energy source for cities only much later, during the first half of the twentieth century in a few cities, then globally after World War II. During the twentieth century, cities also began to draw electricity from nuclear and hydroelectric plants.

The urban consumption of materials and energy produces waste. While mills process ores into desirable metals (iron and steel, for instance), they also produce slag, slurry, and wastewater. Urban residents (human and animal) benefit from the food that is brought into a city, but they also produce excreta, which has created major health problems for cities throughout history. Cities use energy for productive purposes, and its utilization generates pollutants and toxins. All of this waste has to go somewhere. Some waste is deposited inside a city's boundaries, in which case city residents have to tolerate it as a nuisance. In the case of some waterborne pollutants and airborne toxins, residents are forced to suffer potentially deadly consequences.

But for the bulk of urban wastes, cities require sinks outside their borders. Many cities sit along rivers and use them as waste dumps. Where cities are located along coastlines, the oceans and seas often are afforded the same treatment (until the 1930s, for instance, much of New York's garbage was dumped at sea). Waste can also find its way into the soils surrounding the city. Finally, burning fuels produces waste that we call air pollution. Indoor air pollution, still a major problem in poorer cities, arises from burning fuels such as wood, coal, kerosene, and dung in domestic stoves and fireplaces. Local air pollutants include toxic gases produced in metallurgic operations, smoke and soot from coal (an enormous problem through much of the nineteenth and twentieth centuries), and ground-level ozone from automobile exhaust. Urban air pollutants can be a regional problem as well, due to the wind. Acid rain and the deposition of toxins onto soil far away are two examples of pollution on a regional scale. By the second half of the twentieth century, cities had also become significant sources of global air pollution, contributing heavy amounts of chlorofluorocarbons and greenhouse gases to the atmosphere.[2]

The relationship between cities and their surroundings is not a simple one. Cities are dynamic entities, "ever-mutating systems" in the words of one environmental historian, that grow and contract depending on myriad factors. Their human and animal populations as well as their economic and political bases are in constant flux. This extends to their claim on extraterritorial sources and sinks, which can also shrink and expand as conditions change. In such a fluid context, cities have struggled for millennia to secure and maintain access to critical resources. Medieval Nuremberg, for example, imposed municipal control over nearby forests and systematically pushed out rivals in order to preserve the city's fuel supply.[3]

Cities transform nature. They interfere with natural water cycles. Pavements keep water from percolating into the Earth, resulting in more water running off into rivers and sewers. Drawing water from wells depletes aquifers. Canalization of rivers changes streamflows. Most importantly, cities dump masses of pollution into nearby waterways. Streams, rivers, and coastal waters close to cities therefore suffer from many types of degradation, such as decreased biological diversity and eutrophication. Cities' impact upon air quality is simpler than that upon water quality: they pollute it and to a small degree warm it up as well. Cities alter land use and soil characteristics, too. Farmland required to feed growing cities replaces forests and grasslands with simplified, managed, and less diverse ecosystems. Mines dug to satisfy urban demand for metals and fossil fuels often damage surrounding landscapes with pollution and tailings. Urban growth also creates "edges" that have dramatic effects on wildlife habitat and numbers.[4]

The relationship between cities and nature is more nuanced than this roster of direct effects suggests. Cities, of course, have been centers of ingenuity, creativity, and wealth since their origins more than five thousand years ago. If well designed, they can require fewer resources per capita than rural areas. Higher population densities in cities can translate into the more efficient production and distribution of goods and delivery of social services. Densely packed populations require less fuel to keep warm (or to keep cool). Moreover, cities help lower fertility rates. Although the decision to have children is always a complex one involving many factors and there is substantial variation across time and place, women who live in cities tend to have fewer children than their country cousins. Urban couples have better access to birth control, and urban women have greater economic, educational, and social opportunities compared with women in rural areas. By and large, children in urban settings can perform less useful labor for their families and require larger and longer expenditure to raise (and educate). So urban populations choose to have fewer of them.[5]

The Rise of Cities

Cities were unusual prior to the onset of the Industrial Revolution. Few of the world's inhabitants lived in them. Before 1800 only a very small number of cities had ever approached a million inhabitants. Ancient Rome might have come close for a century or two at the zenith of its empire. The same might have been true for a very small number of cities thereafter: Baghdad during the ninth century CE, Beijing from the sixteenth, and Istanbul from the seventeenth, for example. Few, if any, had been able to sustain these populations for very long. Even as late as the eighteenth century, only a handful exceeded a half million residents. About the only cities that could reach large size before the modern period were imperial centers, whose trajectories waxed and waned with political fortunes, and mercantile centers that depended on over-seas trading networks.[6]

There were some basic reasons why there were few large cities, and few cities at all, for that matter, before the modern period. Cities depend on an agricultural surplus to survive. For much of human history, low agricultural productivity required that most people engage in growing and harvesting food, hence most lived on the land. Limited transportation technology compounded this constraint, making it costly to ship goods such as food over long distances. Cities located along navigable rivers or coastlines had a distinct advantage, in that ships, boats, and barges were the easiest and cheapest means of transport. This was especially true for bulky goods. Timber, for example, could be floated downriver to cities at low cost but was very expensive to move short distances overland or upriver. Cities required the agricultural surplus of areas far greater than their own to survive. And they needed the fuel, typically in the form of wood and charcoal, of an even larger space. They were like big carnivores in any ecosystem: they drew their sustenance from over a large space and therefore could only be few in number.[7]

Cities were also unhealthy places. Generally cities suffered from unsanitary conditions and crowding. The result typically was higher mortality in cities than in rural areas. Early death was routine, in particular for infants and toddlers from childhood diseases and, for the general population, from epidemics that ravaged cities with frightening frequency. For centuries cities had little recourse to countermeasures other than quarantine. Owing to their connections with the outside world, trading cities were often struck first and hardest by epidemics. During the early nineteenth century, cholera spread from the Indian subcontinent to port cities across Europe and North Africa. Bubonic plague also struck ports and cities generally more severely than villages. It is important to note that not all cities were alike in their lethality.

Japanese cities in the seventeenth and eighteenth centuries, for instance, may have been substantially healthier than their European or Chinese counterparts. Their systems for water supply and sewerage were more advanced, and their cultural practices were more hygienic. Japanese cities suffered from fewer epidemics as a result.[8]

After 1800, however, cities broke through the many constraints on their growth. The world's richest countries urbanized rapidly in the nineteenth century. The first megacities appeared during this period. London led the way, growing from fewer than a million people at the start of the century to more than five million at its end. New York's growth was even more impressive, from a small city in 1800 to the second largest in the world a century later; by 1930 it was the first metropolitan area in world history to have ten million residents. Its pace so impressed H. G. Wells that he expected New York would be home to forty million people by the year 2000.[9] London owed much of its growth to its role as political center of the world's leading imperial power. It benefited greatly from Britain's centrality in a rapidly growing global economy, allowing it to acquire goods from all over.[10] As Europeans built their empires, they also created new cities in their colonies. The British, for example, founded the East Asian trading cities of Singapore and Hong Kong and most of the major Australian settlement cities during the first half of the nineteenth century. As with so many aspects of colonization, locals played little part in siting cities. Nairobi sits where it does because the British found the location suitable for a refueling depot on their railway between Uganda and Mombasa.[11]

But the Industrial Revolution, rather than imperialism, drove most nineteenth-century urbanization. Agricultural modernization in Great Britain during the seventeenth and eighteenth centuries had increased food production. This meant that more people could eat, but it also created surplus labor in rural areas. Landless and jobless people fled to the cities, where by 1820 the Industrial Revolution was in full swing. Places such as Manchester became major cities almost overnight, driven by a combination of rural-to-urban migration and factory output powered by cheap British coal. Similar processes occurred a bit later in mainland Europe, in particular where coal was found in abundance. Politics spurred industrialization in still other places. While Japan was already one of the most urbanized countries in the world, the 1868 Meiji restoration initiated a period of heavy industrialization encouraged by the state. Huge numbers of people were drawn into the cities during the decades that followed. In 1868 about 10 percent of Japan's population lived in cities; by 1940 this percentage had nearly quadrupled. Japan in 1940 had forty-five cities with populations over one hundred thousand, and four of these (Tokyo, Kyoto, Nagoya, and Osaka) had more than a million.[12]

The Industrial Revolution also brought significant changes in transportation. The steamship allowed faster and cheaper oceanic transport, which bolstered global trade among cities. The steamship also enabled mass transoceanic migrations in the second half of the nineteenth century, which contributed greatly to urban growth in the United States, Canada, Argentina, Brazil, South Africa, and Australia. Perhaps even more important was the railroad, which like the steamship went from being a curiosity at the beginning of the nineteenth century to having become a dominant means of transport at the end. By dramatically reducing overland shipping costs, the railroad allowed cities to extend their geographic reach well beyond the constraints imposed by the horse, foot, and wagon. Chicago's unparalleled growth after 1850, for instance, owed much to the fact that it became the hub of a railroad network extending far to its north and west. (Wells in 1902 also thought that Chicago, like New York City, would one day top forty million inhabitants.)[13] The railroad enabled the city to develop long-distance trade in the grain, livestock, and timber of North America's vast heartland. Chicago parlayed this geographic reach into enormous power, dominating a region that extended for hundreds of miles around. Chicago thus played an important role in organizing and transforming the forests and grasslands of this region into the highly productive, thoroughly commodified, and ecologically simplified landscapes of the American Midwest.[14]

Industrialization had a number of other important consequences for cities. It increased urban wealth but it also in the short run aggravated the problems of pollution, filth, disease, squalor, and crowding. The scale and rapidity of growth itself caused massive problems. The industrial working class, newly arrived from rural areas, most often had no choice but to live packed together in dank and dingy housing. New York's infamous tenements and Berlin's equally notorious *Mietskasernen* (literally, "rental barracks") were among the worst examples, but substandard housing accompanied industrialization nearly everywhere. Housing problems were overlaid upon a backdrop of intense pollution and poor sanitation. Working-class housing stood in the shadow of factories, which spewed coal smoke into the air and dumped toxic sludge into streams and rivers. Tanneries, slaughterhouses, and meatpacking houses operated in the very center of cities, adding all manner of chemical and organic pollutants to urban water supplies. Waste disposal became an even more nightmarish problem. Few cities had municipal services for collecting and disposing of solid wastes, which left streets littered with myriad wastes, including horse manure and dead animals. Rudimentary systems for collecting and disposing of human waste soon became overwhelmed by the scale of urbanization that came with industrialization.[15]

Public authorities struggled to address these problems resulting from swift urban growth. Sanitation became an important public goal in Europe and North America from the middle of the nineteenth century. Reformers such as Britain's Edwin Chadwick, who strove to establish an empirical relationship between cleanliness and disease, drove the process. During the 1850s Chadwick's influence led London and other British cities to build and improve sewage systems. French planners did the same. Baron von Haussmann's famous reconstruction of Paris in the 1850s and 1860s included a thorough rebuilding and upgrading of the city's water supply and sewer systems. Public sanitation measures received another boost from the bacteriological discoveries of the 1880s, which substantiated the germ theory of disease. Bacteriology overturned the prevailing understanding of disease origins and transmission, and gave scientific legitimacy to sanitation efforts, in particular attempts to clean and purify water. After 1880, American cities made major investments in public water supply and sewer systems.[16] The modern discipline of city planning also emerged in the late nineteenth and early twentieth centuries, as planners searched for ways to improve the industrial city. America's Frederick Law Olmsted, Britain's Ebenezer Howard, Scotland's Patrick Geddes, Austria's Camillo Sitte, and Germany's Reinhard Baumeister were a few of the iconic figures in the early history of city planning and related disciplines.

In the first decades of the twentieth century, automobiles started to reshape urban spaces in North America, while big cities began to proliferate on every continent. The United States and Canada built a booming automobile industry. Oil became an increasingly important energy source after enormous quantities were discovered in Texas in 1901, while Ford's Model T (introduced in 1908) greatly reduced the cost of the private automobile. Mass motorization, and with it the emergence of the automobile suburb, began in the United States during the interwar decades. Meanwhile, urbanization was accelerating in other parts of the world. Larger cities began to emerge in Africa, Latin America, and Asia, driven by processes not unlike those already experienced in Europe and North America. Cairo, for example, began to grow faster than Egypt as a whole during and after World War I. Migration to Cairo picked up, due mostly to economic depression in rural areas, at the same time as improved sanitation caused urban mortality rates to fall. By 1937 the city had 1.3 million people, more than three times its size of a half century before. Thanks in part to immigration from Europe, Buenos Aires mushroomed from under 200,000 people in 1870 to 1.5 million in 1910 and 3 million by 1950. Mexico City experienced similar growth at about the same time. Migration from rural areas to most Mexican cities sped up during the revolutionary period (1910–1920), driven by political conflict, changes in the rural economy, and industrialization. By 1940 the greater Mexico City area was more than twice its size of 1910.[17]

Cities since 1945

The period after World War II witnessed a crescendo of urbanization. The share of the world's population living in cities jumped dramatically, from 29 percent in 1950 (730 million people) to slightly more than half in 2015 (roughly 3.7 billion people). This was one of the signal characteristics of the Anthropocene: the majority of humankind now lived within environments of its own creation. Our species had become, in effect, an urban animal. Cities grew faster than rural areas in every part of the world. In 1950 there had been only two cities with populations greater than ten million; by the end of the century there were twenty such megacities.[18] Urbanization thus occurred everywhere, but the pace, nature, and consequences were different depending on location.

The most spectacular theater of urbanization in the postwar era was in the developing world. The share of people living in cities in the developing world more than doubled between 1950 and 2003, from 18 percent to 42 percent of the population. This represented an absolute increase of nearly two billion people (from 310 million to 2.2 billion). From 1950 to 1975, the urban population in the world's poorer countries grew at an average annual rate of 3.9 percent. This was a rate nearly double that of cities in the rich world and more than double that of rural areas in the developing world. For the period 1975–2000, this disparity was even more pronounced. Even though the annual growth rate for poor cities declined to 3.6 percent, it was still about

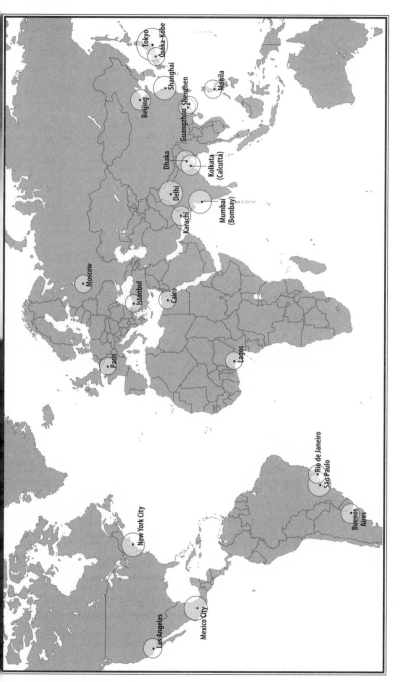

Urban areas with populations of more than 10 million people, 2011.

four times that of rich cities (0.9 percent) and more than three times that of poor rural areas (1.1 percent).[19]

Migration from rural areas fueled urban expansion in the developing world after 1945. Agricultural modernization drove many peasant farmers off the land. They had nowhere else to go but cities. The possibility of finding employment was one attraction, although opportunities were often few and sometimes only in the informal sector. Another attraction was access to social services such as schools and hospitals, however limited in the cities of the developing world. Familial ties and other social networks in cities smoothed the path for many rural migrants.[20]

Economic, political, and military developments had an influence on the process of urbanization as well. Burgeoning economies in some regions drew in urban populations. Villages in the oil-rich Persian Gulf, for instance, mushroomed into cities almost overnight, especially after the 1973–1974 oil price hikes brought enormous revenues into the region. Showcase cities such as Dubai and Abu Dhabi emerged, characterized by immense wealth and in-migration from nearby rural areas and from abroad, especially South Asia. National politics influenced urbanization processes, as in China both before and after the 1949 Revolution. The state's policies sometimes drew people into the cities, as was the case in the 1950s when Chinese ambitions focused on industrialization, and at other times deliberately slowed urbanization, as occurred during the Cultural Revolution. Wars (both international and civil), independence struggles, and guerrilla insurgencies also played a role. These made rural areas less secure, helping to spur migration to cities in some places. Karachi, for example, received several hundred thousand Muslim refugees fleeing sectarian violence in the wake of Indian independence in 1947.[21]

As was true of the Industrial Revolution in the nineteenth century, these processes led to rapid urban growth on a scale that overwhelmed local governments. Dhaka in Bangladesh, to give only one example, grew from a small city of four hundred thousand people in 1950 to over thirteen million in 2007. Poor migrants to Dhaka and other such cities found insufficient housing, and what did exist was often unaffordable for them. A great many thus were forced to squat on any marginal land they could find—on abandoned lots, alongside roads or railroad tracks, next to swamps or city dumps, or on steep hillsides. Developing cities all over the poor world teemed with squatter settlements, which commonly housed a third or more of all urban residents. The absolute numbers of people living in such settlements reached astonishing proportions: over nine million in Mexico City and three million in São Paulo around 1990, for instance. In Mumbai, over half the population was housed in these settlements, and anywhere from three hundred thousand to a million people lived on the streets. Many cities exhibited extreme spatial segregation, as the relatively few rich sought to insulate themselves from the many poor. In Karachi the wealthy began segregating themselves with renewed determination after squatters settled in large numbers in the 1960s and 1970s.[22]

In these settlement conditions, health and environmental problems deepened. Again these issues were similar to those in nineteenth-century Europe and North America. Substandard housing combined with inadequate public infrastructure meant wretched living conditions for large numbers of people in developing cities. Many squatter settlements had little or no access to clean drinking water, proper sanitation, or refuse services. Public infrastructure systematically favored wealthier residents. In Accra during the 1980s, for example, poor households had much worse service provision than richer ones. A majority of poor households had to share toilets with many other households, a condition the rich did not have to tolerate. There were predictable health effects of these types of arrangements. While the overall disease burden in the world's poor cities was slowly shifting from communicable to chronic diseases by the end of the century, communicable diseases maintained their grip on the poorest residents and were major causes of mortality. Infectious and parasitic diseases continued to strike poor children particularly hard. Every squatter settlement suffered these grim circumstances, but each had its own particular character.[23]

Over time, conditions in many settlements improved. Jerry-built housing gradually evolved into permanent neighborhoods. Residents converted flimsy structures made out of cardboard or plastic into more durable ones made out of metal, wood, and concrete. Local and national governments managed over time to extend public services—including electricity, sewers, piped water, paved roads, and schools—to many settlements. Where politics involved elections, politicians quickly figured out that many votes could be won by providing these basic services to squatter settlements. A prime minister and later president of Turkey, Recep Tayyip Erdoğan, made his political reputation by delivering water, electricity, and sewerage to urban neighborhoods while mayor of Istanbul (1994–1998). Where these improvements took hold, older settlements had fewer problems than newer ones.[24]

All neighborhoods, old and new, in the burgeoning cities of the developing world suffered from air pollution. Because coal remained a cheap fuel, rapidly growing countries turned to it for industry and electric power generation. In the last decades of the twentieth century, Asian megacities in particular became notorious for severe air pollution from burning coal. Beijing and Shanghai suffered very high soot and sulfur dioxide concentrations, due in large part to coal combustion. Xi'an and Wuhan were worse still. Unfortunate geography compounded air pollution problems for yet other cities. Mexico City developed some of the worst air pollution in the world partly because it was ringed by mountains and sat at high altitude. Similar geography plagued Bogotá. Coal-based pollution dogged thousands of cities, Delhi most of all.[25]

Cities in the developing world suffered from the environmental consequences of both extreme poverty and concentrated wealth. Often these existed cheek by jowl, as in Jakarta. Once the sleepy capital of the Dutch East Indies, Jakarta (then known as Batavia) became a boomtown after Indonesian independence in 1949. Two aspects of growth characterized its recent history. On the one hand, as Jakarta was Indonesia's capital, the country's leadership saw it as an economic engine and the site for large show projects. The government invested heavily in Jakarta's infrastructure and encouraged rapid industrial and commercial development. Over time Jakarta came to possess all the trappings of the most modern and global of cities—many industries, an extensive highway system, and a glittering downtown of office towers and luxury hotels. On the other hand, Jakarta's growth attracted millions of new and poor migrants from the countryside. Many of these were obliged to live in *kampungs* (squatter settlements or "villages"). Together, these elements shaped Jakarta's environmental history after 1949. The city's poor suffered from the unsanitary conditions found in squatter settlements everywhere. Although the government made some progress in upgrading conditions in them (especially under Jakarta's governor Ali Sadikin during the 1970s), its policies also worked at cross-purposes, as when it cleared some *kampungs* to make room for commercial development and real estate speculation—driving squatters into the now more crowded remaining *kampungs*. Meanwhile new industries poured pollutants into the city's waterways while cement factories coated parts of it in a fine dust. Increasing wealth, plus the government's heavy investment in highways, led to increasing motor vehicle use, which became the chief cause of Jakarta's thick air pollution. All these factors led to significant health problems for Jakarta's residents.[26]

As in Jakarta, in cities of the richer parts of the world, increasing prosperity fueled urban environmental problems after 1945. Urban growth continued in absolute terms. Between 1950 and 2003, the number of city dwellers in the rich world grew from 430 million to 900 million.[27] But population growth arguably was less important in environmental terms than was the transition to the consumer society.

Reformers in industrializing countries had made sporadic efforts at air pollution control during the nineteenth century, but for several reasons their efforts bore fruit only after World War II. Widespread public pressure for reform intensified during the 1950s on both sides of the Atlantic, driven by increased impatience with coal smoke and mounting concern about the health effects of pollution. Several high-profile air pollution disasters that took human life, one in Donora, Pennsylvania, in 1948 and the far worse one in London in 1952, also helped to shape public opinion. At about the same time, some coal cities launched the first significant regulatory reforms. Just before and during the war, St. Louis and Pittsburgh began regulating coal smoke through civic ordinances that mandated smokeless fuels or smoke-reducing equipment. These reforms had immediate effects, which in turn helped to animate the first stirrings of reform elsewhere. West German bureaucrats, for example, watched with much interest, as did a good many in the West German press. During the 1950s that country began taking pollution control more seriously, as in the heavily industrialized Ruhr.[28]

In rich cities, fuel switching from coal to oil changed the nature of air pollution. Over the postwar era, air pollution in rich-world cities shifted from sulfur dioxide and suspended particulate matter (smoke and soot) to nitrogen oxide, ground-level ozone, and carbon monoxide. These shifts occurred mostly during and after the 1960s and 1970s. Deindustrialization and the movement of industry from city centers to peripheries combined with fuel switching to propel these air pollution changes. By the 1970s as well, national air pollution legislation had become the norm in the world's wealthiest countries, adding to the local-scale regulatory reforms begun a few decades before.[29]

As pollution from coal smoke started decreasing, that from auto exhaust grew, accounting for an increasing share of rich cities' air quality problems. Photochemical smog was first identified in Los Angeles during World War II. Within a decade the city's smog had become famous and Los Angeles had become synonymous with the problem.

Jakarta, May 1963. The surge of migration from villages to cities in the second half of the twentieth century caused explosive growth in the world's shantytowns. Jakarta had about six hundred thousand people in 1945 and about three million when this photo was taken. Today, greater Jakarta is home to twenty-five to thirty million people. (Time & Life Pictures/Getty Images)

As the automobile became much more common everywhere, so too did smog. In London, New York, and Tokyo, air pollution generated by cars increased even as other air pollution problems began to abate. Especially after regulatory interventions in the early 1970s, automobile exhausts became much cleaner in many places, hence air pollution levels in many cities fell. But the growing absolute numbers of vehicles on the roads also meant that photochemical smog remained a significant air pollution problem. By the last decades of the twentieth century, pollution from automobiles had become a serious problem in developing-world cities too, as in Jakarta, Beijing, and São Paulo. Even some of the world's poorest cities, such as Addis Ababa, suffered from automotive smog.[30]

Pollution from auto exhaust increased during the postwar era for two primary reasons. Motorization—meaning the share of the population owning an automobile—was the first of these. Before the nineteenth century, people traveled within cities on foot or by horse. During the early nineteenth century, omnibuses (horse-drawn trolleys) began appearing in Europe, then by the end of the century the electric tram. The first automobiles appeared at about the same time, but owing to their high price and impracticality they remained an extravagance for the rich. While several countries began investing in high-speed automobile highways during the interwar period (such as the Italian autostrada and the German autobahn), auto ownership remained low everywhere except the United States and Canada. After World War II, America's wealth, increasing suburbanization, and massive public highway investment entrenched this pattern. North Americans owned far more cars than anyone else, both per capita and in absolute terms, and American automakers dominated the global market. For consumers elsewhere in the world, the American car culture became an object of fascination; for engineers, American transportation planning was an object for emulation. The car became a mass consumer item in Western Europe, Japan, and Australia in the 1950s to the

1970s, later than in the United States and Canada. By 1990 Americans still led the world in car ownership, but other rich nations were not far behind.[31]

Suburbanization was the second reason automotive pollution rose in rich cities after World War II. Though suburbs had existed long before 1945, mass motorization was the primary reason they multiplied so after the war. Again there were significant differences across national contexts. The United States set the precedent in terms of scale and cultural weight. The large, freestanding house with a yard and one or two cars became the iconic and global symbol of suburbia. In 1950 around two-thirds of the American urban population lived in central cities, with a third in suburbs. Forty years later these figures had switched. Over the same time period American cities more than doubled in physical size. Predictably, given the amount of available land, North American, Canadian, and Australian cities also grew outward faster and at lower densities than cities elsewhere. European suburbs were more than three times as dense as North American and Australian suburbs. Japanese cities decentralized as well, but their densities remained far higher than those in other wealthy countries. Japan's mountainous terrain meant that cities had to be concentrated onto narrow stretches of coastal land. Despite this constraint, Japan's private automobile fleet still increased dramatically; Tokyo's alone leaped by 2.5 million from 1960 to 1990.[32]

Together, suburbanization and auto ownership had important consequences. Increased driving was the first and most predictable. Driving was most common in North America, owing to the extent of suburbanization, low average suburban densities, plus other factors such as the low price of gasoline relative to other industrialized countries. In 1990, on average, Americans traveled more than twice as far per year in private cars as Europeans, and significantly farther than Australians. Conversely, Americans walked, bicycled, and used public transit far less often than other peoples, especially compared to urban Europeans.

Nor was this all. American (and Canadian) cars were also consistently larger than those elsewhere throughout the twentieth century. Their larger size and weight made them less fuel-efficient. American motorists thus consumed more fuel and produced far more carbon dioxide than their counterparts anywhere else.[33]

Increasing wealth had a number of other consequences in the world's rich cities. While rapid outward growth consumed only a small percentage of available land in sparsely populated rich countries (Canada, Australia, and the United States), it still transformed millions of hectares of rural land into cityscapes. In places that were already crowded, such growth carried with it heavier consequences for a country's rural heritage. These places tended to have tougher land-use controls and allowed planners more say in how land was allocated, as in Great Britain after 1945. Urban wealth also increased the demand for energy and water, as people acquired the creature comforts that were developed during the postwar era. Only a very small part of the huge American appetite for residential water was for drinking and cooking. Water for lawns, cars, household appliances, showers, and flush toilets accounted for almost all of the rest in cities. The automatic dishwasher alone could increase household water use by up to 38 gallons (144 liters) a day. Finally, the consumer economies of the postwar world also generated tremendous amounts of garbage. Again the United States generated the most in per capita and absolute terms. Wealth was a major factor in increasing the amount of garbage, as were new materials (especially plastics) that became more important in the consumer economy. Cities therefore produced rising tides of garbage, forcing local governments to search endlessly for disposal solutions.[34]

In Search of the Green City

From the 1970s onward, more and more people increasingly sought to revisit the basic ecological arrangement of cities. They wondered whether modern cities must continue to be the grasping, all-consuming metropolises characteristic of the twentieth century, or whether they can be transformed in some way to reduce or eliminate the environmental damage they cause. The urban claim on global resources had increased many times over since the onset of the Industrial Revolution. Cities now acquired enormous amounts of resources from every part of the globe: Brazilian soybeans, American corn, Saudi Arabian oil, Bangladeshi cotton, Australian coal, Malaysian hardwoods, South African gold. Cities had also globalized their waste streams, becoming the source of most anthropogenic carbon emissions.[35]

In the early 1990s the ecologist William Rees, working at the University of British Columbia, and his Swiss student Mathis Wackernagel formulated the "ecological footprint" idea to give conceptual and quantitative expression to the global reach of cities. Every city, Rees argued in an early (1992) and groundbreaking paper on the concept, "coopts on a continuous basis several hectares of productive ecosystem for each inhabitant." Rees estimated that every resident of his own city, Vancouver, required 1.9 hectares of productive agricultural land for food. Rees calculated that the city consumed enough resources (including food, fuel, and forest products) and emitted enough wastes to "occupy" a land area about the size of South Carolina or Scotland. He thus demonstrated that Vancouver, by most standards one of the greenest cities on Earth, had an enormous ecological footprint.[36]

Despite challenges on theoretical and practical grounds to the ecological footprint concept, nonetheless it conveyed a fundamental idea—and anxiety—about cities that was becoming more common. Ecologists and planners such as Rees and Wackernagel had begun to ask whether there was enough nature to go around in a world increasingly dominated by cities. Rising concerns about climate change, ozone layer depletion, and other global environmental issues prompted much of this anxiety. So too did the rash of international environmental conferences that occurred at about this time, most especially the Earth

Summit in Rio de Janeiro of June 1992. Similar concerns inspired some urban planners to call for refocusing their profession around environmental themes and some architects to develop green building standards.[37]

A fair number of cities, especially in central and northern Europe, had been experimenting with wide-ranging green policies since the 1970s. They built efficient cogeneration plants (these recycled waste heat from electrical generation) and encouraged alternative energy. They funneled new urban growth to designated areas adjacent to existing cities. They tried to increase, rather than reduce, densities in new developments. They created programs for recycling, community gardening, green roofs, and ecosystem restoration.[38]

Many of these initiatives became common practice in Europe, as in Freiburg (in southwestern Germany). Now recognized as one of the world's environmental leaders, Freiburg began emphasizing solar energy production in the 1990s as central to the city's long-term economic development. The city government installed solar panels on public buildings, made land available to solar firms at low cost, introduced solar power as a theme in public school curricula, and established cooperative programs with local research institutions. The city integrated solar power into new residential development, including high-profile green showcases such as the Vauban district on the city's outskirts. Freiburg's identity now reflects its great success in establishing itself as a solar city. The city markets itself as Germany's greenest city, where solar energy makes good business as well as environmental sense.[39]

After 1970 a number of European cities also broke with postwar planning trends centered on the automobile. For political or cultural reasons these cities decided to encourage other means of transportation in order to preserve their historic centers and avoid the worst consequences of auto-centric development, especially air pollution and sprawl. During the 1970s and 1980s, for instance, Zurich's leaders decided to expand and improve the city's tram system, which significantly increased ridership while slowing growth in auto use. Because the trams enlivened the streetscape, the effort also helped to revitalize the city center. Other European cities arrived at similar ends using different tactics, as was the case in some Dutch, Danish, and German cities with the bicycle. Popular support for bicycling in cities like Amsterdam and Copenhagen spurred their city governments to invest in cycling infrastructure, contributing to widespread usage of the world's most energy-efficient transportation machine.[40]

Environmental innovation was not limited to wealthy cities, as the case of the southern Brazilian city of Curitiba shows.[41] From the early 1970s, when it began implementing some innovative planning ideas, the local government created a city that won praise worldwide for its environmental credentials and high standard of living. Curitiba's government tried innovative approaches to just about every problem, preferring to focus on practical, low-cost projects over the expensive showpieces that characterized most other developing cities. For instance, the government took an unusual approach to tackling chronic flooding in Curitiba. Instead of building levees alongside the rivers running through the city, it constructed small dams to create lakes. The areas surrounding the lakes were then turned into large urban parks. This approach had two effects. The lakes absorbed the summer rainfall, reducing flooding in the city, and the amount of public green space increased dramatically.

While Curitiba could boast many other programs just as innovative and as important in burnishing the city's international reputation, its most famous success story was its bus transit system. Curitiba's decision to prioritize public transit in the 1960s flew in the face of the dominant planning trends of the period. City planners all over the world, including Brazil, were designing or redesigning cities around the automobile. Curitiba's planners rejected this model, believing it favored the wealthy motorist over the majority of the city's inhabitants. In addition, they thought the model would create traffic congestion and destroy the vibrancy of the city's historic center. They opted instead to revamp the city's bus network, beginning in the early 1970s. Five main axes running into the city center were identified as express transit routes, upon which only buses were allowed; cars were shunted off to side streets. An efficient system of color-coded feeder routes completed the network. Simple but ingenious design improvements were added. One of these innovations, the elegant glass-and-steel "tube stations" that enabled buses to be loaded much more quickly, became iconic symbols of the city's success. Curitiba's planners complemented these efforts through land-use regulations (allowing housing densities to be higher along the bus routes) and building infrastructure in the city center for pedestrians and bicyclists. These measures quickly generated results. By the early 1990s Curitiba's residents owned more cars per capita than the Brazilian average but the bus system carried a large share of the city's traffic, well over a million passengers a day. The city's residents also used less fuel and created less air pollution than would otherwise have been the case.

In Havana, inadvertent measures rather than deliberate planning provided an example of the greening of a developing city.[42] Like other countries, socialist Cuba had built its agricultural economy on mechanization (tractors and trucks), chemicals (artificial fertilizers and pesticides), and specialization in cash crops for export. By the 1980s Cuba imported a large share of its food while producing and exporting sugar. The country relied on Soviet oil and markets, both of which disappeared immediately after the USSR vanished. A sudden and dramatic decline in imports of all kinds, including oil, agricultural equipment, and fertilizers and pesticides, meant that Cuba could no longer produce enough sugar to afford imported goods. This was an even more serious problem given the continuing American trade embargo. Put simply, the country faced starvation, as it was not self-sufficient in food production.

With little choice, starting in the 1990s Cuba embarked on a massive experiment in organic agriculture. Farms shifted from tractors to oxen and from artificial fertilizers and pesticides to organic ones. Both generated unexpected positive developments. Oxen, for instance, did not compact the soil the way tractors had, and organic pesticides were far less toxic than chemical ones. With little oil for long-distance transportation, Cubans had to produce food closer to where it was eaten. Facing hunger, Havana's two million residents took matters into their own hands and began planting gardens on every square meter of land they could find. Over the decade, habaneros created thousands of such rooftop, patio, and backyard gardens. Neighborhood cooperatives emerged to acquire and garden larger parcels of land, such as baseball diamonds and abandoned lots. Recognizing a good thing, the state made tools, land, seeds, and technical advice available to Havana's residents, and allowed the formation of street markets. By 2000 these efforts had paid off. Havana and other Cuban cities produced a large share of the food they needed to survive.

Havana's experiment is astonishing for the rapidity and scale of its agricultural transformation, but "urban agriculture," as it has come to be known, is widespread globally. In the last decades of the twentieth century, as poor cities expanded, the scale of urban agriculture grew rapidly. Often unable to afford food provided through commercial systems, the urban poor turned to informal production and food networks. During the 1990s the United Nations estimated that some 800 million people worldwide depended on informal urban agriculture for sustenance or income, supplying a sizable share of all food consumed in poorer cities. At century's end, urban agriculture provided Accra with 90 percent of its fresh vegetables, Kampala with 70 percent of its poultry, and Hanoi with about half of its meat.[43]

Cities such as Freiburg and Curitiba are cases of real progress. They show again that cities are not uniform and can be places of enormous ingenuity and problem-solving creativity. Yet even these examples are not beyond criticism. Skeptics question whether any city can be made ecologically benign. The urbanization process has not stopped. Most cities will continue to grow in absolute terms well into the twenty-first century. In addition, increasing wealth around the world will mean that cities will continue to demand a wide range of luxury goods that they cannot possibly create within their own boundaries. The world's supply of automobiles, for example, is predicted to increase several times over, driven by rising prosperity in countries such as India and China. Improved technologies and approaches to design have bettered environmental conditions in many cities (not just in the greenest examples cited here), but the question is whether these efforts will be enough to alter the trajectory that cities have followed for centuries. As centers of population, consumption, and industrial production, they have long had an impact on environmental change far out of proportion to their size. As centers of creativity and innovation, they have lately also had a disproportionate role in checking human environmental impacts.[44]

Ecology and the Global Economy

In terms of ecological consequences, the most important feature of the second half of the twentieth century was the performance of the global economy. After World War II the global economy rebounded from the severe problems of the interwar period and embarked on a long period of unprecedented growth. In the half century after 1950, the global economy grew sixfold. Annual economic growth averaged 3.9 percent per year, far outstripping the estimated historical averages for the industrial age up to that point (1820–1950) of 1.6 percent per year and for the "early modern," post-Columbian world (1500–1820) of 0.3 percent per year. Growth peaked between 1950 and 1973, a period that has been labeled the "golden age," a *Wirtschaftswunder*" (economic miracle), "*les trentes glorieuses*" (the thirty glorious years), or "the long boom," depending on the nationality of the observer. For several reasons, including increased oil prices and higher inflation, world economic growth slowed but did not stop after 1973. The economic growth of the postwar era led to a resurgence of global trade, communications, and travel, increased international migration, and technological advances. The era was marked, at different points in time, by the integration or reintegration of large parts of the formerly colonized and socialist worlds into the advanced capitalist economy. Large swaths of Asia became much wealthier over the half century, to the point where levels of prosperity and occasionally political influence began to rival those of the historic economic leaders (mainly Western Europe, the United States, Australia, Canada, and Japan). After the revolutions of 1989–1991 in Central and Eastern Europe, former Soviet Bloc states also began this reintegration process, with varying levels of success. However, the era was also characterized by increasing gaps between the wealthiest parts of the world and those regions that remained poor.[45]

Several factors combined to sustain the postwar era's rapid economic growth. On a political level, the onset of the Cold War quickly reorganized much of the world into two major blocs. Each of these was ruled by a superpower that had an enormous incentive to stimulate economic recovery and growth, albeit using very different methods. By the late 1940s the Cold War and global reorganization were fully under way. American leadership provided the basis for the larger and what would prove to be more dynamic of the two systems, the capitalist order. During World War II the Western Allies (led by the United States and Great Britain) had laid the groundwork for this system. Fearing a return of the Great Depression, the Allies created a series of institutions designed to encourage cooperation in finance, trade, and politics and to discourage autarkic solutions. These institutions included the United Nations and those that grew out of the Bretton Woods Conference in 1944—the International Monetary Fund and the

International Bank for Reconstruction and Development, later the World Bank. They were designed to help finance the reconstruction of national economies ravaged by the war. Within a few years negotiations also produced the General Agreement on Tariffs and Trade (GATT), designed to reduce tariffs, quotas, and other trade restrictions.

The political and economic position of the United States made all this possible. America had emerged from the war with an intact economic base and undamaged cities, in contrast to Japan, China, the Soviet Union, and Europe. It had suffered only a fraction of the human losses endured by all of its potential rivals. As after World War I, it had emerged from the second global war as a creditor rather than a debtor nation. Perhaps most importantly in an economic sense, American industrial power was unmatched. The American economy had overtaken Great Britain's decades before and had since extended its advantage. The country's vast resources and large population contributed to this lead, as did the vigor and innovativeness of its industry. Its firms had perfected the assembly line technique, for example, starting in the early twentieth century, while the relatively high wages these firms offered allowed the world's first mass consumer society to emerge, even before the American entry into the war in 1941. In the immediate postwar world, when the United States alone accounted for more than one-third of the global economy, its financial strength allowed the United States to underwrite a massive worldwide reconstruction program that had the dual aims of stabilizing the global economy and containing communism. America's huge financial resources meant that it could funnel billions of dollars in aid to reconstruct both Europe (via the Marshall Plan) and Japan, thereby stabilizing both and contributing to their rapid economic takeoff during the 1950s, while simultaneously building political and military alliances around the world. On top of all this, the strength of the dollar stabilized the global financial system, at least until the early 1970s.[46]

The story was a bit different in the socialist world after 1945. The Soviet Union suffered the most of all major combatant nations during World War II, having lost upward of twenty million people. With Russia and the Soviet Union having been on the receiving end of three invasions from the west in a bit more than a century, Stalin was in no mood to withdraw the Red Army from Eastern Europe at war's end. The Soviet Union, like the Western Allies, therefore set out to mold its sphere of influence. Among other things, the Soviets attempted to forge an economic bloc in Eastern Europe through the creation of the Council for Mutual Economic Assistance (COMECON), established in 1949. COMECON sought to coordinate economic development among member countries, but unlike the relatively free trading regime eventually established in the West, the organization scarcely furthered economic integration. Rather, it served to facilitate bilateral trade between the Soviet Union and its Eastern European clients.[47]

During the interwar period, the Soviets' crash program in state-led, centrally planned gigantism—the hurried, even frenetic, construction of huge metallurgical complexes, dams, mines, new industrial cities, enormous collectivized farms, and the like—had enabled the country to transform itself quickly from a low level of industrialization to a relatively high level, sufficient to defeat Nazi Germany when war came. This development model therefore had been a success, if one defines success narrowly in a productivist sense and ignores the violence to human beings and the natural world that state-driven industrialization on such a vast scale and in such a compressed time frame seemed to require.

After World War II the Soviets continued to follow the same model. They rebuilt those parts of their industrial base that had been ravaged during the war, a cause helped by their ability to extract reparations from their former enemy (in the form of heavy machinery and equipment that was hurriedly stripped from occupied Germany and shipped eastward). Moreover, they continued to focus on increasing the country's heavy industrial output, concentrated in large state enterprises, as opposed to developing a more flexible, consumer-driven economy like the West's. This was in part a result of ideological preferences, which fetishized heavy industrial output (such as iron and steel production), and in part a result of the Cold War, which required massive and continued investment in armaments. But part of the explanation also rested on the success and prestige of the Soviet model, which had led to industrialization and defeat of the Nazi war machine. Although from a much smaller total base, the Soviet Bloc economy grew nearly as fast as the West's during its golden age. Annual per capita GDP growth averaged 3.5 percent in the East versus 3.7 percent in the West (including Japan). From 1928 to 1970 or so the USSR was an economic tiger—war, terror, purges, and state planners notwithstanding. As there appeared to be little reason to alter their system, during these decades Soviet leaders continued to emphasize heavy industrial development via top-down, bureaucratic, and highly centralized planning.[48]

Global economic growth everywhere also depended on a critical physical factor, energy. Over the twentieth century, energy use and economic expansion proceeded in lockstep, meaning that economic growth required expanding energy inputs. During global economic booms such as the periods before World War I and after World War II, global energy use also increased at high rates. During periods of slower economic growth or contraction, as during the interwar decades, energy use likewise increased much more slowly. During the decades after 1945, the enormous scale of the global economy required energy inputs far in excess of all previous periods.[49]

There were large regional variations in the production and use of energy. The leading producers benefited most of all from good geological fortune. In the nineteenth century, its huge coal reserves helped to make Great Britain the world's largest fossil fuel producer. From the 1890s, however, the vast coal, oil, and natural gas reserves of the United

States enabled it to surpass Great Britain, a position it has never relinquished. After World War II, the Soviet Union also overtook Great Britain and held on to second place behind the United States until the USSR disappeared in 1991. At century's end, China, Canada, and Saudi Arabia joined the United States and post-Soviet Russia as the largest energy producers.

Energy consumption was another story, bearing scant relation to geology. Generally speaking, more wealth required more energy for comfortable levels of consumption, while at the same time more energy deployed productively led to more wealth. In 1950 the rich industrialized world consumed the vast majority (93 percent) of the commercially produced energy on Earth. This percentage fell over time as industrial production, accompanying wealth, and population increased in other regions of the world. By 2005 the proportion was down to a bit more than 60 percent. Nonetheless, throughout the postwar period absolute levels of energy consumption were always highest in the world's richest countries. Canada and the United States stood atop the list in annual per capita energy use for most of the period after 1945, joined lately by some small states of the Persian Gulf. Energy consumption did not always depend on possession of fossil fuels. Japan, for instance, has almost nothing in the way of coal or oil, yet it remains toward the top end of the global scale in energy consumption. At the opposite end were the world's poor countries, with energy consumption rates a tiny fraction of those of the world's richest countries.[50]

The contrast between Canadian and Japanese energy use points to another important issue: efficiency. At the end of the twentieth century, Japan required about a third of the energy needed to produce a dollar's worth of GDP, compared with Canada. European economies were almost as efficient as Japan. At the other extreme were rapidly industrializing countries, including China and India, whose economies were five to six times less efficient than Japan and two to three times less efficient than Canada and the United States. Such figures underscore two distinctions. First, the energy efficiency of national economies has tended to follow a historical pattern. The typical economy's energy use per GDP (energy intensity) rose quickly as it entered a period of rapid and heavy industrialization. This spike in energy intensity would normally be followed by a long and gradual decline as the economy began to use energy more efficiently. This was the historical experience of Great Britain, which peaked in the 1850s, Canada (peaked around 1910), and the United States (peaked around 1920). Not all economies have functioned in this fashion, however. Japan's economy maintained stable but comparatively low energy intensity throughout much of the twentieth century. Second, significant efficiency variations *within* the rich world showed that it was possible to become wealthy using energy at much lower levels than did Canada and the United States. There were many factors that explained why national economies in the rich world diverged, ranging from industrial mix to regional climate to suburbanization patterns. Comparative data showed that core quality-of-life indicators (including infant mortality, life expectancy, and food availability) did not improve substantially beyond annual energy consumption levels of roughly one-third to one-quarter those of the United States and Canada.[51]

As we have seen, the postwar era also saw the highest rates of sustained population increase in world history. Rising populations help explain global economic growth, almost by definition: more people usually meant more economic activity. But otherwise the relationship was not straightforward. In some places at some times, population growth occurred within countries that were experiencing strong economic growth. But in other times and places, population growth rates were so high as to cause problems, wiping out any per capita economic gains. If any generalization can be made about the relationship, it is that rapid industrialization and modernization and their effects, including urbanization and wealth accumulation, tended to reduce fertility rates, and thus population growth rates, over the long run. In

1945 this process had been ongoing in the rich world for a century or more. In the postwar era it continued, resulting in societies with slow population growth or none at all. This occurred despite longer life expectancy. Australian life expectancy increased from 69.6 years in 1950 to 76 years in 1987. Sweden's increased by six years, Italy's by ten, Japan's by almost twenty. Rich world economies thus had to face the economic complications associated with aging populations, including higher social security payments and fewer young workers to support the elderly. Declining population growth rates also marked the trajectories of those poorer societies that were undergoing rapid economic change. Large pools of cheap labor initially were of great assistance to economies in East Asia (South Korea and Taiwan, for instance), but over time their economic success led to lower population growth rates as well.[52] Thus, population growth both underwrote economic expansion after 1945, as it had done before, but when fast enough also imperiled per capita gains. When it slowed after 1975, issues of intergenerational equity (mainly unsustainable pension commitments) loomed ominously, at least in the rich world.

Technology, Economy, and Nature

Improved technology also enabled the rapid economic growth in the postwar period. Periods of intense technical innovation had marked the Industrial Revolution since its origins. Scientific research and its technical application to the postwar world, driven by both public and private investment, acted as an important spur to the global economy. Some postwar innovations, such as satellites and the Internet, were completely new; others simply improved upon earlier designs. The humble shipping container is a perfect example. Before World War II, ocean-going freighters were loaded with odd-size cargo that required legions of stevedores and considerable time to load and unload. After the war, however, shippers began improving the container, a device that had been invented but not used widely before the war. The container's great advantage was that it allowed odd-shaped cargo to be packed beforehand into a standardized box, which could then be loaded and unloaded by crane operators at much greater speed, without longshoremen. This dramatically increased shipping efficiency, hence greatly lowered costs. After 1965 the container became the standard means of shipping manufactured cargo, and probably did more to promote international trade than all free trade agreements put together. Eventually the container was married to railroad and trucking systems and to information technologies that allowed the millions of individual containers to be tracked in real time. By 2000 there were some 6.7 million containers in operation worldwide. The reduction in shipping times achieved through containerization proved especially critical to the rise of export-oriented economies in East Asia that were literally oceans away from their markets.[53]

Postwar technological innovation also created new types of environmental difficulties. Scientific and technological advances during the nineteenth century had produced a range of synthetic chemicals, compounds, and substances. But during the twentieth century in general, and the postwar period in particular, the use of artificial substances greatly proliferated. Laboratories churned out countless new chemicals, ranging from household cleaners to industrial lubricants to agricultural pesticides, herbicides, and fungicides. Because there was little awareness of the possible health and environmental consequences of so many new substances, a great number of these were originally used without any precautionary testing or regulation. This began to change only during the 1960s and 1970s, with the emergence of the mass environmental movement.[54]

The production and use of plastics provided a good example. Polymers (molecular compounds consisting of linked chains of simpler molecules) based on natural materials such as cellulose had been invented in the late nineteenth century. Synthetic polymers were created shortly after 1900. Then during the interwar period they were manufactured and marketed on larger scales. During the 1950s and 1960s, rapid advances in the laboratory enabled large chemical firms such as DuPont in the United States and Imperial Chemical Industries (ICI) in the United Kingdom to create a slew of improved synthetic polymers, enabling their rapid proliferation. Before 1960 the manufacture and use of plastics during these decades appeared to cause little, if any, anxiety about environmental consequences. As was typical of the period, this form of technical achievement was embraced without much reservation. A 1959 article in *The Science News-Letter* (an American publication), for example, gushed about polymer research. Polymers, the author wrote, would provide "lighter, stronger components for missiles and space vehicles and automobile bodies that are more rugged pound for pound than those in current use." In deference to the prevailing faith in (male) expertise to overcome any difficulty, the author argued that any problems could be solved by "technical men" who were "confident that important progress" was being made. The link between the technical mastery of plastics and social progress was considered a given; environmental considerations remained minimal. Global plastics production exploded at midcentury. World production rose from less than 50,000 tons in 1930 to 2 million tons in 1950 and 6 million tons a decade later. New types of plastics flooded the marketplace. Plastics substituted for materials such as glass, wood, and paper in existing goods or became the key substance in a huge array of new consumer goods.[55]

Production in such quantities invariably meant that plastics began to show up in the world's ecosystems. By the early 1970s the previously sunny narrative about plastics darkened as the mass environmental movement began to alter the way in which people thought about introducing artificial substances into the environment. Observers started filing disconcerting reports about plastics dumping, in particular in the world's waterways and seas. In 1971 the Norwegian adventurer Thor Heyerdahl caused a stir when he published a book containing the claim that the Atlantic Ocean resembled a vast garbage dump. The subjects of the book were the 1969–1970 transatlantic voyages of Heyerdahl's papyrus rafts *Ra* and *Ra II*, voyages that were similar in design and purpose to the 1947 *Kon-Tiki* expedition in the Pacific that had made the author famous. The transatlantic voyages had shown him that the ocean had become laced with oil and all manner of refuse, notably plastics. The Atlantic of the late 1960s, Heyerdahl said, was infinitely dirtier than the Pacific he had sailed in the late 1940s. "I had seen nothing like this when I spent 101 days with my nose at water level on board the *Kon-Tiki*," he wrote. "It became clear to all of us [on board the *Ra*] that mankind really was in the process of polluting his most vital wellspring, our planet's indispensable filtration plant, the ocean." A couple of years later, a large-scale study of the Caribbean Sea and western Atlantic Ocean, undertaken by scientists at America's National Oceanic and Atmospheric Administration (NOAA), confirmed the accuracy of Heyerdahl's claims.[56]

Yet the newfound concern for protection of the environment from plastics did not reduce the use of plastics in the following decades. The range of applications and general utility of plastics outweighed environmental concerns, so that by 2000 the world produced some 150 to 250 million tons of plastics annually (estimates vary), some 75 to 125 times as much by weight as in 1950 and perhaps 3,000 to 5,000 times as much as in 1930.[57] Despite some environmental regulation in some places, plastics continued to accumulate in the world's oceans and seas, not to mention its landfills (globally, in the early twenty-first century plastic constituted about a tenth of all garbage).

Early in the twenty-first century, scientists and sailors reported a new and frightening variant of the plastics saga, consisting of gigantic floating trash middens that plagued the world's oceans. One of these concentrations, a massive plastic soup slowly twirling in the Pacific Ocean between Hawaii and California, contained a good share of the last sixty years' worth of plastic production, much of it apparently from

A pile of trash removed from the North Pacific Gyre, October 2009. Ingenious chemistry in the twentieth century led to ever more durable plastics, but many plastic items end up in the world's oceans, bobbing in the waves for decades. (UIG via Getty Images)

Japan. (No one knew its exact size, but by 2010 some estimates put it at twice the size of Texas.) The bulk of the gyre consisted of tiny fragments of plastic, sodden petrochemical confetti. But there were also rubber dinghies and kayaks, condemned to endless drift voyages, like the *Flying Dutchman* of yore. The South Pacific, Indian Ocean, and North and South Atlantic had their own, smaller patches of floating plastic. Although scientists do not know how ocean plastics affect ocean biology, it is well attested that seabirds and marine mammals get tangled up in plastic and often eat it. All recently examined seabirds of the North Sea contain plastic, as do a third of those in the Canadian Arctic. Tiny bits of plastic work their way through the food web of the oceans, collecting in the top predators such as killer whales and tuna fish. Happily, most plastics are not toxic, and only a few are dangerously so. Some birds have learned to use plastic pieces in making nests. It is early days yet in the history of plastics, but chemists expect the contents of the marine middens to last centuries or millennia, so the oceans' flora and fauna will for a long time be subject to a new selection pressure—compatibility with plastic.[58]

The history of plastics indicates that technologically driven economic change had enormous environmental consequences. But the relationship between technology, economy, and environment often was more complex than the plastics example showed. New technologies occasionally could be less destructive of the environment compared with what preceded them. On the other hand, such technological innovations might not have net environmental benefits if economic growth swallowed the gains. The history of electronic appliances such as refrigerators provides an apt illustration of this contradiction.

Modern refrigerator technology dates to the early twentieth century, in particular the 1920s, after a cheap and apparently harmless category of refrigerants, CFCs, was discovered in the laboratory. This discovery was the key that allowed refrigerator prices to fall rapidly in the United States, where the appliance was in half of all homes even before World War II. Postwar mass consumerism in the rich world drove sales of the appliance strongly upward for decades. After it had become clear in the 1970s and 1980s that CFCs were thinning the Earth's ozone layer, an insight that led to the signing of the 1987 Montreal Protocol, the world's largest refrigerator manufacturers embarked on campaigns to "green" their appliances and to market them as such. During the 1990s they phased out CFCs as other refrigerants came onto the market and began designing and building appliances that contained less material, used energy more efficiently, contained fewer toxic chemicals, and were more recyclable. In addition, firms worked with regulatory agencies and nonprofit organizations to create environmental standards and performance benchmarks. All of this activity had a real effect: the typical refrigerator made in 2002 consumed nearly

80 percent less energy than a unit produced in 1980. Meanwhile, global refrigerator sales expanded throughout the period. Households in the developing world, especially East Asia, bought their first refrigerators, while some households in the rich world acquired their second or third units. The environmental benefits of the improved refrigerators, in fact, became a key part of the marketing strategies of the major manufacturers and contributed to higher global sales. Eventually even a fivefold reduction in energy use per refrigerator was offset by the growing number of refrigerators in use, boosting total energy consumption. In China refrigerators account for 15 percent of total electricity demand. Household appliances are now enormous consumers of electricity on a global level.[59]

Regional Economic Shifts

In 1945 the great majority of the world's population lived outside of the consumer-driven, high-energy, and materials-intensive global economy that now characterizes much of the globe. The story of the succeeding seven decades was one of the incorporation of ever-larger parts of the world into this economy. Only North America had emerged from the war in a condition that allowed a quick return to a peacetime consumer economy. The war itself had almost leveled the economies of both Western Europe and Japan, both of which had been at a much lower level of consumer development than the United States and Canada before the war. But these economies also transitioned quickly to mass consumerism, beginning with the onset of the "golden age" in the 1950s. Other world regions started their integration into this economy at still later dates. Perhaps the most important were Southern, Southeastern, and East Asian countries, beginning with the "tigers" Taiwan, South Korea, Singapore, and Hong Kong. These small economies utilized low labor costs and other advantages to service the richer parts of the world in an export-led strategy. Their success induced other states in the region to follow their example. China was the biggest and most significant of these later participants. It began a transition in the late 1970s from a statist, centralized, autarkic economy to one that incorporated some key capitalist features, a choice that by the 1990s began to produce some spectacular results. The socialist economies of Eastern Europe and the Soviet Union would have to wait until the revolutions of 1989–1991 to begin their transitions to a consumer society. Latin America and Africa also increasingly integrated into global circuits of trade and investment, but with mixed results that permitted only a narrow expansion of consumerism.

After some difficult initial years following the war, the economies of Western Europe began to grow quickly. Under the American security umbrella, European elites could focus on the linked processes of refashioning their economies around consumer-driven growth and on increasing the political and economic integration of the continent. They were successful on both fronts. The major European economies of the Western alliance—West Germany, France, Italy, and Great Britain—grew quickly after 1950, owing to a combination of government activism in guiding and stimulating the economy, high savings and investment rates, skilled workforces, and full access to the enormously wealthy American market. Economic activity was also enhanced by the spread of cheap energy, in particular oil, which gave European economies the basis for their postwar transition to high-consumption societies. After 1973, Western European economies ran into considerable difficulty thanks in large part to higher oil prices. But over several decades, from the 1950s to the 1990s, Europe's politicians and Brussels's bureaucrats managed to bind the continent's economies tightly together in the European Union, helping to underpin continued economic growth into the twenty-first century.[60]

Japan followed a similar growth trajectory. Flat on its back in 1945, Japan's economy under the American occupation soon rebounded to prewar production levels. By the early 1950s rapid growth was well under way, spurred by American military contracts as a result of the Korean War. Over the next two decades the country grew faster than any other in the world, averaging eight percent per year. Japan's success owed much to its well-educated workforce, high levels of savings and investment, and close cooperation between the government and big business on economic policy and technological development—for instance, through the powerful Ministry of Trade and Industry (MITI). Growth in Japan slowed after 1973, as it did nearly everywhere else, but it remained higher than in Europe or the United States into the 1990s. Mass consumerism reflected a rising Japanese standard of living. Within a few decades after the war, the typical Japanese household went from possessing almost no large durable goods to owning most of those goods that characterized the high-consumption economy. For instance, in 1957 only 3 percent of Japanese households owned an electric refrigerator. By 1980 nearly all of them did. In 1957, 20 percent of households owned an electric washing machine and just 7.8 percent a television set. In 1980, nearly all Japanese households had both these items. Automobile ownership also skyrocketed: from 22 percent in 1970 to 57 percent just a decade later. Japan by 1980 had joined the mass-consumption club.[61]

The European and Japanese economic revivals demonstrated the pull of American consumer culture. Europeans had alternatively feared or embraced the "Americanization" of their continent in the interwar period, but during the postwar era American cultural and economic power on the continent attained unprecedented levels. The broad-based prosperity enjoyed by Europeans enabled many more people to consume products and services that were exported by the United States. Even more critically, large numbers of Europeans had the desire and the means to approximate the high-energy, materials-intensive American lifestyle, embodied in the automobile, household appliances, the freestanding house in the suburbs, and everyday consumer products. Nor was this experience confined to Western Europe.

The Japanese also had their version of Americanization, having been directly exposed to American culture through the postwar occupation. As Japanese workers earned higher wages during the miracle decades, they eagerly snapped up the fashion, food, entertainment, and clothing that were regarded as quintessentially American. Advertisers discovered this taste for American products and tailored their messages and products to fit demand. Like Italians or Britons, the Japanese found new methods of consumption that mirrored American practice. By the late 1950s, for example, supermarkets had found their way into Japanese cities, as did 24-hour convenience marts and fast-food restaurants about two decades later. Americanization, it should be noted, is a construct that historians have debated for decades. Scholars now consider the historical production, transmission, and reception of American culture abroad to be highly complex, nonlinear, and constantly evolving. Nonetheless, it is reasonable to argue that it was a key factor in stimulating consumer desires around the globe.[62]

However, mass consumerism had little to do with the socialist economies of the USSR and, after 1949, the People's Republic of China. Mao Zedong had developed a worldview that in some respects mirrored that of Soviet leaders in the interwar years. He had a commitment to rapid industrial development, driven by a fear of Western encirclement and by a desire to catch up with and eventually overtake the Soviet Union itself. Mao believed that the Chinese Communist Party, through the force of superior organizational skill and a willingness to engage in mass mobilization, could force China to develop from a nation of poor peasants to an industrial power almost overnight. It was true that China did industrialize after 1949, a process that by the time of Mao's death in 1976 had both enlarged the country's economy and nearly doubled its per capita GDP (albeit from a low initial level).[63] Yet, as did the Soviet Union, China paid a heavy price for this in human and environmental terms, as we shall see.

Around 1960 the Soviet Union's economy appeared to be in better shape than China's. But by the 1970s it began to show signs of major structural problems. The constant emphasis on heavy industry and military spending worked to the detriment of the consumer economy, empowering central planners, the military, and large state producers rather than individual consumers. The Soviet economy thus was capable of churning out huge quantities of materials, including some categories of consumer items, but these rarely matched consumer preferences. The system provided factory managers with few incentives to use materials and energy sparingly and laborers with little reason to work hard. Moreover, despite having outstanding scientists, the Soviet economy seemed unable to keep up with Western technological improvements, at least in areas such as computerization that were beginning to reshape the global economy. In agriculture, collectivized farms proved grossly inefficient. The small plots that peasants were allowed to cultivate for themselves were far more efficient, because peasants could sell produce from them on the market. Large agricultural projects, such as Khrushchev's "Virgin Lands" scheme (1956–1963), wasted untold amounts of valuable resources, including soil and fresh water. On top of all this the Soviet Union faced serious social problems that hampered the economy, such as chronic alcoholism.[64]

In the 1970s, despite these problems, the Soviet leadership proved unwilling to engage in any serious reforms. Part of the reason stemmed from what appeared to be the system's success. The Soviet economy had been propped up by the discovery of enormous oil and natural gas deposits in the 1960s. This generated huge revenues for the state, in particular after the 1973 OPEC oil embargo caused global fuel prices to skyrocket. Oil prices stayed high through the 1970s, allowing the Soviets to paper over their system's shortcomings. While several Western countries, including the United States and Great Britain, were forced to engage in painful restructuring of their heavy industrial sectors during the 1970s, the Soviets did no such thing. The aging Soviet leadership, dominated by men who had come of age under Stalin, also refused to reconsider the country's increasingly difficult geopolitical position. The Cold War imposed a military spending burden on the country that was far larger than in the West in terms of the share of GDP spent on defense. The Soviet Union's sphere of influence contributed to the problem. Eastern Europe was as much a drain on resources as it was a benefit. Unlike the Western alliance, the Soviet Bloc had been held together through coercion more than anything else, as the violent uprisings in East Berlin and Poland (1953), Hungary (1956), and Czechoslovakia (1968) had shown, and as later mass resistance movements such as Poland's Solidarity would again demonstrate.[65]

By the 1980s the Soviet Union was in desperate straits. At mid-decade a global collapse in oil prices took away the state's windfall revenues, exposing the glaring weaknesses of the Soviet economy. In March 1985 things appeared a bit brighter after the fifty-four-year-old Mikhail Gorbachev became general secretary of the Communist Party, displacing the Kremlin's old guard. Having long recognized the shortcomings of the Soviet system, Gorbachev immediately embarked on a program of fundamental political, economic, and diplomatic reform. Glasnost opened up the Soviet Union's political system to freer exchange of information. Perestroika reforms were intended to reshape the economy. Gorbachev also sought a new relationship with the West that included deep cuts in nuclear arms, a decision motivated as much by Gorbachev's recognition that military spending was a major part of the Soviet Union's economic weakness as it was by a desire to defuse Cold War tensions. While these reforms produced positive results in a number of areas, in aggregate terms they backfired. Soviet citizens reacted to the unceasing reports of the state's incompetence and corruption with widespread cynicism and anger. Glasnost became a boon to nationalists in the country's peripheral republics. After Gorbachev allowed the Eastern European revolutions to proceed in 1989, the political integrity of the Soviet Union itself withered. Worse still, the economic reforms proved to be only halfway measures and failed to reinvigorate the economy. Attempts to stimulate consumerism and introduce profit motives to state-owned firms were more than offset by the system's bureaucratic inertia and by long-standing corruption.[66]

Gorbachev's efforts to remake the Soviet Union therefore succeeded, but not in the way he had hoped. He intended for his reforms to reinvigorate a moribund socialism, but what occurred was the end of the Soviet system. In 1991 the Soviet Union disappeared and a set of new republics took its place. During the 1990s all of these underwent very difficult transitions to market-based economies. So did those of the former Soviet Bloc, although some, such as Poland's, experienced fairly high growth. Russia, the core of the former Soviet Union, was hit the hardest, in part because it presided over the largest collection of obsolete heavy industrial plants, most of which could not compete in the global marketplace. A host of other problems beset Russia during the 1990s, including elites' redirection of much of the country's remaining wealth into their own hands. The Russian economy collapsed, shrinking by as much as 40 percent during the decade, although no one really knew the true extent, owing to reporting irregularities and the country's vast black market.[67]

China followed a much more successful path. By the mid-1970s China had gone through a series of convulsions, including both the Great Leap Forward and the Cultural Revolution, which had left the country exhausted. To make matters worse, China had become economically and politically isolated. Deepening ideological differences with China's Soviet mentors had resulted in Soviet withdrawal of aid in 1960, signaling an era of escalating tensions between the largest, most important, and most militarily powerful regimes in the communist world. Soviet withdrawal also effectively cut China off from its remaining political and economic allies. This began changing in the early 1970s, when both China and the Western powers began seeing opportunities for a realignment of global geopolitics. American policy had been antagonistic toward China for two decades. But in the early 1970s, seizing the advantage presented by the Sino-Soviet split of 1958–1960, the Americans and the Chinese opened diplomatic relations. Economic reintegration with the global economy had to wait another half decade, until Mao's death in 1976. His successors, searching for ways to revitalize China's dormant economy, began reforms, including opening regions along the country's southern coastline to foreign investment and trade.[68]

Several neighboring economies had shown China the merits of capitalism. South Korea, Taiwan, Hong Kong, and Singapore, the "tiger" economies of the 1970s and 1980s, had engaged in a developmental strategy focusing on exports of manufactured goods. Starting in the 1960s these economies had benefited from a favorable strategic environment. The Cold War ensured continuous American attention to the region, in places such as Taiwan, Japan, the Philippines, and South Korea, as well as billions of dollars in economic aid. At about the same time, firms from the rich world came in search of low-wage investment opportunities. Japanese firms were the first to do this, becoming the most important external economic force in the region. For their part, the four tigers found ways to attract external investment, offering among other things cheap and well-educated labor plus stable, if frequently undemocratic, politics. The tiger economies grew quickly, becoming globally important in industrial sectors such as metallurgy and electronics. Average wages in the tiger economies rose, so other countries in the region with lower wage scales could now attract foreign investors. The process was thus repeated in Southeast Asian economies such as Thailand, Malaysia, and Indonesia.

By the 1990s China was a full participant as well. The Chinese leadership skillfully maneuvered the country into position to benefit from export trade, using its huge, low-wage population to attract massive foreign investment from all over the rich world. Since then the Chinese economy has mirrored the Japanese golden age, except on a far larger scale. China since 1995 has featured very high economic growth rates, rising per capita wealth, increasing technological capabilities, and an expanding consumer market. As in the other success stories, the state was critical to the success of the Chinese venture. Unlike the Soviet leadership during the 1980s, the Chinese Communist Party also showed it could retain tight control of the country's politics.[69]

Many developing countries suffered from a poor structural position in the global economy, wherein they exported primary commodities in exchange for finished (manufactured) goods from the rich world. This was in large part a legacy of the colonial era, when imperial powers' investment in their colonies went to little more than extractive enterprises such as plantations and mines. The commodities-for-manufactured-goods swap continued after decolonization swept across the world from the 1940s to the 1960s. Selling raw materials was no recipe for economic prosperity. Among other things, it could quickly devastate the natural resource base of a developing economy, undermining itself over the long term. Also, the rich world's demand for these commodities fluctuated. Changing consumer tastes half a world away had strong influence over the fortunes of entire countries. World prices for commodities, from bananas to copper to cocoa, fluctuated dramatically, imposing great uncertainty and reversals upon the economies of producing countries.[70]

Political leadership in the developing world struggled to find ways to escape from this primary commodity trap. Import substitution was one solution pursued in Asian, African, and above all in Latin American countries. This strategy was based on the theory that global trade systematically discriminated against poor countries. Developing countries therefore needed to build their own domestic manufacturing bases through protection from rich world competition. After much experimentation, this strategy proved largely unsuccessful. Yet the export-led growth model of the kind used by the East Asian tigers also was difficult for many developing countries to emulate, because they could not attract the high levels of foreign investment necessary to repeat the tigers' experience. Nor could many poor countries benefit from geography as favorable as that of the entrepôt economies of Singapore and Hong Kong.[71]

After decolonization, per capita GDP growth rates in Africa lagged behind other regions, although they were still around 2 percent per year. After 1973, however, the continent ran into more serious difficulties. Africa's problems became severe, with per capita GDP growth slowing to almost nothing between 1973 and 1998. Problems included high external debt levels, rampant official corruption, ramshackle educational systems, and political instability, including several civil wars. Africa's transport systems proved a particular obstacle to economic improvement. A good portion of the continent also faced severe social problems, including high illiteracy rates and public health crises such as HIV/AIDS. None of this encouraged foreign investment. The demographic dividend so important to East Asia's per capita growth was conspicuous by its absence in Africa, where fertility generally remained exuberant. But like other regions, Africa was and is a heterogeneous place. Some countries, such as Botswana, Namibia, and Côte d'Ivoire, were wealthier and more stable than others.

Latin America had a better record of success in the postwar period. Again the golden age witnessed relatively strong per capita economic growth (about 2.5 percent per year), based mainly on rising world demand for minerals, oil, wheat, beef, coffee, sugar, and other primary products but also on the early success of protected industries. Between 1973 and 1998, however, this rate dropped to around 1 percent. Inflation and heavy external debt quickly became major problems for many countries in Latin America. Sharp economic inequalities within Latin American societies limited the scope for the emergence of domestic markets for manufactured goods, and few segments of Latin American manufacturing proved internationally competitive. By the 1990s, economic stagnation inspired most countries to do as Chile had already done, and experiment once again with more open markets and less state direction. This helped the export trades to benefit from rising commodity prices (after 2000) associated with the roaring demand of the Chinese economy for raw materials and food.[72]

While considerable variation existed from one place to another, and from one decade to another, the conspicuous trait of the world economy after 1945 was fast growth. Cheap energy, technological change, and market integration all helped generate per capita growth never seen before in human history. No three consecutive generations ever experienced anything remotely like what those alive in the sixty-five years following 1945 witnessed. That spectacular growth raised the consumption levels of several billion people, and the aspirations of most of the rest.

Economy, Ecology, and Dissent

During the postwar era, dissenters emerged who saw the ecological consequences of, and social injustices in, the global economy. Two sets of critiques among many can serve as illustration. The first set fell under the heading of ecological economics. Its central idea was, and remains, that the global economy is a subsystem within the Earth's ecosystem, which is finite and nongrowing. The laws of thermodynamics were foundational concepts in this field. Energy, according to the first law of thermodynamics, can be neither created nor destroyed. While the first law implies that the Universe is in a state of perpetual stability, the second law does not. Rather, it states that matter and energy deteriorate from initially concentrated and more capable states (low entropy) to diffuse and weaker states (high entropy). Therefore, while the first law means that the total amount of energy in the Universe will always be the same, the second means that that energy is inevitably heading toward a less usable form. The ecological economists who applied these laws to human endeavors argued that any system that depends on infinite growth is impossible, for eventually it will exhaust the finite quantities of low-entropy matter and energy on Earth. At the same time, and for exactly the same reason, any such system will pollute the Earth with high-entropy waste. For ecological economists, the only question is how long the process will take.[73]

Although ecological economics had important intellectual roots in the late nineteenth and early twentieth centuries, it was not until the 1960s and 1970s that a coherent body of thought coalesced around these insights. Part of this coalescence was due to pioneering work by economists who had a dissenting view of their field's obsession with economic growth. These included the Romanian expatriate Nicholas Georgescu-Roegen, the English-born Kenneth Boulding, and the American Herman Daly, all of whom worked at American universities. Another part of the coalescence was due to the emergence of the mass environmental movement, which allowed this otherwise obscure intellectual exercise to gain some traction during the 1970s. It was not until the 1980s that a self-conscious field of study, defining itself as "ecological economics," came into existence. By the end of that decade the field had established an international society with affiliates in numerous countries around the world, a specialist's journal, and key texts introducing the field to outsiders. Over the course of the 1990s it developed rapidly. Scholars added to the field's theoretical bases and also developed alternative measures of economic performance that included the societal and ecological costs of growth. One well-known study, published in the journal *Nature* in 1997, attempted to estimate the total economic value of indispensable ecological "services" such as pollination, nutrient cycling, genetic resources, and soil formation. All of these are provided by the Earth free of charge to humans but are not priced in markets. The authors estimated these seventeen services were worth $33 trillion per year. Although the study aroused criticism for its attempt to put a price on nature, the point nonetheless had been made: the global environment provides humankind with enormous hidden and undervalued benefits.[74]

A second set of criticisms fell under the heading of sustainable development. While it had important intellectual linkages to ecological economics, the concept of sustainable development evolved mainly outside of academic circles, hashed out in countless international forums by practitioners, diplomats, and social and environmental activists. It was thus a political idea that eventually found its way into mainstream thinking. Since its inception, most iterations of the sustainable development concept have combined two big ideas: first, that the global economy as it operated in the postwar era was socially unjust, in particular for the world's poor; and second, that the global economy threatened to outstrip ecological limits, mainly due to the patterns of consumption in the rich world. Beyond these basic components, the idea has been redefined countless times.

As with ecological economics, one can trace the intellectual roots of sustainable development back to the nineteenth century, but its direct origins lay in recent decades. The paradigm's basic linkages between wealth, poverty, and ecology emerged out of the many environmental and development conferences held during the 1970s, in particular those under the aegis of the United Nations. The term *sustainable development* came into vogue in 1987 with the publication of *Our Common Future*, a report issued for the UN by the Brundtland Commission (named for its chair, Norwegian prime minister Gro Harlem Brundtland). Its definition of sustainable development as "development that meets the needs of the present without compromising the ability of future generations to meet their own needs" became the archetypal expression of the concept. The Brundtland report also helped to institutionalize sustainable development at the 1992 Rio Earth Summit and subsequent international negotiations.[75]

Yet despite the seriousness of these and other critiques, at the beginning of the twenty-first century the global economy operated in much the same fashion as it had since 1945. Billions of people in the developing world strove to attain the levels of comfort enjoyed by those in the rich world, while the latter sought to increase their wealth. These aspirations undergirded the continuity of the postwar global economy. In the decades after 1945, hundreds of millions of people, including most Japanese and Spaniards, and quite a few Brazilians and Indonesians, attained levels of consumption unimaginable to their ancestors. Although billions more remained on the outside looking in, this represented a major shift in human history. In some respects all of this amounted to great progress, as it lifted many out of poverty. But at the same time the global economy's aggregate effects on the planet became all too apparent, and that economy was deeply dependent on the use of nonrenewable resources such as fossil fuels and minerals. A central question for the current century is whether styles and patterns of consumption can be altered to fit within a finite ecological system.[76]

CHAPTER FOUR

Cold War and Environmental Culture

While historians, like the Cold Warriors before them, argue about who started the Cold War and when, its general outline is simple enough. During or soon after World War II, the victorious Allies quarreled and quickly found themselves enemies. Josef Stalin's Soviet Union and its Eastern European satellites formed a contiguous bloc in Eurasia stretching from the Elbe to Vladivostok. The Americans formed a rival, larger, but looser coalition, involving European allies, notably Britain and West Germany, Middle Eastern ones, especially Iran and Turkey, and East Asian ones, particularly Japan. The chief theaters of the Cold War were those of World War II: Europe and East Asia. While the Cold War featured many moments of peril and political shifts that at the time seemed portentous, it was remarkable for the stability that it brought, especially after the victory of Mao Zedong and the communists in the Chinese civil war in 1949 settled the question of the alignment of the world's most populous country.

Cold War Priorities

It was a stability of armed and arming camps. One of the distinguishing features of the Cold War was its sustained militarism. In modern history, most countries, after major wars, reduced their military spending sharply, stopped buying mountains of materiel, and cashiered most military personnel. The United States and USSR did this—briefly—after 1945. During the Cold War, however, the major powers maintained high levels of military spending decade after decade. They sustained their military-industrial complexes, indeed nurtured them, even though this was extremely expensive. Probably it could only have been done because of the spectacular economic boom of 1945–1973. In the Soviet Union during the Cold War, for example, as much as 40 percent of all industrial production was military. A tenth of the world's commercial electricity production went to the building of nuclear weapons.[1]

The Cold War also justified, or seemed at the time to justify, heroic commitments of money, labor, and planning to gigantic state-sponsored infrastructure projects and development campaigns. The United States in 1956, for example, authorized unheard of sums for the world's largest engineering project. The building of the interstate highway system reshuffled American landscapes, hastening suburbanization and altering wildlife migrations, among other effects. Like most acts of government, this decision had many motives behind it, but prominent among them was military preparedness in expectation of war with the USSR.[2] In 1958 Mao's China launched a frenetic campaign to overtake Britain and the United States in economic production within only a few years, a quixotic quest known as the Great Leap Forward, and in 1964, as we will see, it undertook to build a new military-industrial complex from scratch. After the Sino-Soviet split, the Soviet Union for its part built a second Siberian railroad line, which provided a more secure link to its Pacific ports because it stood farther back from the Chinese border than the old Trans-Siberian Railway. This rail line opened up vast new possibilities for accelerated harvesting of timber, furs, and minerals in the Soviet Far East.[3]

The Cold War context also helped to motivate sustained efforts at economic self-sufficiency in China and the USSR; these carried environmental consequences. This ambition never became a priority for the United States, which relied on its navy and its allies to keep sea lanes open and goods flowing internationally. But Stalin and Mao usually felt they needed to be able to make everything they might need within their borders, a sentiment that US embargoes, sanctions, and quarantines reinforced. Both regimes went to great lengths to do so. In the late 1950s, for example, after Stalin's death, his successors chose to convert dry swaths of Central Asia into cotton land. This required massive irrigation works drawing water away from the rivers that fed the Aral Sea, so that by the early 1960s that salt lake began to shrink. Today it stands at a tenth of its 1960 size and is divided into several salty puddles. The strangulation of the Aral Sea evolved into one of the twentieth century's signature environmental disasters, what with vanished fisheries, desiccated delta wetlands, a tenfold increase in the seawater's salinity, airborne salt blown onto croplands by dust storms arising from newly exposed lake beds, and a dozen other problems. But the Soviet Union needed cotton, and in the Cold War context importing it from India or Egypt entailed risk that Stalin's successors wished to avoid.[4]

Equally attracted by the vision of economic autarky, Mao's China concocted the ambition to grow rubber in the rainforest corner of Yunnan Province called Xishuangbanna, a prefecture in the Mekong River watershed near the border with Burma and Laos. In the early 1950s the USSR had requested that China provide rubber in the spirit of socialist solidarity. Rubber, derived from an Amazonian tree, could not grow in the frosty climes of the USSR. It was a strategic good, necessary for tanks and aircraft (all airplanes use natural rubber tires). Inconveniently for Moscow and Beijing, most of the world's rubber came from Malaya, then a British colony, and Indonesia, ruled by anticommunist generals allied to the United States. The first plantings in Xishuangbanna took place in 1956; after the Sino-Soviet split, the Chinese wanted all the rubber they could get for their own military purposes. Much of the brute labor involved was done by youths sent to the frontier during the Cultural Revolution to improve their political outlook. In China's most biologically diverse region, they cut trees over thousands of square kilometers, destroying animal habitat and obliging the local Dai population to migrate to higher elevations, which put

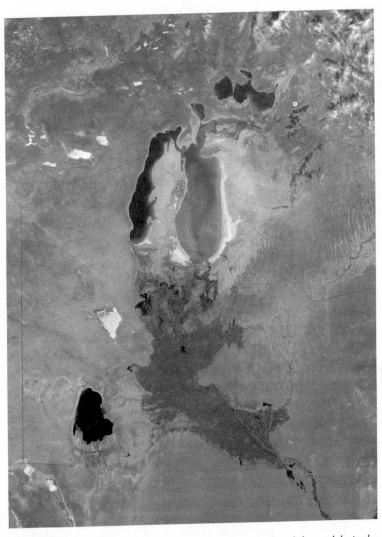

The Aral Sea, as seen from space in October 2008. Once the fourth-largest lake in the world, by 2008 the Aral covered less than 10 percent of its former area. Soviet irrigation projects built in the 1960s deprived the sea of most of its inflowing waters. (Getty Images)

them in conflict with other minorities. The rubber trees often froze because Xishuangbanna lies on the northern climatic margin of the possible range for the Brazilian tree, but eventually these efforts did manage to provide China with the prized supply of rubber. As the Chinese economy boomed from the 1980s, its demand for industrial rubber skyrocketed, and monoculture plantations spread over more and more of the region. After 2000 China needed ever more rubber for its own burgeoning fleet of automobiles. The replacement of forest by rubber plantations over an area the size of Lebanon even altered local climate, bringing a sharper cycle of drought and flood and far fewer days of fog. Rubber processing also filled the nearby rivers and lakes with chemical pollution, all of it destined for the Mekong River. The early quest for military self-sufficiency prepared the way for a thorough environmental transformation of Xishuangbanna.[5]

The Cold War also sparked and sustained guerrilla wars around the world. The United States and the USSR especially, but also China, Cuba, France, and South Africa from time to time, thought it cost-effective to support separatists, revolutionaries, resistance movements, and their ilk wherever that could weaken their rivals. Thus, in places such as Angola, Mozambique, Ethiopia, Somalia, Vietnam, Afghanistan, and Nicaragua, the Cold War superpowers waded into local power struggles, backing their preferred factions with arms, training, money, and occasionally troops. Guerrilla struggles normally involved a large component of environmental warfare—burning forests and crops, slaughtering livestock, flooding fields—because one side or the other typically used forests as cover, and because peasant populations had to be punished for supporting (or merely tolerating) one's enemies. Moreover, these wars produced legions of refugees, people fleeing combat zones or on the move because militias and armies had destroyed their livelihoods. Refugee movements, like other migrations, brought environmental changes both to the lands people left and to those where they settled. The section below on Southern Africa and Vietnam will explore some of these matters.

For its sustained militarism, its military-industrial complexes, its heroic efforts to mobilize or alter nature for political ends, its fueling of guerilla wars—for all these reasons the Cold War contributed to the environmental tumult of the post-1945 decades. None of it will have a longer-lasting imprint on the biosphere than nuclear weapons programs.

Nuclear Weapons Production and the Environment

Cold War anxieties motivated the United States to build about 70,000 nuclear warheads and to test more than a thousand of them from 1945 to 1990. The USSR built about 45,000 and tested at least 715. Meanwhile, Britain after 1952, France after 1960, and China after 1964 built hundreds more. Nuclear weapons require either enriched uranium or plutonium (made from uranium). The nuclear weapons industry led to a rapid increase in the volume of uranium mining around the world after 1950, especially in the United States, Canada, Australia, central and southern Africa, East Germany, Czechoslovakia, Ukraine, Russia, and Kazakhstan. In the early Cold War years, when safety regulations were few, miners routinely received abundant doses of radiation that shortened thousands of lives.[6] All nuclear powers developed atomic archipelagoes, networks of special sites devoted to nuclear research, uranium processing, and weapons manufacture and testing. These were shielded from public scrutiny by Cold War secrecy, and to some extent, especially in Russia and China, they still are. In the United States, this archipelago involved some three thousand locales, including the Savannah River Site in South Carolina and the Rocky Flats Arsenal in Colorado, both central to the bomb-making effort. The jewel in this crown, the Hanford Engineer Works (later called the Hanford Site), some 600 square miles of dusty, windy, almost-empty sagebrush steppe on the banks of the Columbia River in south-central Washington state, opened in 1943.[7]

Hanford was the principal atomic bomb factory in the United States throughout the Cold War.[8] In a little over four decades of operation, Hanford generated 500 million curies in nuclear wastes, most of which remained on site, and, both by accident and design, loosed 25 million curies into the environment, much of it into the Columbia River. Often the quantities in question exceeded those thought to be safe at the time (the limits of what is deemed safe have been ratcheted downward over time). For comparison, the 1986 explosion at Chernobyl released some 50 to 80 million curies into the environment, all of it into the atmosphere. The environmental and health dangers of radioactivity releases and wastes seemed large enough to require constant secrecy and, by some accounts, occasional dishonesty on the part of the responsible officials, but to decision makers the dangers also seemed small enough to be an acceptable cost for the acquisition of more nuclear weapons. Most officials believed Hanford's operations posed minimal risk to people and to local ranching operations, and in the early years at least did not concern themselves with broader ecosystem effects.[9]

The murky story of the Green Run shows the degree to which urgency and haste shaped the history of Hanford. The largest single release of radioactivity, known as the Green Run, took place in December 1949. It is still not entirely clear whether this was fully intentional or somehow got out of control (some pertinent documents remain secret more than sixty years later). It was probably an experiment prompted by the detonation of the USSR's first nuclear weapon, which registered on radioactivity monitoring equipment in western North America. American officials had reason to assume the Soviets were using "green" uranium, only sixteen to twenty days out of the reactor. If so, it indicated accelerated production schedules for Soviet enriched uranium. To test the hypothesis, it seems, they decided to release green uranium from

Hanford's smokestacks and then see how accurate their monitoring might be. Some engineers involved now suggest the experiment went awry. In any case, the Green Run released radioactivity on a scale never matched before or since in the United States, quietly spattering down-wind communities in iodine-131 (a radionuclide potentially dangerous to humans and implicated in cases of thyroid cancer). The radioactivity secretly released in the Green Run was about four hundred times that which escaped in the Three Mile Island accident of 1979, which put an end to the construction of nuclear power plants in the United States for three decades. The affected people learned of the Green Run only in 1986, after persistent effort to get the federal government to release relevant documents. The secret experiment vividly indicates the risks American officials felt obliged to run in the dark days of the early Cold War.[10]

Remarkably, in retrospect, statesmen often took a relaxed attitude toward radiation risks. In Oceania, the Americans, British, and French tested nuclear weapons beginning in 1946, 1957, and 1966, respectively. Atomic explosions shook various remote atolls again and again. The appeal of Oceania for atomic experimentation was that population was sparse, so testing did not immediately imperil many people—and most of the imperiled people were not citizens of the United States, Britain, or France. They were Polynesians and Micronesians with little formal education or political voice, which made it easier for statesmen to take risks with their health. Beginning eleven months after the end of World War II, American nuclear testing exposed the islanders of Bikini and adjacent atolls to repeated dangerous doses of radiation. Their experiences provided useful information about the susceptibility of the human body and its genes to radiation-related illness and muta-tions. They, and some US military personnel, were essentially human guinea pigs in the early days of atomic testing.

The French program of nuclear testing in the Pacific also occasionally put safety below other concerns. In 1966 General Charles de Gaulle, then president of France, ventured to Polynesia so he could personally witness a test on the Moruroa Atoll. Adverse winds that meant radiation resulting from the test would be scattered over populated islands held matters up for two days. De Gaulle grew impatient, and citing his busy schedule demanded the test proceed regardless of the winds. Shortly after the explosion, New Zealand's National Radiation Laboratory recorded heavy fallout on Samoa, Fiji, Tonga, and other population centers of the southwest Pacific. De Gaulle returned to Paris and state business forthwith. Since 1966 Polynesians have compiled a long list of grievances against the French nuclear program in the Pacific, as Marshall Islanders have against the American program since 1946.[11]

The Soviet nuclear weapons complex operated with even greater nonchalance toward environmental risks and human health. Stalin declared the creation of nuclear weapons to be "goal number one" as the Cold War began, and by 1949 he had what he wanted. The Soviet atomic archipelago consisted of uranium mines (in which hundreds of thousands of prisoners died), secret cities built for nuclear research, fuel-processing sites, bomb factories, and test sites. The chief plutonium- and weapons-making centers were near Chelyabinsk in western Siberia, and Tomsk and Krasnoyarsk, both in Central Siberia. These secret facilities were often cryptically referred to by their postal codes, such as Tomsk-7 and Krasnoyarsk-26. Their histories remain for the most part sealed in secrecy. Chelyabinsk-65, which also went by the name of Mayak (lighthouse) is the best known. Chelyabinsk region, once a landscape of birch and pine groves amid thousands of lakes, became a main cog in the Soviet military-industrial complex during World War II, when it produced half the tanks used by the Red Army. It was far from the vulnerable frontiers of the country and had plenty of water, as well as metallurgical and chemical industries, all of which recommended it for nuclear weapons production. For fifty years it has been the most dangerously polluted place on Earth.[12]

The Mayak Chemical Complex opened in 1948, creating the USSR's first plutonium. Over the years, at least 130 million curies (the official figure—others say billions of curies)[13] of radioactivity has been released at Mayak, affecting at least half a million people. Most of that occurred in its early years, especially 1950–1951, when nuclear wastes were dumped into local rivers, tributaries to the Techa from which thousands of people drew their drinking water. Several thousand villagers were evacuated; those who remained apparently suffered from elevated rates of leukemia.[14] As a result of an explosion in a high-level radioactive waste tank in 1957, about 20 million curies of radioactivity escaped and 2 million showered the Mayak vicinity. Some ten thousand people were evacuated (beginning eight months after the accident) and 200 square kilometers were ruled unfit for human use.[15]

A bit more radioactivity spattered regions downwind of Lake Karachay. A small and shallow pond used after 1951 as a dump for nuclear wastes, Lake Karachay is now the most radioactive place on Earth. It contains about twenty-four times as much radioactivity as was released in the disaster at Chernobyl in 1986. Today, standing at its shore for an hour would provide a fatal dose of radiation. As it is situated in an often dry landscape, its water level frequently subsides, exposing lake bed sediments. Fierce Siberian winds periodically scatter the radioactive dust, most damagingly in a 1967 drought. In addition to the 1957 and 1967 tragedies, several other accidents have befallen the Mayak complex. In all, the contamination from Mayak affected about 20,000 square kilometers.[16]

The human health effects of Mayak's contamination, if official Soviet and Russian studies are to be believed, were modest.[17] However, a local politician, Alexander Penyagin, who chaired the Supreme Soviet's Subcommittee on Nuclear Safety, once said the mess at Mayak was a hundred times worse than Chernobyl. Evidence offered by journalists and anthropologists who visited the region implies serious and pervasive human health problems.[18] So do some epidemiological studies, although their conclusions are often inconsistent.[19] In one especially hard-hit village, life expectancy in 1997 was twenty-five years below the Russian national average for women and fourteen years below for men.[20] The true human costs remain elusive at Mayak, and health effects of nuclear contamination are much in dispute, even where data are more complete.[21]

The atomic archipelagoes consisted of much more than Hanford and Mayak. Nuclear test sites, such as those in Oceania, Nevada, Kazakhstan, and the Arctic island of Novaya Zemlya, were especially active in the 1950s and early 1960s—and radioactive ever since. Atmospheric tests (of which there were more than five hundred) scattered about four hundred times as much radioactive iodine-131 to the winds as did Chernobyl. The Soviet navy used dumping sites at sea for its spent nuclear fuel and contaminated machinery, polluting inshore waters of the Pacific and the Arctic Oceans, especially around Novaya Zemlya. Surprisingly, perhaps, the world's most radioactive marine environment was not Soviet responsibility, but Britain's. The Windscale site (renamed Sellafield in an attempt to shed notoriety), which produced weapons-grade plutonium for the United Kingdom's nuclear arsenal, released radioactivity into the Irish Sea, especially in 1965–1980. The Irish Sea's currents do not disperse pollutants quickly, so the radioactivity lingers and turns up in British seafood. Windscale also caught fire in 1957, which the British government eventually acknowledged in 1982 and blamed for thirty-two deaths and a further 260 cases of cancer.[22]

The nuclear weapons industry created several "sacrifice zones" in a half dozen countries. The security demands of the moment seemed, to those in power, to justify lethally contaminating chosen areas for millennia into the future. Of all the mines, bomb-making plants, test sites, and waste dumps, none were sacrificed more thoroughly than the grasslands, birch groves, streams, ponds, and villages of the Mayak region, which was still in the twenty-first century acquiring additional radioactive contamination.[23]

In one of the many ironies associated with the Cold War, some of its nuclear weapons development sites became de facto wildlife preserves. The Savannah River Site, for example, produced plutonium and tritium, and its 300 square miles were kept free of routine human activities. As a result of banning humans in the interest of building bombs, ducks, deer, snakes, 250 species of birds, and the largest alligator ever found in Georgia (not an atomic mutant) flourished despite 35 million gallons of high-level nuclear waste scattered around. The Rocky Flats Arsenal in Colorado, which produced plutonium until the mid-1990s, became a prairie wildlife preserve, a protected home where the deer and the antelope play under the watchful eye of up to a hundred bald eagles. The Hanford stretch of the Columbia, where the first atomic bombs were built, hosted the healthiest population of chinook salmon anywhere along the River.[24]

In a further irony, one of the world's first international environmental agreements arose from nuclear testing. As evidence mounted that atmospheric testing sprinkled all ecosystems and earthlings with extra doses of fallout, as test explosions grew bigger and bigger, and as expertise in radiation medicine accumulated, politicians and scientists by the late 1950s developed some doubts about the prudence of continued testing. In some countries, where such things were permitted, citizen action helped to build pressure for a ban on atmospheric testing. In all countries the fear of nuclear annihilation, intensified by the Cuban Missile Crisis of October 1962, added to this pressure. In late 1963 the USSR, United States, and United Kingdom signed a partial test ban (meaning no atmospheric testing), and many other countries soon followed, although not France or China, each of which prized its own independence in matters of nuclear politics. As a result of the partial test ban, people born after 1964 carried much smaller quantities of strontium-90 and other radioactive isotopes in their bones than did their elders. Everyone alive in the 1950s and early 1960s, even those living in remote Tasmania or Tierra del Fuego, keeps a signature of the Cold War atomic weapons programs in their teeth and bones.[25]

In sum, the nuclear weapons programs of the Cold War probably killed a few hundred thousand people, at most a few million, slowly and indirectly, via fatal cancers caused by radioactivity releases.[26] Almost all were killed by their own governments in a Cold War version of friendly fire. French president François Mitterrand is credited with saying that the most essential quality for any statesman is indifference. He meant that leaders must at times take decisions that result in death and suffering for others. During the Cold War, leaders, including scientists heading atomic weapons research and development programs, made such decisions repeatedly. Some no doubt acquired troubled consciences in the process, but they all felt the politics of the moment required them to do as they did, even when it involved the likely sacrifice of some of their own subjects or fellow citizens.

Nowhere, not even at Mayak, did radioactive pollution kill many millions of people and lay waste to broad regions. Cigarettes killed far more people during the Cold War than did nuclear weapons programs. So did air pollution and road accidents. Cooler heads prevailed over those who wanted to use nuclear weapons to blast instant harbors in Alaska or new canals through Panama.[27] When an American B-52 exploded in midair and dropped four H-bombs on the coast of southeastern Spain in 1966, the bombs did not explode and only a little plutonium splashed on the countryside.[28] So one is tempted to conclude that the health and environmental effects of Cold War nuclear weapons programs were therefore modest.

But the story is not over yet. It will not end for at least one hundred thousand more years. Most radioactivity decays within hours, days, or months and quickly ceases to carry dangers for living creatures. But some radioactive materials used in nuclear weapons, such as plutonium-239, have half-lives of up to twenty-four thousand years. Some wastes created in nuclear weapons manufacture will remain lethally radioactive for more than a hundred thousand years. This is a waste management obligation bequeathed to the next three thousand human generations. If not consistently handled adroitly, this will elevate rates of leukemia and certain cancers in humans, especially children, for a long time to come.

To reflect on the significance of this obligation, it may help to remember that twenty-four thousand years ago was the height of the last ice age, long before cities or agriculture or the first arrival of humans in North America or Oceania. One hundred thousand years ago, mastodons, wooly mammoths, and giant saber-toothed tigers roamed the future territories of the USSR and United States, while hominins were just beginning their migrations out of Africa. Long, long after only a few historians know anything about World War II or the Cold War, people will either manage Cold War nuclear wastes through all the political turmoil, revolutions, wars, regime changes, state failures, pandemics, earthquakes, megafloods, sea level rises and falls, ice ages, and asteroid impacts that the future holds, or inadvertently suffer the consequences.

China's Great Leap Forward and the Third Front

Few, if any, Cold War leaders felt that the political climate justified manipulations of nature more strongly than did Mao Zedong. Mao came to power in 1949, self-educated in a Marxist tradition in which nature exists to be conquered by labor. The prestige derived from his success as a revolutionary leader, and his skill at destroying rivals, gave him an unusually powerful hand within China for most of his career as helmsman of the ship of state (1949–1976). Like many men whom luck and talent propelled to the heights of power, he acquired a firm faith in his own wisdom and was not easily swayed by evidence or apparent failure. His determination to outstrip the economies of capitalist enemies, for example, helped inspire him to disregard basic laws of chemistry, biology, and physics, not to mention human nature, in a campaign known as the Great Leap Forward, launched in 1958. In January of that year Mao announced, "There is a new war: we should open fire on nature."[29]

Scholars have yet to forge a consensus on the priority of motives behind the Great Leap Forward. But it surely involved, on Mao's part, a twin ideological urge to industrialize China as fast as possible and to build communism sooner than the "revisionist" Soviets, and a geopolitical ambition to make China strong in a hostile world. Scholars also disagree about the human toll it took: estimates of the number who starved to death as a result of the grain requisitioning and other features of the Great Leap Forward range from fifteen million to fifty million, some 2 to 7 percent of the Chinese population.[30]

For Mao, steel production had a special talismanic quality. It bespoke modernity and power. When confronted with disappointing economic performance in his first five-year plan (1953–1957), Mao made steel production a centerpiece of the second, fantasizing about overtaking British and American steel production in just a few years. When Soviet premier Nikita Khrushchev, visiting China in 1958, expressed doubts that China could meet its steel targets, Mao raised them.[31] His secret speeches to party cadres in 1958 reveal a persistent fascination with steel tonnage and China's rank among great powers in steel production.[32] Because China lacked the capital and technology to build modern steelworks, Mao insisted that each peasant commune and urban neighborhood would make steel with "backyard furnaces." Mao's lieutenant and sometimes rival, Premier Zhou Enlai, personally organized the students and faculty of Peking University for steel production. Nationwide, the scale of mobilization was heroic: ninety million people smelted steel and iron in six hundred thousand backyard furnaces, melting down cooking pots, bicycle frames, and doorknobs. Through stupendous effort they doubled China's steel output. Most of it, however, was brittle and worthless.[33]

Unsurprisingly, making steel in this fashion was extremely inefficient in terms of fuel and dangerous in terms of pollution. In those parts of China with plentiful coal, decentralized steelmaking simply meant wasted coal. Elsewhere it meant that all rail lines were clogged with coal and ore shipments, and that any and all wood and shrub was reduced to charcoal and fed to the furnaces. In Yunnan, Sichuan, and perhaps across the whole country, some 10 percent of extant forests vanished within a year. In some provinces, Hunan and Guangdong, for example, half or a third of forests were felled. This was surely the fastest retreat in the long history of shrinking Chinese forests.[34] Equally unsurprisingly, wherever backyard furnaces burned charcoal, they emitted intense air pollution. The city of Suzhou, near the mouth of the Yangzi, recorded a fall of 400 tons of soot and dust per square kilometer, and some places more than double that. Breathing air so laced with particulate matter, not to mention sulfur dioxide, did no one any good.[35]

The grain harvest was a second priority in the Great Leap Forward. Appropriately enough, Mao thought China needed to produce more food. However, he wanted it done instantly, and promoted quack science to that end. Party officials assigned peasant communes wildly unrealistic production targets, which the communes usually claimed to meet for fear of punishment. Peasants drained marshes and lakes to plant more rice and wheat. They terraced mountains up to the summits and plowed China's northern grasslands. They followed instructions to plant seeds close together because Mao believed plants of the same species would not compete with one another for water and nutrients but would somehow grow in harmony. In some parts of the country, the peasants plowed furrows deeper than they were tall, on the theory—another of Mao's passing enthusiasms—that this enhanced soil fertility and encouraged larger root systems. Everywhere they constructed jerry-built dams and dug new wells for irrigation water. Mao wanted each commune to collect and store its own water: as the slogan went, "Each piece of land has its own piece of sky." People who voiced doubt about the production targets and the absurd farming methods invited swift retribution.

Linked to the struggle for grain was a campaign against creatures deemed parasitic or unhealthy. Slogans urged Chinese as young as kindergartners to eliminate the "four pests"—rats, mosquitoes, flies, and sparrows. (Mao was under the impression that Japan had rid itself of insect pests.)[36] Party officials assigned communes and neighborhoods quotas of rats and sparrows—even flies—to be killed and counted. In seven months in 1959, the Chinese killed nearly two billion sparrows, whose crime was eating grain.[37]

All this frantic urgency brought fiasco.[38] Millions of peasants starved to death while party cadres requisitioned more and more grain for the cities, the army, and export. The agricultural policies were fully abandoned only in 1961 (when grain was purchased from Canada and Australia). The deep plowing, planting on mountainsides, and cultivating the steppe brought more erosion and dust storms. The hastily built dams often burst. The wells depleted groundwater in some places while reservoirs raised the water table in others, bringing salts to the surface and salinizing fields. In the North China plain in the late 1950s, the area damaged by salinization grew by 40 percent, mainly due to hastily engineered water impoundment schemes.[39] The assault on sparrows reduced predation on many kinds of insects, leading to infestations of crop pests (so in 1959 bed bugs replaced sparrows on the most-wanted list). In the city of Jilan, on the lower Yellow River, a successful antisparrow campaign was followed by a plague of caterpillars.[40] Pests of all sorts gobbled up a tenth of the grain harvest in Zhejiang Province in 1960; locusts helped themselves to a sixth of the rice crop in Hubei Province in 1961. In addition to short-run starvation, the agricultural policies of the Great Leap Forward hampered China's long-range agricultural potential.[41]

The failures of the Great Leap Forward dimmed Mao's star for a few years. But by 1964 he again had assumed the reins (which some historians believe he held all along from behind the scenes). Soon he launched another militarized, top-down campaign, the construction of the "Third Front." By late 1964 Mao concluded that China's international position had worsened. The Sino-Soviet rift, brewing in 1956–1960, had become a full breach by 1962, turning his patron and ally into an enemy. The Americans were preparing a massive escalation of their combat forces in Vietnam. Mao felt that China needed to prepare for all-out war. In particular, he felt China needed a new military-industrial complex deep within the country, well away from American bombers based in Taiwan, South Korea, or Okinawa, and well back from the Soviet frontier. The Soviet invasion of Czechoslovakia in 1968 and the weeks-long border clashes in 1969 further convinced Mao that Moscow might well unleash its Red Army—of which twenty-five full divisions were stationed on the border—into China.

To withstand this anticipated assault, Mao chose to build a secret armaments industry with all the trimmings in Sichuan, Guizhou, and Yunnan Provinces. It would include mines, smelters, steel mills, chemical plants, hydroelectric stations, and more, all linked by new railroads. In the 1930s the Chinese Nationalists had tried to build industry in Sichuan when the Japanese Imperial Army occupied China's coastal regions. Mao admired Stalin's response to the German invasion of the USSR in 1941, in which the Soviets had removed hundreds of factories behind the Urals. Now Mao would do the same thing, only before being attacked, on a much larger scale, and into much more remote and rugged country. Siting military industry in Yunnan had the added attraction that it would ease Chinese support of their North Vietnamese allies against the Americans: Yunnan had a rail link (its only rail link before 1965) to Hanoi.

Mao, not a man given to half measures, wanted this military-industrial complex built overnight. Beginning in late 1964, industrial plant in coastal provinces was disassembled, transported to the interior, and put back together again. In addition, just about all Chinese investment in new industry in the years 1965–1971 went to the Third Front. Construction brigades from the People's Liberation Army worked around the clock, laying railroad track, blasting tunnels, and building factories. Where possible, factories were put in caves and steep-sided valleys to make them less vulnerable to attack from the air. Altogether, the Third Front was the most intensive commitment ever made by any country to military industry. The centerpiece of this crash program was a giant steel mill at Panzhihua.[42]

Panzhihua, near the border of Sichuan and Yunnan provinces, sat atop mother lodes of minerals with military uses, including the world's biggest reserves of titanium. It had all the iron ore and coal needed for steelmaking. Its inhabitants before 1964 were mainly an ethnic minority, the Yi, who had long history of fractious relations with Han Chinese. Starting in 1965, hundreds of thousands of migrant workers flooded into Panzhihua. An indication of its priority in Chinese politics was that Premier Zhou Enlai assumed direct responsibility for getting Panzhihua up and running. By 1971 it was making steel—probably of better quality than that made thirteen years before under Zhou's direction by the faculty and students of Peking University.

In these frenzied times, no thought could be spared for the environment. Little enough was spared for safety: during its construction, upward of 5 percent of Panzhihua's workforce died each year. The steel mill generated vast clouds of air pollution. Its location in a steep-sided valley with frequent temperature inversions meant that sulfur dioxide and particulates sometimes accumulated for weeks before being swept off by the wind. In 1975 particulate matter at times reached concentrations three hundred times the national standard. A location that made sense from the military and mineralogical points of view proved a dismal choice from the air quality standpoint. The mill also poisoned the local rivers and soils. No environmental regulation took place at Panzhihua until 1979, well after the international situation had changed, China's isolation had ended, the Americans had left Vietnam, and no strategic logic remained for locating military industry in the remote interior of the country. Today Panzhihua is China's fourth largest steelmaking center, a quirk of economic geography derived (like the rubber plantations of Xishuangbanna) from the exigencies of the Cold War.[43]

In the campaigns of the Great Leap Forward and the Third Front, a sense of urgency pervaded everything. In the first case it derived only partly from Cold War international considerations. In the second, the Chinese sense of impending war with the Americans or the Soviets, or both, was the sole reason to build the Third Front. This urgency meant that environmental implications counted for nothing.

Mao was not always blind to environmental matters, however. He favored afforestation, and at least once wondered aloud how it might affect groundwater supplies.[44] One of his stated reasons for trying to raise grain yields was so that one-third of Chinese farmland could be converted to forest, a proportion recommended for Russia by a Soviet agronomist whose work had come to Mao's attention. But Mao's outlook was normally what is sometimes called "instrumentalist." He took interest in the environment insofar as it provided resources for the political agendas that mattered to him. What few environmental regulations China did have were declared "capitalistic, inhibiting, and revisionist" at the outset of the Cultural Revolution in 1966 and duly jettisoned.[45] Only in 1972–1973 did China's leadership start to develop doubts about its neglect of the environment—largely inspired apparently by the first international environmental conference in Stockholm.[46] But China's efforts to control environmental problems to date have been overwhelmed by the hectic urbanization and industrialization of the decades after 1980, a true great leap forward in economic terms. By 2015 China had far surpassed Mao's reckless dream of 1958, milling roughly ten times as much steel as the United States. Thanks to his penchant for autarky and his campaigns of mass peasant mobilization, Mao took a great toll on the environment of China. But perhaps by inadvertently delaying the economic rise of China by a generation, he postponed a larger impact upon China's environment, and the global environment as well.

Hot Wars and Environmental Warfare in Southern Africa and Vietnam

Mao fretted about the designs of the imperialist camp in the 1950s and 1960s, but most of its members proved to be paper tigers as imperialists. They could not maintain their grip on their Asian and African territories. A surge of decolonization (1947–1975) resulted, changing the landscape of world politics. Decolonization presented the Cold War powers with an opportunity, or, as they saw it, an obligation, to compete for the loyalties of newly created countries. The Soviet Union in particular tried to portray itself as the champion of anti-imperialism, and often supported liberation movements seeking to end British, French, or Portuguese colonial rule. Mao did the same, and in the 1960s and 1970s China overtly competed with the USSR for the mantle of anti-imperialist champion.

In southern Africa, the Cold War intruded deeply into the politics of decolonization. Ongoing political and sometimes guerrilla struggles took shape in the 1960s, aiming to end Portuguese rule in Angola and Mozambique, white settler rule in Rhodesia (now Zimbabwe), and South African rule in what has since become Namibia. In addition, groups formed to contest white rule and apartheid in South Africa itself. The Portuguese, white Rhodesians, and white South Africans sought to portray their causes as anticommunist crusades, hoping for assistance from the United States and its allies.

In 1974–1975 a staunchly anticommunist Portuguese dictatorship collapsed at home and Portuguese colonial rule in Africa collapsed with it. Civil wars heated up in Angola and Mozambique, and competing factions found willing sponsors in the Cold War rivals. In Angola, the USSR, Cuba, China, the United States, and South Africa all got involved, supporting various factions. Here, and in other cases too, Cold War logic was only part of the motivation for foreign involvement. The South Africans, although they often offered anticommunism as the rationale for their incursions into Namibia, Angola, and Mozambique, and although they were in some cases egged on by the United States, were also fighting to preserve racial apartheid at home and to prevent the triumph of movements hostile to it in neighboring lands. Fidel Castro, although in many respects dependent on Soviet support, sent tens of thousands of Cuban soldiers to Angola without consulting Moscow and had his own agenda of promoting African revolution. The outside support, whether directly or indirectly motivated by Cold War strategies, made the wars in southern Africa more destructive than they could otherwise have been. Foreign powers supplied Angola with fifteen million land mines, eventually producing the world's highest rate of amputees.

In Ovamboland, a densely populated floodplain region of northern Namibia and southern Angola, warfare raged from 1975 to 1990 with frequent South African involvement. The South Africans were trying to destroy a Namibian militia that enjoyed support from an Angolan faction that itself was supported by Cuban soldiers and Soviet weaponry. Militias and armies terrorized the farming populations of Ovamboland for years, burning homes and farms, butchering livestock, and flattening orchards. The main grain crop, millet, grew tall enough to give guerrillas excellent cover, so anti-guerrilla strategies featured systematic burning of stands of maturing millet. Thousands fled, allowing their fields and homesteads to return to nature (often a dense cover of thornbush, of little use to man or beast).

In southern Mozambique, where the anti-Portuguese struggle also gave way to civil war starting in the mid-1970s, rival factions again enjoyed outside support—from China, the USSR, South Africa and, after 1980, Zimbabwe. In some districts so many refugees fled that population fell by half. The refugee totals ran into the millions. Again, farms went untended and the bush encroached. Bush encroachment in Mozambique often led to infestation by tsetse flies, the carriers of sleeping sickness and nagana (a livestock disease). The widespread use of land mines discouraged people from returning to their farms after the fighting ended in the early 1990s, so the land-use patterns of the region continued to bear the imprint of war.

In Ovamboland, in southern Mozambique, and indeed throughout the zones of guerrilla war in southern Africa, fifteen or more years of fighting changed the land by making routine human management of it—pruning back the bush, tending flocks and herds, cultivating fields and orchards—too dangerous. Instead, fire, used to punish or intimidate, or to deny cover to enemies, became the principal tool of—often accidental—ecological management. Armies and militias frequently operated in parks and nominally protected areas, because they offered easy hunting and plentiful meat for armed men without secure supply lines. Moreover, animals such as elephants that offered marketable parts (such as ivory tusks) made inviting targets for cash-strapped forces. Refugees, too, often flooded into protected areas and survived as best they could off of wildlife and the fruits of the land. Wildlife and livestock both suffered in the independence war in Zimbabwe, because anthrax and rabies ran wild in the absence of veterinary services disrupted by war. The southern African wars proved very hazardous for the animal kingdom, human and nonhuman alike.[47]

In Vietnam, the clashes were more deadly and the involvement of Cold War powers more thorough than in southern Africa. After 1945 Vietnamese nationalists (some of whom were also communists) redoubled their effort to achieve independence from France. The French tried to hold on, but after a major defeat in 1954 they increasingly invited the Americans to help resist communism in Vietnam. Despite some ambivalence about ground wars in Asia, the United States in 1964–1965 committed itself heavily to preserving its flimsy client state in South Vietnam and combating the forces of North Vietnam, which was ruled by its communist party and supported by both China and the USSR. To President Lyndon Johnson, and initially to most Americans, Vietnam was worth fighting over mainly because it seemed to be part of the Cold War chessboard.

American firepower made it an asymmetrical conflict. While there were phases of conventional warfare, at most times and places the North Vietnamese forces, and their Viet Cong allies in South Vietnam, had to fight guerrilla style. In turn, the Americans fought anti-guerrilla campaigns, something in which they had scant recent experience. They converted their more traditional capital- and equipment-intensive way of war to the circumstances they faced, using the latest technologies against their enemies.

Much of Vietnam was tropical forest, which afforded good cover for guerrillas. The North Vietnamese even carved out supply lines hundreds of kilometers long through the jungle, such as the famous Ho Chi Minh trail, part of which traversed neighboring Laos. They inflicted damage on the Americans via ambush, snipers, booby traps, using the terrain and especially the vegetation to their advantage. To counter these tactics, the Americans turned to defoliants, various chemical agents that killed trees, bushes, and grasses. The most notorious of these—Agent Orange—contains dioxin, a particularly nasty and persistent chemical compound. This form of chemical warfare had been pioneered on a small scale in the British campaign against communist rebels in the 1950s in Malaya. The Americans used it far more widely. Conveniently, airplanes could spray these chemicals cheaply and easily over vast tracts. The United States sprayed about 80 million liters of defoliants on an area the size of Massachusetts (about 8 percent of

Vietnam, mainly in the Mekong Delta) to try to save US soldiers from surprise attacks. Today the Vietnamese government claims four million people suffer from the effects of dioxin.

The United States also used mechanical means to try to deny forest cover to its enemies in Vietnam. Fleets of Rome plows, giant bulldozers wielding two-ton blades for scything down trees, could make short work of most vegetation. The United States developed them specifically for conditions in Vietnam, and used them especially for clearing the land alongside roadways. Rome plows shaved about 2 percent of South Vietnam's land area starting in 1967. From at least the time of the caesars, anti-guerrilla and counterinsurgency efforts had often involved deforesting strips adjacent to roads, but no one before could do it with the efficiency and thoroughness of the Americans with their Rome plows. Between the defoliants and the mechanical devices, the United States cleared about 22,000 square kilometers of forest (the size of New Jersey or Israel), roughly 23 percent of Vietnam's 1973 forest cover.[48]

In contrast to the wars in southern Africa, the conflict in Vietnam also featured a large bombing campaign, larger than all those of World War II combined. The US Air Force dropped over 6 million tons of bombs on Vietnam over nine years, leaving about twenty million craters, more than the moon has acquired in 4.5 billion years of bombardment by bolides. Some of these craters now serve as fish ponds. Some bombs, nicknamed "daisy-cutters," exploded aboveground and, when they worked properly, cleared away everything over a patch about the size of four football fields. They were designed to create openings in the forest for helicopter landing sites or field artillery emplacements.

Thanks to its firepower and technology, the US military was able to make rapid changes to the environment of Vietnam. No doubt the North Vietnamese and Viet Cong made some too, burning crops and villages when it suited them. But they did not have the Americans' technological capacity, or the persistent motive, to clear and poison forests.[49]

In addition to obliterating a goodly chunk of Vietnam's flora, the Vietnam War altered conditions for Vietnam's fauna. Scavenger species probably flourished thanks to extra servings of corpses. Rats, too, because of military food storage. Elephants, however, suffered, because the Americans often strafed them from the air, suspecting them of aiding and abetting the enemy as beasts of burden. The Viet Cong and other guerrillas tried to kill dogs, which might alert their enemies to impending surprise attacks. Forest animals lost habitat because in the wake of defoliation many landscapes supported only tough *imperata* grass, which few creatures can eat. Herbivores ate grass and leaves laced with toxins. Minefields selected for lightweight animals and against large ones (and continue to do so decades afterward). As in Southern Africa, in Vietnam warfare was hard on many animal species, if helpful for a few.[50]

In earlier centuries warfare had often created refuges in which wildlife could flourish, because people found it too dangerous to settle where violence reigned. In the late twentieth century, the effect of warfare on wildlife seems to have changed. Weapons had become so powerful and accurate that men with even minimal hunting skills could easily bag big game. And after 1945, most warfare involved informal forces, militias, guerrillas, and so forth, which needed to live off the land because they had no bureaucracy of quartermasters and supply chains to rely on. Thus, theaters of war in recent decades became wildlife killing zones. Moreover, the effects of wars tended to linger on, and not merely in the form of land mines. The end of warfare might remove some of the immediate motives to hunt wildlife, but the postwar profusion of guns and vehicles, and in some cases a newly pervasive culture of lawlessness, often meant that edible or marketable fauna enjoyed no peace dividend.[51]

All in all, the Vietnam War, like the struggles in southern Africa, involved a large quotient of environmental warfare and much destruction of flora and fauna. This, it should be remembered, was probably

Fires burn a cluster of huts following napalm bombing by American planes, Vietnam, January 1966. Anti-guerrilla warfare often involved intentional deforestation in efforts to deprive enemies of cover. (Time & Life Pictures/Getty Images)

true of all guerrilla conflicts around the world, those connected to the Cold War and those not. In the post–Cold War decades, insurgencies and guerrilla campaigns have diminished somewhat, but Congo, Somalia, Liberia, Sierra Leone, Iraq, Afghanistan, and a few other unfortunate lands have seen their share of unconventional warfare with collateral damage to the biosphere.

From Iron Curtain to Green Belt

The Cold War also created a few war-zone wildlife refuges. These were not combat zones but corridors in the shadow of the Iron Curtain. Churchill in 1946 famously called the line that separated zones controlled by the USSR from those of the West "the Iron Curtain." It ran from the Baltic coast, where West and East Germany met the sea, to the Adriatic, although the defection of Yugoslavia from the Soviet camp made the southern reaches of the Iron Curtain no more formidable than tin foil. But from the border of Hungary with Austria all the way to the Baltic, the Iron Curtain was a no-go zone for forty years, bristling with barbed wire and military observation towers. Unauthorized human visitors risked their lives by entering.

As a result of exclusion of ordinary human activity, the Iron Curtain gradually became an unintended nature preserve, a north–south wildlife corridor in the heart of Europe. Border police served unwittingly as park wardens, maintaining ecosystems and wildlife through exclusion of humans. Rare insects survived because no pesticides were used. Deer and boar proliferated. Along the Baltic shores, where the Iron Curtain met the sea, coastal species flourished. Thanks to Cold War distrust, the Drava River, separating Hungary and Yugoslavia, remained in a more natural state, undredged and unstraightened, preserving aquatic life, floodplains, oxbows, meanders, and the wild, channel-shifting character of the river. The Rhodope Mountains form the border between Bulgaria and Greece, another prohibited corridor during the Cold War. Consequently, the mountains hosted a wealth of rare and endangered species, with perhaps the greatest biodiversity in the Balkans. In Berlin the area immediately around the wall became a de facto sanctuary for urban species.

When the Berlin Wall fell and the Iron Curtain parted in 1989, a German doctor gathered allies to campaign for the preservation of the unusually rich environment the Cold War left behind. With the help of nature conservation organizations in Germany, and eventually the IUCN, long stretches of the former frontier have been set aside as parkland in a project known as Europe's Green Belt.[52]

The same thing could conceivably happen in Korea. Since the end of the Korean War in 1953, a demilitarized zone (DMZ) has separated North Korea from South Korea. It amounts to about half a percent of the peninsula's area and is about 4 kilometers wide, a narrow belt across Korea's waist, guarded by barbed wire, booby traps, about one million land mines, and armed men instructed to shoot to kill. Farmed for more than five thousand years and then abandoned for more than fifty, the DMZ became another accidental nature preserve. It contains a broad cross-section of Korean ecosystems, from coastal marshlands to mountain moors. It is home to dozens of endangered species, some fifty mammals in all, including bear, leopard, lynx, and a very rare mountain goat. It hosts still more species of birds and fish. Many of East Asia's migratory birds, including several kinds of majestic cranes, use the DMZ as a rest stop on their travels between Siberia and warmer climes. Red-crested cranes, now exceedingly rare, are symbols of good luck and longevity in Korea and throughout East Asia. The DMZ, the last frontier of the Cold War, has given them a new lease on life.

Since 1998 a group of Koreans (and some foreigners) have sought to prepare for the day when the two Koreas reunite and the DMZ's ecosystems are no longer protected by political standoff. They fear, not unreasonably given the environmental records of both North and South Korea, that upon reunification the DMZ might be stripped of its wildlife and sheathed in asphalt and concrete. Their organization, DMZ Forum, proposes to convert the DMZ from an accidental nature preserve to a deliberate one, a peace park. Perhaps in Korea, as on the western edge of the old Iron Curtain, one of the environmental legacies of the Cold War will be a ribbon of nature sanctuary.[53]

During the tense decades of the Cold War, leaders of the great powers normally felt that their survival, and that of the populations they led, hung by a thread. Any and every action that seemed to promise improved security appealed to them, as did anything that promised to enhance the prosperity that underwrote expenditures on security. In this political circumstance, they thought it was justifiable, even necessary, to sacrifice select places such as Mayak or Hanford and to risk the health and livelihoods of many people, such as uranium miners or the Dai people of Yunnan. World leaders found it easy enough to summon the necessary indifference to the environment to act upon their plans to bolster security and prosperity.

Until the late 1960s their populations did too. But the Cold War, paradoxically, indirectly helped spawn a surge of modern environmentalism. Anxieties about fallout from nuclear testing in the early 1960s filtered into a broader environmentalism. Beyond that, the years of détente (ca. 1972–1979), when Cold War tensions abated somewhat, opened a window of opportunity for people to voice environmental concerns. In Western Europe, North America, and Japan, and in the less regimented parts of Eastern Europe, more and more people expressed doubts about nuclear weaponry and unrestrained industrial development. Détente made them more likely both to think about the environment as an important issue and to feel more free to say so. Even after the end of détente, conventionally dated to the 1979 Soviet invasion of Afghanistan, the genie of environmentalism was out of the bottle. It could not be put back in when the Cold War entered a new frosty phase in the 1980s, despite the best efforts of some political and business leaders—such as the Bavarian politician who referred to the German Green Party as the "Trojan horse of the Soviet cavalry."[54]

The Cold War left its imprint on the biosphere on every continent and in every ocean. Many of its effects, such as the destruction of crops and villages in guerrilla wars, proved fleeting. Some effects will linger for generations still, such as the desiccation of the Aral Sea. Others will be with us, and our descendants, for time out of mind.

The Environmental Movement

The rise of the global environmental movement was one of the great stories in twentieth-century history. While there were many reasons why it occurred, not least anxieties about nuclear testing, the best explanation might be the most obvious. Economic expansion threatened environmental conditions in a great many places. This caused a reaction among those concerned about their lives, health, and livelihoods. A global economic thesis generated its own antithesis, environmentalism.

The beginning of the mass environmental movement in the United States is often tied to the publication of Rachel Carson's *Silent Spring* in 1962. Songbirds, Carson argued, were caught in a chemical web of contamination that might lead to their elimination. But behind the book's evocative imagery of lost birdsong stood a stark message for humankind, namely, how chemicals such as DDT were destroying the very basis of life itself. Modern chemistry was leading humanity to its own doom. This was the message that resonated with readers around the globe. The book made Carson famous overnight, both in the United States and in many other parts of the world (the book was translated into well over a dozen languages). It made DDT notorious. Before *Silent Spring*, the chemical had been considered a godsend in the twin battles against crop pests and insect-borne diseases. After, it became a symbol of humankind's ecological hubris.[55]

But as environmental historians point out, it is a gross oversimplification to pin the emergence of a mass, heterogeneous, and global movement on a single book.[56] Over half a century before Carson, the United States had gone through a debate about the proper use of public lands, in particular forests. It had created national parks and had busily expanded that system throughout the twentieth century. So had several European countries, both at home and in their colonies. Debates about industrial pollution also extended well back into European and North American history. In the United States, Progressives fretted about coal smoke from the end of the nineteenth century, leading to smoke control efforts in some of the country's biggest cities. After World War II, West German engineers followed the examples of St. Louis and Pittsburgh, in the hope that West Germany might also reduce smokiness for regions such as the industrial Ruhr.[57]

Moreover, the times were ripe for the message in Carson's book. The first two decades after the war had witnessed a blind faith in technology and a headlong quest for affluence. Nearly every state on Earth, rich or poor, bought into this consensus. Yet even at its height the consensus had shown signs of cracking. Anxieties about technology such as nuclear testing had crept into international discourse well before *Silent Spring*. During the 1950s the superpowers' atmospheric testing helped to create the initial wave of global fears about radioactive fallout and its effects on human health. Testing during the 1950s not only provoked much unease but also spurred some, such as Barry Commoner, to start thinking systematically about the relationships between technology and the natural environment. By 1960 some influential Americans were becoming increasingly uncomfortable with the side effects of prosperity. One was the Canadian-born economist John Kenneth Galbraith, whose best-selling book *The Affluent Society*, published in 1958, argued among other things that wealth entailed adverse effects upon nature. Grassroots groups across the country, many led by women, were linking suburbanization, the ultimate expression of American postwar prosperity, to the destruction of the countryside.[58]

Mass environmentalism in affluent countries emerged out of this background and in tandem with the "new social movements" (antiwar, students, women, hippies) of the late 1960s. The emergence of mass unrest in so many areas of life was critical for launching the nascent environmental movement from the margins of public consciousness into the forefront. All around the world, people began to question all types of authority, objecting to everything from racial injustice to gender relations to American behavior in Vietnam. Ironically the most materially comfortable generation in world history (to that point) was also the most revolutionary (at least while young). It did not take long for many in these mass movements to shift attention to the postwar consensus and its environmental consequences. Many of the youth involved in student and antiwar demonstrations ended up providing environmentalism with both energy and leadership.[59] But environmental protest did not take the same form everywhere, was not motivated by identical problems, and was not always a youthful phenomenon. Students and hippies may fit the stereotype of 1960s/1970s activism, but these were not the only participants in the new mass environmental movement. Middle-aged women had been among the vanguard at various times. So too, in many places, were intellectuals of all stripes. People of all social ranks around the world were occasionally aggrieved by the environmental degradation of their immediate surroundings, by the consequences of greater economic activity, and by inappropriate technology—and enlisted in environmental movements.

Japan provides a cogent example. After the flattening of Japanese factories in World War II, a ruling elite in government and big business joined in a headlong rush to reindustrialize the country. Their efforts met with spectacular success. Over three decades the Japanese economy grew fifty-fold, to about 10 percent of the entire global economy in the mid-1970s. Massive new industrial complexes drew huge numbers of people into Japan's cities. Unfortunately these also generated some of the world's worst air, water, and soil pollution. By the early 1960s, local opposition had emerged in several industrial cities, driven almost entirely by residents frightened for their health and lives. Toxic traces of lead, copper, mercury, zinc, asbestos, and other contaminants were widespread in industrial areas and were reliably linked to diseases and grotesque birth defects. Japan's economic miracle came at a hefty price. Citizen complaints induced some bureaucratic response, but it was not nearly enough, and by the end of the decade pollution had been turned into a national political issue. Motivated in part by the examples set by environmental protesters abroad, Japanese groups became an important factor in inducing the national government to enact tough pollution control legislation from the 1970s. By and large, Japan's environmental movement focused tightly on pollution and human health, rather than embracing concern for forests, wildlife, fisheries, or ecosystems generally.[60]

Global environmental activism intensified rapidly after 1970. For the first time, environmentalists could mobilize large numbers of people in mass demonstrations. While the most famous of these might have been the first Earth Day (April 22, 1970) and the mass protests against nuclear power in Western Europe later in the decade, such demonstrations occurred in a great many places and for a great many reasons. Older conservation organizations were put on the defensive as more confrontational groups formed, motivated by frustration over tactics and a more critical outlook based in the ecological sciences. David Brower resigned the Sierra Club presidency in 1969 to begin Friends of the Earth, a global organization dedicated to what he believed would be more radical social and environmental change. In the early 1970s a new wave of publications appeared that questioned economic growth itself. *The Limits to Growth*, a report issued in 1972 by the Club of Rome (a group formed in 1968 by Aurelio Peccei, an Italian industrial magnate), was by far the most significant of these. It sold twelve million copies in thirty languages and helped to trigger an intense debate among intellectuals about industrial society, pollution, and environment that would last for decades.[61]

The Cold War also fueled countercultural environmentalism. Although the 1963 Partial Test Ban Treaty had eliminated atmospheric testing, all the nuclear powers continued undersea or subterranean testing programs. In 1971 a small group of Canadian and American environmentalists sailed a boat toward a nuclear testing site in the Aleutian Islands, causing the US government to cancel a planned detonation there. Out of this act emerged a high-stakes brand of direct environmental activism and a new transnational environmental group, Greenpeace. Over the following years the group continued its confrontational methods in opposition to Pacific nuclear testing, a strategy that brought it into open conflict with the French government. This resulted in the 1985 sinking of the Greenpeace ship *Rainbow Warrior* by French intelligence agents in the harbor of Auckland, New Zealand.[62]

The first Earth Day, New York City, April 22, 1970. In the course of the 1960s, environmentalist social movements became increasingly popular around the world. The Earth Day tradition was launched in the United States by Gaylord Nelson, a Wisconsin senator outraged by a California oil spill. Earth Day eventually became a global observance, officially supported by the United Nations. (© JP Laffont/Sygma/CORBIS)

The Cold War's nuclear shadow, not merely testing, motivated environmentalists. The many ecology or green parties that sprang up across Western Europe found common cause with the peace movement. This alliance became much stronger in the late 1970s and early 1980s, in particular after NATO's decision in 1979 to station Pershing II and cruise missiles in Europe, causing a dramatic escalation in popular fears of nuclear war. West Germany's Green Party became the exemplary case of the marriage between the peace and environmental movements, with the party's early history marked as much by its steadfast pacifism as its environmentalism.

Environmentalism of the Poor

The same developmental forces that had created the postwar consensus in rich countries were also at work in poorer ones. The rapid global economic growth from the 1950s required ever-increasing quantities of raw materials and foodstuffs—metals, oil, coal, timber, fish, meat, and agricultural commodities of all types. Heightened demand for these pushed commodity frontiers ever outward, into parts of the world that were not yet wholly integrated into the modern economy. This demand was matched by the goals and policies of national elites in poor countries, almost all of whom subscribed to the same ideology of economic growth as prevailed in wealthier parts of the world.

Economic intensification had practical and often very negative consequences for poor people in rural areas. More metals required more mines in more places, more timber required more felling in more forests. As extractive industries began their operations (or intensified existing ones), the worst outcomes fell on the poor residents of these places. These outcomes were of two types. One resulted from extraction processes, which produced all manner of unpleasant and even deadly problems. Mines produced huge piles of tailings and polluted drinking water for miles around. Timber extraction denuded steep mountain slopes, leading to soil erosion and mudslides. Hydroelectric projects flooded large areas where rural people lived. A second outcome concerned access to natural resources. The rural poor depended for their existence on the very same resources that were now being extracted by far more powerful (and rapacious) industries. Fishing villages that had relied on small boats and low technology, for example, were now confronted by industrial trawlers able to wipe out entire fisheries.[63]

These outcomes fueled what is known as "the environmentalism of the poor." The idea originated during the 1980s, when Indian intellectuals subjected environmentalism in the richer parts of the world to intense scrutiny. In their view, environmentalism in the United States and other wealthy countries had been motivated by concerns for idealized (and constructed) forms of nature such as wilderness. Thus, it failed to address the root causes of environmental degradation—in particular, consumption—whether in their own countries or other parts of the world. In addition, some North American and European intellectuals had subscribed to a "postmaterialist" theory of environmentalism's origins. According to this theory, people in the West had become environmentalists only because their basic needs had been securely met. Environmentalism, so this theory went, had begun in the rich world because wealth allowed people there to stop worrying about their next meal and start caring about whales, bears, and wilderness. Poor people in poor countries had other environmental priorities because they were busy trying to stay alive.[64]

The Indian critics refuted the notion that the poor had no awareness of nature, no desire for protection of their environment. Much of their intellectual ammunition stemmed from a deep understanding of protests that had been lodged by the rural poor in their country. The vigor and effectiveness that the Indian poor had brought to environmental issues not only had attracted scholarly attention to their cause, it also had helped to force a rethinking of environmentalism as an intellectual problem. The formative case occurred in the Indian Himalayas in the early 1970s, when villagers in the northern state of Uttarakhand pitted themselves against foresters selling timber concessions. State-supported logging had cleared forested hillsides, leading to flooding, and had also encroached on villagers' long-standing claims to forest access and use. Hence, logging threatened villagers' lives, property, and economic livelihoods. Things came to a head in 1973 when a group of villagers, including women and children, stopped a timber operation by threatening to bind themselves to the trees. This act gave the movement both its name, Chipko (roughly, "to hug") and everlasting renown. Chipko's initial successes allowed it to expand for a time to other parts of the Himalayas, after which it faded. Besides earning environmentalists everywhere the "tree-hugger" moniker, Chipko provided the iconic example of the environmentalism of the poor.[65]

Details and circumstances differed in every case, but around the world stories very similar to Chipko abound in postwar history. No global coordinated movement existed, but these examples had much in common. Many were localized protests that did not receive much attention elsewhere. A few attracted significant notice internationally. Almost all were rooted in struggles over access to nature's bounty. In the 1980s and 1990s the Indian cause célèbre shifted to protest over dams on the Narmada River. Other instances included indigenous people's uprisings over forests in Indonesia, Buddhist monks protesting deforestation in Thailand and Burma, and villagers' objections to gold mining in Peru. Several cases have ended in tragedy. The rubber tapper Chico Mendes became a global icon after he was murdered in 1988 for organizing opposition to ranching in the Brazilian Amazon. A further example was the case of the Nigerian playwright Ken Saro-Wiwa, who led his Ogoni people in mass protest against the degradation of the Niger Delta caused by oil drilling. The Nigerian government, threatened by the attention brought to the deplorable state of the delta, arrested Saro-Wiwa and his associates. In 1995, after a short show trial, they were all executed, against international objections.[66]

The environmentalism of the poor also extends to the plight of poor people who live in rich countries. Laborers and their families in grimy landscapes had protested sporadically against the pollution of air and water since the dawn of the industrial age. But they rarely had the power to achieve their goals, partly because their organizations typically were small, local, and short-lived, attuned to specific examples of environmental degradation rather than to the broader phenomenon. In the late twentieth century this too began to change. A key event occurred in 1982, when the governor of North Carolina decided to locate a toxic waste dump in the poor and mostly African American community of Afton. This triggered mass protest, out of which was born the environmental justice movement. Rejecting mainstream environmentalism as a middle-class white phenomenon with no interest in the poor, advocates in the movement sought to link environmental health and civil rights. They stressed the fact that toxic waste dumps and power plants, for example, were placed in poor minority communities much more often than in wealthier ones. Since the 1980s, environmental justice has become increasingly integrated into mainstream environmentalism in the United States. Elsewhere, shorn of its emphasis on racism in the American context, the concept of environmental justice has flourished in several of the many places where ecological sins seem disproportionately visited upon the poor, upon minorities, or upon indigenous peoples.[67]

Environmentalism and Socialism

Socialist regimes took the correction of nature's mistakes as a duty and put environmental protection near the bottom on their list of priorities. Ideology had much to do with it. Socialist orthodoxy simply defined environmental degradation as a capitalist problem. Pollution occurred under capitalism because profit-maximizing firms foisted their pollution on society as a way to save costs. Soviet theorists maintained that pollution could not exist under socialism.

Such blinders had consequences for the real existing socialist environment. Soviet orthodoxy after World War II defined population control, for example, as a reactionary concept. All such proposals were said to stem from Thomas Robert Malthus, a Briton who had explained poverty in demographic terms and had thus committed the sin of failing to blame capitalist exploitation. Mao Zedong refused to be concerned about China's rapidly growing population in part because he accepted Soviet orthodoxy on the matter. In the mid-1950s China's leading demographer, Peking University president Ma Yinchu, had warned of catastrophe if the country did not bring growth under control. Mao, sensing the hand of a dead Englishman, branded Ma a rightist, thereby silencing him and ending all talk of population control until the early 1970s. By that time, alarm about overcrowding overwhelmed socialist orthodoxy, and the state resorted to increasingly strict family planning measures, culminating in the desperate one child per family policy in 1978 (discussed above).[68]

Resistance to environmental protection stemmed from the theoretical underpinnings of Marxism and its twentieth-century variants. Marx had formulated a progressive theory of human history, running from feudalism, through capitalism, to socialism, before culminating in communism. Industry was the key to the last three stages of the process. Capitalist industrialization was necessary and good, but by definition socialist industry had to be better. When this theoretical perspective was combined with the very real imperative to match Western powers militarily, socialist regimes could not resist emphasizing industrialization as much as possible.

The result was a narrow and utilitarian view of nature. Although nature conservation had prospered in the Soviet Union's first decade, by the time of Stalin's first five-year plan (1929–1934) state policy had begun to shift dramatically toward using all available resources for productive purposes. Mining and logging operations began to encroach on the nation's extensive system of protected areas (*zapovedniki*), the collectivization of agriculture began in earnest, and the country's best conservationists were purged. After 1945, states within the Soviet orbit went to work on gigantic and, in retrospect, ill-conceived projects of all sorts. Engineers in Eastern Europe built countless hydroelectric projects and steel mills. Their Soviet counterparts dreamed of redirecting Siberian rivers from the north, where they emptied into the Arctic Ocean, to the south, where they were to be put to work irrigating Central Asian cotton fields. The Cuban government drew up plans to construct gigantic dikes between the mainland and surrounding islands, thereby walling out the Caribbean and allowing the interior to be drained for farmland. The biggest of these projects would have increased Cuba's land area by more than 15 percent. Lack of funds, rather than concern for ecology, shelved these plans to improve upon nature.[69]

Against this backdrop it was not surprising that environmental protection had a very low priority under state socialism. But *environmentalism* existed in a kind of netherworld in these states. Having defined environmental degradation as a capitalist phenomenon, socialist regimes could hardly acknowledge, let alone publicize, the severity of their own shortcomings. Instead their public rhetoric embraced environmental protection even as they suppressed information about environmental problems. Socialist regimes often claimed superior treatment of nature as a way of showing their merits to the rest of the world. As proof they would occasionally cite legislation that contained stricter standards than anything found in the West and trumpet the existence of state-directed or state-sponsored environmental organizations having enormous membership. Both types of claims were usually groundless. More often than not, environmental legislation was ignored in practice, while state-sponsored environmental organizations often had inflated membership lists and servile governing boards.[70]

In the dictatorships of the proletariat, speaking frankly on the environment could be a costly undertaking, but it was not always so. In the right circumstances, the authorities found it preferable to tolerate the few environmental organizations that emerged during the Cold War. As long as such groups remained small in size and apparently apolitical in goals, they did not constitute much of a threat. Even episodes of genuine national anxiety about the environment, as occurred in the case of the pollution of the pristine Lake Baikal in the Soviet Union from the late 1950s, could be kept in check. The Soviet government concealed information about Baikal's condition while permitting some public dissent about pollution in the "pearl of Siberia." Environmental critiques concerning Lake Baikal were deemed tolerable: they focused on a very limited geographic area and did not call into question state control of the economy.[71] Further, some regimes avoided harsh treatment of environmentalists out of a desire to maintain domestic peace. This was the case in East Germany, where a small environmental movement managed to form from the early 1970s. It originated within the Protestant church, one of the very few institutions in the country that had had enough power to negotiate some independence from the state. While the secret police, the Stasi, kept an eye on environmentalists' activities and tried to contain or deflect them, the state allowed the movement to survive because it feared a showdown with the church.[72]

In parts of the Soviet Bloc in the 1980s, the policy of containment of popular environmentalism failed. By the beginning of the decade, large swaths of Eastern Europe and Russia had been conspicuously degraded by air, water, and soil contamination. In the Soviet Union, the first ecology groups without official recognition started to form. Influential writers such as Valentin Rasputin and Sergey Zalyagin publicly questioned the state's handling of environmental issues. The biggest change followed in the wake of Mikhail Gorbachev's arrival and his political reforms, which allowed people to voice concerns about the environment openly and without prior approval. These voices became a chorus after Chernobyl in 1986, after which hundreds of new environmental groups emerged. Many originated in the Soviet Union's outlying republics, where environmental degradation became associated with the unaccountability of the Soviet state. In places such as Latvia and Estonia, environmentalism was put in the service of nationalism, thereby contributing to the eventual breakup of the Soviet Union. In Hungary and Czechoslovakia, too, in the 1980s, popular environmentalism escaped the control of officialdom and became a vehicle for the expression of political dissent.[73]

The 1980s also marked an important shift in China. Again the key change was the creation of space for an independent civil society. The economic reforms of the late 1970s and early 1980s had nudged the Chinese economy toward private enterprise and invited trade with foreigners. This had two effects. The first occurred in the wake of the massive economic growth that started in the 1980s. As had been the case in other countries after 1945, in China the government pursued growth at any price, whatever the environmental consequences. There followed the now-familiar story of China's blackened rivers, eroded soil, and unbreathable air.

The second effect took the form of environmental dissent. It emerged in the 1980s, centered at first in larger cities. By the end of that decade, nationwide networks had surfaced. As in other socialist states, in China the government attempted to channel environmental criticism into state-sponsored organizations. But independent groups managed to form anyway. The sizable and influential Friends of Nature, for instance, decided to register itself in 1994 with the state's Academy of Chinese Culture. This act defined the Friends of Nature as a cultural organization, which meant it could avoid conflict with state restrictions on environmental groups. Thereafter, environmental organizations proliferated. By the beginning of the twenty-first century, observers estimated that thousands of groups existed throughout China, in cities of every size and in rural areas as well. These groups became increasingly bold. When supported by China's Ministry of Environmental Protection (which diverged from the party line on occasion), some groups took up taboo matters such as dam construction. Indeed, during the 1990s the Three Gorges Dam project became a preeminent focus of Chinese environmental activism.[74]

Institutional Environmentalism

The early 1970s were marked, nearly everywhere, by a significant upswing in governmental activity on the environment. Within the OECD member states, the number of major environmental laws doubled in 1971–1975, compared to the previous five years. West Germany alone crafted some two dozen pieces of new legislation during this period. In 1970 the United States created the Environmental Protection Agency (EPA) and the United Kingdom reshuffled its bureaucracy to create a cabinet-level Department of Environment. Such changes were not limited to rich countries. Mexico, for example, passed comprehensive pollution control legislation at about the same time as Japan and the United States. A large number of Latin American countries followed, establishing environmental protection ministries, many of which were based on the EPA.

In the 1970s, governments of all political hues enacted progressive environmental policies. Richard Nixon, for example, was a Republican president who embraced environmentalism to help him win reelection in 1972. West Germany's Hans-Dietrich Genscher, of the centrist Free Democratic Party, made environmentalism his own partly to steal support from the enormously popular Social Democratic chancellor, Willy Brandt. Right-wing dictatorships had no such electoral motives, but some tried environmental reform anyway. In the case of Brazil's military government before 1985, early reforms were largely hollow, undertaken as much to look modern to the outside world as anything else. But reforms under the Dominican Republic's dictator Joaquín Balaguer, who reversed some of his predecessor's destructive forestry policies, were more substantial.[75]

International organizations of all types matched this flurry of national environmental policy making. Governments had held conferences and formalized treaties as early as the nineteenth century on such matters as wildlife conservation. This picked up a bit after World War II. In the late 1940s the youthful United Nations joined with a handful of conservationists to create the IUCN. It later spun off the World Wildlife Fund (WWF). During the 1950s and 1960s the UN oversaw a small spate of conferences, one of which produced the successful biosphere reserve program.[76] By far the most important international meeting of the period was the United Nations global environmental conference, held in Stockholm in June 1972. Attended by delegates from all over the world, the conference appeared to legitimize environmentalism at the highest diplomatic level. It brought some concrete results, such as the creation of the United Nations Environment Programme (UNEP), later headquartered in Nairobi. But the conference also revealed important fissures that would bedevil subsequent environmental diplomacy, as some in poorer countries saw environmentalism as a cynical trick by which rich countries could deny them the means to develop.[77]

After Stockholm, international environmental agreements became routine in global politics. States negotiated agreements on every conceivable topic, including ocean pollution, whaling, endangered species, hazardous waste, Antarctica, forests, regional seas, biodiversity, wetlands, desertification, and acid rain. Admittedly, some of these agreements were weak. Some, however, were not, such as the 1987 Montreal Protocol that laid the foundation for the sharp reduction in CFC emissions, which had depleted the ozone layer. Over the past two decades intergovernmental bodies have become key institutions in directing attention to climate change, which by 2000 was the most important and contested area in global environmental politics. The most significant of these bodies, the Intergovernmental Panel on Climate Change, took shape in the early 1990s under UN auspices. It has sought to digest the plethora of publications on climate change and present its consensus findings in a format suitable for policy makers. Its efforts have resulted in the most authoritative synopses of the relevant science but nonetheless aroused storms of controversy, fed by forces hostile to constraints on fossil fuel use.

The trajectory of the environmental movement intersected with that of national and international political developments. In many cases national environmental movements retrenched after enjoying an initial burst of activism, settling into a long period of institution building. Much activity centered on building the capacity and technical expertise required to deal with increasingly complex scientific and regulatory issues. This was important in some places because industries were becoming much better at organizing against environmental legislation. Yet even after suffering political setbacks due to environmental backlash, as occurred in Japan, Great Britain, and the United States at different points, the environmental movement often managed to retain all or much of its strength.[78] Political engagement by environmentalists also took on new forms with the emergence of ecology parties. New Zealand formed the world's first nationwide ecology party in 1972. A bit more than a decade later, several such parties had become fixtures in the political landscapes of many countries, especially in Europe. In Belgium, a green party won seats in the national legislature in the late 1970s, followed by West Germany's greens in the early 1980s. The Finnish green party took part in a coalition government starting in 1995.

Similar institutionalization occurred within poorer countries' environmental movements. Some environmental groups in these countries enjoyed institutional trajectories that mirrored those found in North America or Europe. A few of these groups grew into large, established organizations having influence well beyond their national contexts. Kenya's Wangari Maathai started planting trees in the 1970s with no more than a little money, a few contacts abroad, and her own formidable talents. Since then, Maathai's Green Belt Movement has planted tens of millions of trees in rural areas around Kenya and in other parts of Africa. The organization grew into a global success story and became a model for emulation, for which Maathai was awarded a Nobel Peace Prize in 2004.[79]

Brazil's environmental movement illustrates the same process but on a larger scale. For much of the twentieth century Brazil had no environmental movement outside of a small number of scientists and conservationists who were concerned about protecting their country's astonishing natural heritage. Most Brazilian elites, including the military regime that ran the country from 1964 to 1985, subscribed to a consensus focusing on rapid economic development.[80] From the late 1970s, however, the regime began to bow to growing domestic pressures for political reform. As in other places, this opened up space for the formation of an environmental opposition. Over the next decade, a growing Brazilian movement widened the scope of its activities and deepened its professional and organizational sophistication. It also began building ties to other parts of the world, as when Brazilian and West German environmentalists started cooperating after their countries agreed to build nuclear plants together. This process received an enormous boost from the second UN-sponsored global environmental conference, held in Rio de Janeiro in 1992. Brazilian environmentalists traveled the globe in the run-up to the conference while groups from all over the world converged on Rio. The result, before and after 1992, was a much deeper integration of Brazilian environmentalism within a global activist network.[81]

The emergence of formal environmental movements, politics, and parties had grown well-nigh universal by 2016. Just about everywhere that electoral politics existed, so did green parties. A loose international coalition of green parties existed from 2001.[82] Unorganized, spontaneous, countercultural environmentalism survived here and there, bubbling to the surface in the aftermath of newsworthy ecological mishaps, such as the nuclear contamination at Fukushima. And environmental institutions disappeared from time to time, as in Russia in 2000 when President Putin abolished the environment ministry. By and large, though, by the twenty-first century environmentalism as a social movement had become a legitimate and institutionalized part of the political architecture on local, national, and international levels all around the world. But it remained, with few exceptions, a small part.

The Mainstreaming of Environmentalism

Environmentalism is now a lasting element in global culture—politically, morally, and socially acceptable to a great many people, although by no means to everyone. Political discourse is infused with environmental rhetoric, while environmentalism itself has become commodified. What are some of the reasons for this mainstreaming?

Disasters have provided nearly continuous fuel for environmentalists and graphic tragedies for public consumption. Some types of disasters, such as oil spills, generate particularly riveting images of destruction—beaches covered in thick black ooze and sea birds in wrenching death throes. One of the most important occurred in 1967 when the supertanker *Torrey Canyon* ran aground in the English Channel off Cornwall. Caught wholly unprepared for oil spill containment, the British government resorted to extreme measures that included aerial bombardment of the wreck in the hopes of setting it afire. This was the world's first catastrophic tanker disaster, drawing global attention to the risks attendant upon the new supertankers.[83]

Many high-profile disasters followed. The 1979 accident at the Three Mile Island nuclear power station in Pennsylvania caused a partial meltdown of a reactor core. Although the incident turned out to be minor in terms of actual damage, the fear it generated was very real. In 1983 in the Brazilian city of Cubatão, an industrial accident killed several hundred poor people living in a nearby shantytown. Ten months later a Union Carbide plant in Bhopal, India, exploded, killing thousands. The most serious and frightful of all, the Chernobyl accident, followed less than two years later. These and many other widely publicized ecological disasters helped to mainstream environmentalism.[84]

Electronic media assisted in the mainstreaming process. Environmental disasters became culturally and politically more important starting in the 1960s because television could beam visceral images into households around the world. But television's influence extended much further than coverage of disasters. Not long after television sets became a mass consumer item in North America and Europe, broadcasters discovered an immense popular interest in nature programming. By the mid-1950s, West Germans could watch *Ein Platz für Tiere* (*A Place for Animals*), a series made famous by Frankfurt's zoo director Bernhard Grzimek. A few years later, Americans were introduced to the world's wildlife via Marlin Perkins and his *Wild Kingdom* series. But it was the French oceanographer Jacques Cousteau who became the most famous. Like Grzimek, in the 1950s Cousteau had produced a color film about nature that earned him public acclaim and an Oscar to boot (Grzimek's film was about the Serengeti, Cousteau's about Mediterranean marine life). Propelled by this success, Cousteau set about plying the oceans, gathering footage for countless films and television documentaries. These were broadcast the world over, turning Cousteau into a global celebrity and solidifying the grip on the public imagination held by the glories of nature.[85]

The Internet and the World Wide Web further entrenched environmentalism in the mainstream of culture and society. The Internet made it far easier for environmental activists to locate one another and make common cause. In addition, their ability to raise funds, research issues, and share legal expertise only grew thanks to the Internet and social media. Moreover, the new electronic media made it more difficult for anti-environmental states to prevent environmental organizing and limit the availability of information. Through the Internet, even under oppressive regimes environmentalism could escape the shadows and slip into the mainstream of societies.

The commodification of the environment has proceeded in tandem with heightened public interest in the subject. Corporations now market themselves and their products in the greenest possible terms. Much of this is simple public relations posturing with little relationship to actual behavior, but a good deal of it consists of a genuine interest in appealing to customers' green sensibilities. This development reflects the increasing power of consumers who demand products that are safe, clean, and energy-efficient. Consumer interest built a burgeoning organic food movement, for example, now big business in many parts of the world.[86] The list of green products and new green industries is almost endless: electric cars, energy-efficient appliances, Earth-friendly clothing, wind turbines, green buildings, solar-powered everything.

In many ways all of this represents a remarkable set of changes from the 1950s or even 1960s. It points to the increased breadth and vigor of environmentalism as a movement and to its staying power at the global, national, and local levels. Environmental awareness and concern have become commonplace nearly everywhere, as have environmental institutions and politics.

What before 1950 was an issue mainly for aristocrats and bluebloods anxious about birds, game animals, and property rights, and typically called "conservation," gradually became broader in its concerns. By slow degrees it became environmentalism and increasingly between 1950 and 1970 a cause of the political left and counterculture, at least in Europe and North America. In the following decades, however, environmentalism evolved into a more generic movement, important to people from various parts of the political spectrum and fully integrated into politics through lobbying groups, fundraising machines, political parties, and the like. Environmentalism continued to draw some energy from young volunteers and grassroots activists, and still had some supporters among the blue-blooded squires and landed proprietors, creating fractious alliances of strange bedfellows.

Despite the unquestioned successes of the environmental movement, the fact remains that the global economy continues to expand in ways that threaten all that environmentalists cherish. The postwar vision of unending economic growth and unbridled technological progress remains intact—if no longer unchallenged.

Modern environmentalism, perhaps, represents a stage in the development of the Anthropocene. For many decades people tinkered with the basic biogeochemical cycles of the Earth without recognizing that they were doing so. As the scale of these unwitting interventions grew, more and more people noticed that, in some ways at least, humans could have an impact on the Earth. By the 1950s, if not before, a few saw that human action could affect matters as vast and important as atmospheric chemistry and global climate. Popular environmentalism from the 1960s prepared the way for a fuller recognition of the scale and scope of human impact, to the point where, in the early twenty-first century, scientists and journalists began to adopt the term "Anthropocene."

So far humankind has influenced basic Earth systems without consciously managing them. It is as accidental by-products of actions undertaken for other reasons that we have our powerful impacts on the global carbon and nitrogen cycles. If we elect to try to manage Earth systems, that is, if we undertake explicit geo-engineering, that will amount to yet another stage of the Anthropocene—whether it goes well or badly.

Conclusion

The Earth is now in a new epoch, the Anthropocene. Human history, likewise, may be in a new period, the Anthropocene, but that is less clear. The reason it is less clear is that the periodization of history is an anarchic business with no set criteria. Global history, in particular, has no consensus scheme of periodization, nor is agreement likely anytime soon. Moreover, in this one respect, the future will shape the past. If, on the one hand, turbulence in global ecology should prove disruptive to human affairs, then the Anthropocene will seem like a period in human history as well as an epoch in Earth history. If, on the other hand, humankind should find ways to pursue its customary routines despite a more turbulent climate and biosphere, then the Anthropocene will seem less like a historical period—even if it seems worthy of recognition as an epoch in Earth history. So, just as the past constrains the future, the future will constrain what we make of the past.

Our best guess is that the Anthropocene, in the fullness of time, will seem worthy both as an epoch in Earth history and as a period in human history, even if geologists and historians understand the term differently. Whether geologists will formally adopt the term Anthropocene will be decided by vote in the International Union of the Geological Sciences, probably in 2016 or soon thereafter. Whether historians will one day find the term and concept appropriate as a period in human history in general will take far longer to decide. However these professional communities decide, we maintain that the Anthropocene in global environmental history has already begun.

As we see it, the Anthropocene began when human actions became the main driving forces behind some basic Earth systems, such as the carbon cycle and the nitrogen cycle, and the general human impact on the Earth and its biosphere lurched upward to new levels. While it is futile to try to pinpoint this moment precisely, the weight of the evidence points toward a date in the middle of the twentieth century, something like 1945 or 1950.

Of course, people affected the environment before 1945. Hominins did so, with fire, before humans existed. Humans did so in the Pleistocene by helping to drive hundreds of species of large mammals to extinction. They did so in the mid-Holocene by clearing forests for farming. Although we do not do so, it is possible to define the Anthropocene so that it begins with any of these activities.

But to our way of thinking, it makes more sense to consider the Anthropocene as launched only by the Great Acceleration of the post-1945 period. Nearly every page of this book contributes to the proposition that the post-1945 period deserves to be marked off as different from what came before in environmental history. The first reason for that conclusion is that only after 1945 did human actions become genuine driving forces behind crucial Earth systems. Our carbon contribution pushed the CO_2 concentration of the atmosphere outside the boundaries of the Holocene–indeed, pushed it to heights not seen in the past 870,000 years, which is as far back as ice core evidence goes. (But 400+ parts per million *probably* is novel for at least the past three million years, since the Pliocene.) We revolutionized the nitrogen cycle, so that it operates in a way unprecedented in the history of our planet (and half the nitrogen in our bodies comes from the Haber-Bosch process). The second reason is that after 1945 the human impact on the biosphere and global ecology ramped up, as shown by the evidence on dam building, city growth, biodiversity loss, ocean acidification, the accumulation of plastic debris, and so on.

Thus, to date, the Anthropocene and the Great Acceleration coincide. But they will not for long. The Anthropocene will last long into the future, barring some calamity that removes humankind from the scene. Indeed, even if every human immigrated to another planet tomorrow, our impacts of the past few generations will linger for millennia in the Earth's crust, in the fossil record, and in climate. But the Great Acceleration will not last long. It need not and it cannot. The burst in human population growth is already coming to an end. And, less clearly but no less surely, the age of fossil fuels will come to an end. These trends should be sufficient to decelerate the Great Acceleration and moderate the human impact on the Earth. That will not end the Anthropocene but will bring it to another stage.

So far humankind has influenced basic Earth systems only by accident, as an unforeseen and unintended by-product of actions undertaken for routine quests for wealth, power, and contentment. Late in the twentieth century many people noticed that humans were doing so, which in some circles seemed imprudent and alarming. Sometime soon people will likely moderate their impact on the Earth, partly by design and partly as an accidental by-product of reduced population growth and a shift away from fossil fuels. No one can say when or how fast such shifts will take place. But when they do, the Anthropocene will have entered a new stage, perhaps a less worrisome one—although one never knows what the future may bring. The history of the twenty-first century should give us a fair idea of what to expect.

Meanwhile, many adjustments to the Anthropocene are in order. Political, economic, and cultural institutions, evolved in a context of dramatic and unprecedented resource use and economic growth, must now evolve into forms more compatible with the Anthropocene—or give way to their successors. Closer to home, for historians, the work of those who claim to make sense of human affairs—social scientists and humanists—needs some updating.

Strangely enough, just as the Great Acceleration was shifting into high gear, academic social scientists and humanists chose to retreat from grimy and greasy realities into various never-never lands. They found all manner of discourses worthy of their studied attention, reveling in the linguistic and cultural "turns." But the extinction of species, the incineration of forests, the concentration of CO_2 in the atmosphere—all this seemed unworthy of their powers, interesting only for the discourses it aroused. Meanwhile, one species of social scientists, economists, jilted reality in favor of a different fantasy, one of ever-more-abstract modeling based on universalizing assumptions of individual behavior and state conduct, casually ripped from all historical and cultural, not to mention ecological, context. Social sciences and the humanities, especially in their most prestigious bastions, showed themselves scarcely more attuned to the advent of the Anthropocene than governments floundering with energy policy and climate politics. The intellectual flight from reality made it slightly easier for those in positions of power to avoid facing up to it.

Happily, recognition of the relevance of reality and the reality of the Great Acceleration has already begun to seep into the humanities and social sciences. Something of an "environmental turn" seemed afoot early in the twenty-first century, and the linguistic turn seemed destined to go the way of all academic fashions. Perhaps any environmental turn will run its course too, but to judge by prior academic twists and turns, it probably has a generation yet to go. Economists, less malleable than most to the whims of fashion, remained wedded to their venerable models, with the exceptions of a few heretics, the ecological economists of Chapter 3.

Societies in general, and their political institutions in particular, showed uncertain signs of adjusting to the Anthropocene. As our discussion of environmentalism explained, since the 1970s most societies found ways to regulate some but not all of their ecological impacts. In a few cases (for example, CFCs), bold and effective action proved to be within reach. With respect to the tougher nuts to crack, such as greenhouse gas emissions, the attitudes and policies of societies remained doubly inconsistent. They were inconsistent in the sense that some (few) societies favored vigorous efforts even at the cost of economic sacrifice, while others sternly opposed any departures from the status quo. And many were inconsistent in the sense that their positions changed from time to time, depending on new information or political winds. But in general, by far the greater part of systems of thought and ideologies, of customs and habits, of institutions and policies, remained firmly anchored in the late Holocene. Adjustment to the Anthropocene, on every level, has only just begun.

This should come as no surprise. Intellectual, social, and political inertia are normally powerful forces. Modern thought and institutions, evolved and nurtured in the late Holocene, fit comfortably with a world of cheap energy and stable climate. That world of roughly 1750 to 1950 was tumultuous in many respects, but people could know what to expect in terms of climate, as existing patterns did not change much. And more and more people found fossil fuels more and more affordable, apparently inexhaustible, and thus infinitely appealing as a centerpiece around which to construct everything else. Now that climate is less stable and the Earth system is charting a new course never experienced before, thought and institutions will evolve in new directions more compatible with the Anthropocene. Since we cannot exit the Anthropocene, we will adjust to it, one way or another.

Notes

INTRODUCTION

1   Paul Crutzen and Eugene Stoermer, "The Anthropocene," *IGBP Global Change Newsletter* 41 (2000): 17–18. An Italian geologist-priest-revolutionary had used the term "anthropozoic" as early as 1873, but it did not catch on. A. Stoppani, *Corso di geologia* (Milan, 1873). Thinking along similar lines, the Soviet Armenian geologist George Ter-Stepanian used the term "technogene" to refer to a transitional geological period in which humans dominated geological processes. "Beginning of the Technogene," *Bulletin of the International Association of Engineering Geology* 38 (1988): 133–142. Scientists as far back as Buffon occasionally entertained kindred ideas.

2   Andrew Glikson, "Fire and Human Evolution: The Deep-Time Blueprints of the Anthropocene," *Anthropocene* 3 (2013): 89–92; Erle Ellis et al., "Dating the Anthropocene: Towards an Empirical Global History of Human Transformation of the Terrestrial Biosphere," *Elementa* (2013), doi: 10.12952/journal.elementa.000018; William Ruddiman, "The Anthropocene," *Annual Review of Earth and Planetary Sciences* 41 (2013): 45–68; Simon Lewis and Mark Maslin, "Defining the Anthropocene," *Nature* 519 (2015): 171–180.

3   Biogeochemical cycles refer to the flows of chemical elements (or compounds) among the atmosphere, oceans, rock and soil, and living things. Important ones for the functioning of the Earth and its climate, in addition to those mentioned, are the water cycle and the oxygen cycle.

4   This term was first used in this sense in a Dahlem workshop discussion in 2005, intended as an echo of Karl Polanyi's 1944 book *The Great Transformation*. Polanyi, a Hungarian American economic historian and polymath, insisted that the market economy was a recent construct, that formal economics misses social context, and that the economy must be understood as embedded in social traditions, customs, and habits of mind. Similarly, the driving forces behind anthropogenic global ecological change are embedded in societies and their traditions, while all human history is embedded in the evolving biogeophysical environment. Thus the logic of the homage to Polanyi. See Kathy Hibbard, Paul Crutzen, Eric Lambin, Diana Liverman, Nathan Mantua, John McNeill, Bruno Messerli, and Will Steffen, "Group Report: Decadal Scale Interactions of

Humans and the Environment," in *Sustainability or Collapse? An Integrated History and Future of People on Earth,* ed. Robert Costanza, Lisa Graumlich, and Will Steffen (Cambridge, MA: MIT Press, 2007), 341–378. Through Will Steffen, the term became well known in the global change science community. See also Will Steffen, Paul Crutzen, and John McNeill, "The Anthropocene: Are Humans Now Overwhelming the Great Forces of Nature?," *Ambio* 36, no. 8 (2007): 614–621.

5 Will Steffen et al., "The Trajectory of the Anthropocene: The Great Acceleration," *Anthropocene Review* 2 (2015): 81–98; to see these figures and more in convenient graphs, visit the website of the IGBP at www.igbp.net/globalchange /greatacceleration.4.1b8ae20512db692f2a680001630.html. The figures on nitrogen and plastics come from Vaclav Smil, *Making the Modern World: Materials and Dematerialization* (Chichester, UK: Wiley, 2014).

1. ENERGY AND POPULATION

1 The next several paragraphs draw on Vaclav Smil, *Energy in World History* (Boulder, CO: Westview, 1994); Smil, *Energy in Nature and Society* (Cambridge, MA: MIT Press, 2008); Alfred Crosby, *Children of the Sun: A History of Humanity's Unappeasable Appetite for Energy* (New York: Norton, 2006); Frank Niele, *Energy: Engine of Evolution* (Amsterdam: Elsevier, 2005).

2 Charles Hall, Praddep Tharakan, John Hallock, Cutler Cleveland, and Michael Jefferson, "Hydrocarbons and the Evolution of Human Culture," *Nature* 426 (2003): 318–322.

3 China figures from IEA/OECD, *Cleaner Coal in China* (Paris: IEA/OECD, 2009), 45–46; For the United Kingdom: F. D. K. Liddell, "Mortality of British Coal Miners in 1961," *British Journal of Industrial Medicine* 30 (1973): 16. In the United States around 2000, some fourteen hundred former miners died annually from black lung. Barbara Freese, *Coal: A Human History* (Cambridge, MA: Perseus, 2003), 175.

4 Chad Montrie, *To Save the Land and People: A History of Opposition to Surface Mining in Appalachia* (Chapel Hill: University of North Carolina Press, 2003).

5 Irina Gildeeva, "Environmental Protection during Exploration and Exploitation of Oil and Gas Fields," *Environmental Geosciences* 6 (2009): 153–154.

6 Joanna Burger, *Oil Spills* (New Brunswick, NJ: Rutgers University Press, 1997), 42–44.

7 On fisheries and ecological effects, see Harold Upton, "The Deepwater Horizon Oil Spill and the Gulf of Mexico Fishing Industry," Congressional Research

Service report, February 17, 2011, available at http://fpc.state.gov/documents
/organization/159014.pdf. On legal aspects, see the symposium "Deep Trouble:
Legal Ramifications of the Deepwater Horizon Oil Spill," *Tulane Law Review*
85 (March 2011). Of the journalistic accounts, the best to date is Joel Achen-
bach, *A Hole at the Bottom of the Sea: The Race to Kill the BP Oil Gusher* (New
York: Simon and Schuster, 2011).

8 The following discussion is based on Anna-Karin Hurtig and Miguel San Se-
bastian, "Geographical Differences in Cancer Incidence in the Amazon Basin
of Ecuador in Relation to Residence near Oil Fields," *International Journal of
Epidemiology* 31 (2002): 1021–1027; and Miguel San Sebastian and Anna-Karin
Hurtig, "Oil Exploitation in the Amazon Basin of Ecuador: A Public Health
Emergency," *Revista Panamericana de Salud Pública* 15 (2004): 205–211. The
cancer claims are disputed by Michael Kelsh, Libby Morimoto, and Edmund
Lau, "Cancer Mortality and Oil Production in the Amazon Region of Ecuador,
1990–2005," *International Archives of Occupational and Environmental Health*
82 (2008): 381–395. See also Judith Kimmerling, "Oil Development in Ecuador
and Peru: Law, Politics, and the Environment," in *Amazonia at the Crossroads:
The Challenge of Sustainable Development,* ed. Anthony Hall (London: Institute of Latin American Studies, University of London, 2000), 73–98.

9 M. Finer, C. N. Jenkins, S. L. Pimm, B. Keane, and C. Ross, "Oil and Gas Projects in the Western Amazon: Threats to Wilderness, Biodiversity, and Indigenous
Peoples," *PLoS ONE* 3, no. 8 (2008): e2932, doi:10.1371/journal.pone.0002932.
For general context, see Allen Gerlach, *Indians, Oil, and Politics: A Recent History of Ecuador* (Wilmington, DE: Scholarly Resources, 2003). The UNDP deal
is explained at http://mdtf.undp.org/yasuni.

10 P. A. Olajide et al., "Fish Kills and Physiochemical Qualities of a Crude Oil Polluted River in Nigeria," *Research Journal of Fisheries and Hydrobiology* 4 (2009):
55–64.

11 J. S. Omotola, "'Liberation Movements' and Rising Violence in the Niger
Delta: The New Contentious Site of Oil and Environmental Politics," *Studies
in Conflict and Terrorism* 33 (2010): 36–54; Tobias Haller et al., *Fossil Fuels, Oil
Companies, and Indigenous Peoples* (Berlin: Lit Verlag, 2007), 69–76. For po-
litical analyses, see the many writings of Michael Watts; e.g., Watts, "Blood Oil:
The Anatomy of a Petro-insurgency in the Niger Delta," *Focaal* 52 (2008): 18–38;
Watts, ed., *The Curse of the Black Gold: 50 Years of Oil in the Niger Delta*
(Brooklyn: PowerHouse Books, 2009).

12 Haller et al., *Fossil Fuels,* 166–167.

13 D. O'Rourke and S. Connolly, "Just Oil? The Distribution of Environmental and Social Impacts of Oil Production and Consumption," *Annual Review of Environment and Resources* 28 (2003): 598.

14 Ibid., 599–601.

15 In the 1990s in the United States, the agency responsible for pipeline safety employed one inspector for every 60,000 kilometers of (oil and gas) pipeline. The ratio was probably less favorable in almost every other country of the world. O'Rourke and Connolly, "Just Oil?," 611.

16 Now Usinsk has a website on the spill: http://usinsk.ru/katastrofa_city.html. We thank Valentina Roxo, of Ludwig-Maximilians University, for bringing this to our attention.

17 G. E. Vilchek and A. A. Tishkov, "Usinsk Oil Spill," in *Disturbance and Recovery in Arctic Lands,* ed. R. M. M. Crawford (Dordrecht: Kluwer Academic, 1997), 411–420; Anna Kireeva, "Oil Spills in Komi: Cause and the Size of the Spill Kept Hidden," www.bellona.org/articles/articles_2007/Oil_spill_in_Komi. See also "West Siberia Oil Industry Environmental and Social Profile," a Greenpeace report, www.greenpeace.org/raw/content/nederland-old/reports/west-siberia-oil-industry-envi.pdf.

18 Marjorie M. Balzer, "The Tension between Might and Rights: Siberians and Energy Developers in Post-Socialist Binds," *Europe-Asia Studies* 58 (2006): 567–588; Haller et al., *Fossil Fuels,* 168–178.

19 B. K. Sovacool, "The Cost of Failure: A Preliminary Assessment of Major Energy Accidents, 1907–2007," *Energy Policy* 36 (2008): 1802–1820.

20 Michelle Bell, Devra Davis, and Tony Fletcher, "A Retrospective Assessment of Mortality from the London Smog Episode of 1952: The Role of Influenza and Pollution," *Environmental Health Perspectives* 112 (2004): 6–8.

21 The blitz of September 1940 to May 1941 killed about twenty thousand Londoners over nine months.

22 Quoted in Devra Davis, *When Smoke Ran Like Water* (New York: Basic Books, 2002), 45.

23 Ibid., 31–54; Peter Brimblecombe, *The Big Smoke: A History of Air Pollution in London since Medieval Times* (London: Methuen, 1987), 165–169.

24 Inferred from data in B. Brunekreef and S. Holgate, "Air Pollution and Health," *Lancet* 360 (2002):1239.

25 Eri Saikawa et al., "Present and Potential Future Contributions of Sulfate, Black and Organic Aerosols from China to Global Air Quality, Premature Mortality, and Radiative Forcing," *Atmospheric Environment* 43 (2009): 2814–2822.

26 M. Ezzati, A. Lopez, A. Rodgers, S. Vander Hoorn, and C. Murray, "Selected Major Risk Factors and Global and Regional Burden of Disease," *Lancet* 360 (2002): 1347–1360. A similar figure was reached by A. J. Cohen et al., "The Global Burden of Disease due to Outdoor Air Pollution," *Journal of Toxicology and Environmental Health* 68 (2005): 1301–1307.

27 Bear in mind that air pollution kills mostly the very young, the very old, and those with respiratory or heart conditions. War mainly kills people in the prime of life. So from an economic point of view, air pollution mortality is much less costly than war mortality, because it chiefly kills those who are easily replaced (infants and toddlers) and those who have already made what contributions they will ever make (the very old). For those who regard all humans as equal, this calculus is of course abhorrent.

28 See John Watt et al., eds., *The Effects of Air Pollution on Cultural Heritage* (Berlin: Springer, 2009) on these issues generally.

29 David Stern, "Global Sulfur Emissions from 1850 to 2000," *Chemosphere* 58 (2005): 163–175; Z. Lu et al., "Sulfur Dioxide Emissions in China and Sulfur Trends in East Asia since 2000," *Atmospheric Chemistry and Physics Discussions* 10 (2010): 8657–8715; C. K. Chan and X. H. Yao, "Air Pollution in Mega Cities in China," *Atmospheric Environment* 42 (2008): 1–42; M. Fang, C. K. Chan, and X. H. Yao, "Managing Air Quality in a Rapidly Developing Nation: China," *Atmospheric Environment* 43, no. 1 (2009): 79–86.

30 Jes Fenger, "Air Pollution in the Last 50 Years: From Local to Global," *Atmospheric Environment* 43 (2009): 15.

31 H. R. Anderson, "Air Pollution and Mortality: A History," *Atmospheric Environment* 43 (2009): 144–145.

32 M. Hashimoto, "History of Air Pollution Control in Japan," in *How to Conquer Air Pollution: A Japanese Experience,* ed. H. Nishimura (Amsterdam: Elsevier, 1989), 1–94.

33 James Fleming, *Fixing the Sky: The Checkered History of Weather and Climate Control* (New York: Columbia University Press, 2010).

34 J. Samuel Walker, *Three Mile Island: A Nuclear Crisis in Historical Perspective* (Berkeley: University of California Press, 2004).

35 March 29, 1986, issue of *The Economist.*

36 A. V. Yablokov, V. B. Nesterenko, and A. V. Nesterenko, "Consequences of the Chernobyl Catastrophe for the Environment," *Annals of the New York Academy of Sciences* 1181 (2009): 221–286. Effects upon animals extended far beyond the Chernobyl exclusion zone. Swedish moose, for example, contained thirty-three times their usual quantities of radioactivity (ca. 1988). Ibid., 256.

37 Jim Smith and Nicholas Beresford, *Chernobyl* (Berlin: Springer, 2005); A. B. Nesterenko, V. B. Nesterenko, and A. V. Yablokov, "Consequences of the Chernobyl Catastrophe for Public Health," *Annals of the New York Academy of Sciences* 1181 (2009): 31–220.

38 The wastes are stored in concrete and steel containers, mainly on reactor sites. Deep geological storage ran into political problems, as had dumping at sea. See the pro-nuclear Nuclear Energy Institute page at www.nei.org/keyissues /nuclearwastedisposal/factsheets/safelymanagingusednuclearfuel/.

39 Useful data and perspectives appear in the April 2012 issue of *Environmental History*, especially Sara Pritchard, "An Envirotechnical Disaster: Nature, Technology, and Politics at Fukushima," *Environmental History* 17 (2012): 219–243. See also J. C. MacDonald, "Fukushima: One Year Later," *Radiation Protection Dosimetry* 149 (2012): 353–354; and Koichi Hasegawa, "Facing Nuclear Risks: Lessons from the Fukushima Nuclear Disaster," *International Journal of Japanese Sociology* 21 (2012): 84–91.

40 For an insiders' view of the blunders, see Yoichi Funabashi and Kay Kitazawa, "Fukushima in Review: A Complex Disaster, a Disastrous Response," *Bulletin of the Atomic Scientists* 68 (2012): 9–21.

41 On the controversies surrounding hydropower development, see R. Sternberg, "Hydropower: Dimensions of Social and Environmental Coexistence," *Renewable and Sustainable Energy Reviews* 12 (2008): 1588–1621.

42 The Rihand Dam in Uttar Pradesh, India, built 1954–1962. E. G. Thukral, *Big Dams, Displaced People: Rivers of Sorrow, Rivers of Change* (New Delhi: Sage, 1992), 13–14.

43 A. G. Nilsen, *Dispossession and Resistance in India: The River and the Rage* (London: Routledge, 2010).

44 Satyajit Singh, *Taming the Waters: The Political Economy of Large Dams in India* (Delhi: Oxford University Press, 1997); John R. Wood, *The Politics of Water Resource Development in India: The Narmada Dams Controversy* (Los Angeles: Sage, 2007); Nilsen, *Dispossession and Resistance.*

45 K. Xu and J. D. Milliman, "Seasonal Variations of Sediment Discharge from the Yangtze River before and after Impoundment of the Three Gorges Dam," *Geomorphology* 104 (2009): 276–283.

46 P. Zhang et al., "Opportunities and Challenges for Renewable Energy Policy in China," *Renewable and Sustainable Energy Reviews* 13 (2009): 439–449.

47 Quotation from a Canadian lumberjack, Arnst Kurelek, cited in R. C. Silversides, *Broadaxe to Flying Shear: The Mechanization for Forest Harvesting East of the Rockies* (Ottawa: National Museum of Science and Technology, 1997), 107.

48 Manfred Weissenbacher, *Sources of Power: How Energy Forges Human History* (Santa Barbara, CA: ABC-CLIO, 2009), 452.

49 On these examples, see A. P. Muñoz, R. S. Pavón, and L. Z. Villareal, "Rehabilitación turística y capacidad de carga en Cozumel," *Revista iberoamericana de economía ecológica* 11 (2009): 53–63; S. Gössling et al., "Ecological Footprint Analysis as a Tool to Assess Tourism Sustainability," *Ecological Economics* 43 (2002): 199–211 (this is about the Seychelles, an interesting case because of its government's effort to preserve the islands' environment while reaping revenues from tourism); G. M. Mudd, "Gold Mining in Australia: Linking Historical Trends and Environmental and Resource Sustainability," *Environmental Science and Policy* 10 (2007): 629–644; M. Cryer, B. Hartill, and S. O'Shea, "Modification of Marine Benthos by Trawling: Generalization for the Deep Ocean?," *Ecological Applications* 12 (2002): 1824–1839; Lawrence Solomon, *Toronto Sprawls: A History* (Toronto: University of Toronto Press, 2007); John Sewell, *The Shape of the Suburbs: Understanding Toronto's Sprawl* (Toronto: University of Toronto Press, 2009).

50 Joel Cohen, *How Many People Can the Earth Support?* (New York: Norton, 1995), 78–79.

51 Adapted from Carlo Cipolla, *An Economic History of World Population* (Harmondsworth, UK: Penguin, 1978), 89.

52 Robert Fogel, *The Escape from Hunger and Premature Death, 1700–2100* (New York: Cambridge University Press, 2004), 21.

53 The successes and failures of malaria control are detailed in James L. A. Webb Jr., *Humanity's Burden: A Global History of Malaria* (New York: Cambridge University Press, 2009). For the agricultural story, see Giovanni Federico, *Feeding the World: An Economic History of World Agriculture, 1800–2000* (Princeton, NJ: Princeton University Press, 2005).

54 According to Fogel, *Escape from Hunger* (40), in Britain the "elite" cohort born in 1875 lived about seventeen years longer than the population as a whole; by 2000 that gap was four years. UN life expectancy data at http://esa.un.org /unpp/p2k0data.asp.

55 Han Feizi, *Han Feizi: Basic Writings*, trans. Burton Watson (New York: Columbia University Press, 2003), 98.

56 The Tertullian quotation is from Cohen, *How Many People*, 6.

57 Leo Silberman, "Hung Liang-chi: A Chinese Malthus," *Population Studies* 13 (1960): 257–265.

58 India's birth rate at the time stood at 36 per 1,000 population and the target was 25 per 1,000, achieved only around 2000, some twenty years later than hoped.

Ramachandra Guha, *India after Gandhi: The History of the World's Largest Democracy* (New York: HarperCollins, 2007), 415–416, 511–514.

59 Yves Blayo, *Des politiques démographiques en Chine* (Lille: Atelier National de Reproductions des Thèses, 2006); Thomas Scharping, *Birth Control in China, 1949–2000* (London: RoutledgeCurzon, 2003); Tyrene White, *China's Longest Campaign: Birth Planning in the People's Republic, 1949–2005* (Ithaca, NY: Cornell University Press, 2006). Susan Greenhalgh, *Just One Child: Science and Policy in Deng's China* (Berkeley: University of California Press, 2008); Greenhalgh, *Cultivating Global Citizens: Population in the Rise of China* (Cambridge, MA: Harvard University Press, 2010). On both India and China, see also Matthew Connelly, *Fatal Misconception: The Struggle to Control World Population* (Cambridge, MA: Harvard University Press, 2008).

60 For recent data on desertification in northern China, see Ma Yonghuan and Fan Shengyue, "The Protection Policy of Eco-environment in Desertification Areas of Northern China: Contradiction and Countermeasures," *Ambio* 35 (2006): 133–134. For historical perspective, see James Reardon-Anderson, *Reluctant Pioneers: China's Northward Expansion, 1644–1937* (Stanford, CA: Stanford University Press, 2005); Peter Perdue, *China Marches West: The Qing Conquest of Central Asia* (Cambridge, MA: Harvard University Press, 2005); Dee Mack Williams, *Beyond Great Walls: Environment, Identity, and Development on the Chinese Grasslands of Inner Mongolia* (Stanford, CA: Stanford University Press, 2002).

61 Mary Tiffen, Michel Mortimore, and Francis Gichuki, *More People, Less Erosion: Environmental Recovery in Kenya* (Chichester, NY: Wiley, 1994). On the Mediterranean, see J. R. McNeill, *The Mountains of the Mediterranean: An Environmental History* (New York: Cambridge University Press, 1992).

62 In 2010 the world's irrigated area came to about three hundred million hectares, some five times the size of Texas or seven times the size of France. Bridget Scanlon, Ian Jolly, Marios Sophocleous, and Lu Zhang, "Global Impacts of Conversions from Natural to Agricultural Ecosystems on Water Resources: Quantity vs. Quality," *Water Resources Research* 43 (2007): W03437, available at www.agu.org/pubs/crossref/2007/2006WR005486.shtml.

63 Dean Bavington, *Managed Annihilation: An Unnatural History of the Newfoundland Cod Collapse* (Vancouver: University of British Columbia Press, 2010).

64 Jason Link, Bjarte Bogstad, Henrik Sparholt, and George Lilly, "Trophic Role of Atlantic Cod in the Ecosystem," *Fish and Fisheries* 10 (2008): 58–87; Ilona Stobutzki, Geronimo Silvestre, and Len Garces, "Key Issues in Coastal Fisheries in

South and Southeast Asia: Outcomes of a Regional Initiative," *Fisheries Research* 78 (2006): 109–118. The depletion of cod, a top predator, has entirely reorganized the marine ecosystems of places such as the Grand Banks.

65 FAO marine fish catch data at www.fao.org/fishery/statistics/global-production /en. FAO data do not go back further than 1950, and are probably more reliable the more recent they are.

66 H. Bruce Franklin, *The Most Important Fish in the Sea: Menhaden and America* (Washington, DC: Island Press, 2007).

67 Anqing Shi, "The Impact of Population Pressure on Global Carbon Emissions, 1975–1996: Evidence from Pooled Cross-Country Data," *Ecological Economics* 44 (2003): 29–42. Further discussion is in John R. McNeill, *Something New under the Sun: An Environmental History of the Twentieth-Century World* (New York: Norton, 2000), 272–273. Historical carbon emission data, 1751–2004, from fossil fuel use only, are available at http://cdiac.ornl.gov/trends/emis/em _cont.html.

68 The plant manufactured pesticides, used in Indian agriculture. Although one might argue that it did so because of population growth in India, this in no way explains the accident, which was a matter of neglected maintenance. A recent account appears in Suroopa Mukerjee, *Surviving Bhopal: Dancing Bodies, Written Texts, and Oral Testimonials of Women in the Wake of an Industrial Disaster* (London: Palgrave, 2010), 17–40.

69 Dirk Hoerder, *Cultures in Contact: World Migration in the Second Millennium* (Durham, NC: Duke University Press, 2002), 508–582.

70 Char Miller, *On the Border: An Environmental History of San Antonio* (Pittsburgh: University of Pittsburgh Press, 2001).

71 Ren Qiang and Yuan Xin, "Impacts of Migration to Xinjiang since the 1950s," in *China's Minorities on the Move,* ed. Robyn Iredale, Naran Bilik, and Fei Guo (Armonk, NY: M. E. Sharpe, 2003), 89–105. The precise numbers of Chinese migrants in Xinjiang are unclear.

72 J. M. Foggin, "Depopulating the Tibetan Grasslands," *Mountain Research and Development* 28 (2008): 26–31; A. M. Fischer, "Urban Fault Lines in Shangri-La: Population and Economics Foundations of Inter-ethnic Conflict in the Tibetan Area of Western China," London School of Economics Crisis States Program Working Paper #42; Hao Xin, "A Green Fervor Sweeps the Qinghai-Tibetan Plateau," *Science* 321 (2008): 633–635. A historically minded study of a region on the eastern Tibetan plateau is Jack P. Hayes, "Modernisation with Local Characteristics: Development Efforts and the Environment on the Zoige Grass and Wetlands, 1949–2005," *Environment and History* 16 (2010): 323–347.

73 Greg Grandin, *Fordlandia: The Rise and Fall of Henry Ford's Forgotten Jungle City* (New York: Metropolitan Books, 2009).

74 A recent assessment is P. M. Fearnside, "Deforestation in Brazilian Amazonia: History, Rates, and Consequences," *Conservation Biology* 19, no. 3 (2005): 680–688. See also Michael Williams, *Deforesting the Earth* (Chicago: University of Chicago Press, 2003), 460–481. A boom in soybean exports to China after 2008 reduced Amazonian deforestation rates sharply, because all available investment went into plowing up the savannas in Goias and other states south of Amazonia. See the web page of Brazil's Institute for Space Research (INPE): www.inpe.br/ingles/news/news_dest154.php.

75 Peter Dauvergne, "The Politics of Deforestation in Indonesia," *Pacific Affairs* 66 (1993–1994): 497–518; J. M. Hardjono, "The Indonesian Transmigration Scheme in Historical Perspective," *International Migration* 26 (1988): 427–438. Logging, plantation agriculture, and much else contributed to Indonesia's rapid deforestation.

2. CLIMATE AND BIOLOGICAL DIVERSITY

1 The following discussion is from Jonathan Cowie, *Climate Change: Biological and Human Aspects* (New York: Cambridge University Press, 2007), 1–16, 22–31, 126–167.

2 For a discussion of the Earth's carbon cycle, see Bert Bolin, *A History of the Science and Politics of Climate Change: The Role of the Intergovernmental Panel on Climate Change* (New York: Cambridge University Press, 2007), chap. 2.

3 Michael R. Raupach et al., "Global and Regional Drivers of Accelerating CO_2 Emissions," *Proceedings of the National Academy of Sciences of the United States of America* 104, no. 24 (June 12, 2007): 10288. For estimates of the effects of tropical deforestation on global carbon emissions, see Wolfgang Cramer et al., "Tropical Forests and the Global Carbon Cycle: Impacts of Atmospheric Carbon Dioxide, Climate Change and Rate of Deforestation," *Philosophical Transactions of the Royal Society: Biological Sciences* 359, no. 1443 (March 29, 2004): 331–343. On deforestation in historical context, see generally Williams, *Deforesting the Earth.*

4 T. A. Boden, G. Marland, and R. J. Andres, "Global, Regional, and National Fossil-Fuel CO_2 Emissions," in *Trends: A Compendium of Data on Global Change* (Oak Ridge, TN: Carbon Dioxide Information Analysis Center, Oak Ridge National Laboratory, U.S. Department of Energy, 2009), doi: 10.3334/CDIAC/00001; Raupach et al., "Global and Regional Drivers," 10288. CDIAC data at: http://cdiac.ornl.gov/trends/emis/meth_reg.html.

5 Joseph G. Canadella et al., "Contributions to Accelerating Atmospheric CO_2 Growth from Economic Activity, Carbon Intensity, and Efficiency of Natural Sinks," *Proceedings of the National Academy of Sciences of the United States of America* 104, no. 47 (November 20, 2007): 18866–18870; Raupach et al., "Global and Regional Drivers," 10288–10292.

6 James Hansen et al., "Global Temperature Change," *Proceedings of the National Academy of Sciences of the United States of America* 103, no. 39 (September 26, 2006): 14288–14293; P. D. Jones, D. E. Parker, T. J. Osborn, and K. R. Briffa, "Global and Hemispheric Temperature Anomalies: Land and Marine Instrumental Records," in Oak Ridge National Laboratory, *Trends*, doi: 10.3334/CDIAC/cli.002; John M. Broder, "Past Decade Was Warmest Ever, NASA Finds," *New York Times*, January 22, 2010, A8.

7 Andrew E. Dessler and Edward A. Parson, *The Science and Politics of Global Climate Change: A Guide to the Debate* (New York: Cambridge University Press, 2006), table 3.1; Edward L. Miles, "On the Increasing Vulnerability of the World Ocean to Multiple Stresses," *Annual Review of Environment and Resources* 34 (2009): 18–26; Ian Simonds, "Comparing and Contrasting the Behavior of Arctic and Antarctic Sea Ice over the 35-Year Period 1979–2013," *Annals of Glaciology* 56 (2015): 18–28.

8 Scott C. Doney and David S. Schimel, "Carbon and Climate System Coupling on Timescales from the Precambrian to the Anthropocene," *Annual Review of Environment and Resources* 32 (2007): 31–66; Miles, "On the Increasing Vulnerability," 26–28.

9 United Nations Environment Programme, *Climate Change Science Compendium, 2009*, 15–16.

10 Jianchu Xu et al., "The Melting Himalayas: Cascading Effects of Climate Change on Water, Biodiversity, and Livelihoods," *Conservation Biology* 23, no. 3 (June 2009): 520–530.

11 M. Monirul Qader Mirza, "Climate Change, Flooding and Implications in South Asia," *Regional Environmental Change* 11, suppl. 1 (2011): 95–107; Katherine Morton, "Climate Change and Security at the Third Pole," *Survival* 53 (2011): 121–132.

12 Bolin, *A History*, chap. 1.

13 Spencer Weart, *The Discovery of Global Warming* (Cambridge, MA: Harvard University Press, 2008), 14–17.

14 Ibid., 19–33. For a recent summary of the Mauna Loa time series, see R. F. Keeling, S. C. Piper, A. F. Bollenbacher, and J. S. Walker, "Atmospheric CO_2 Records from Sites in the SIO Air Sampling Network," in Oak Ridge National

Laboratory, *Trends*, doi: 10.3334/CDIAC/atg.035. Doney and Schimel (2007) write that the Mauna Loa time series is "one of the most iconic data sets in geophysics, if not all of science" (48).

15 Cowie, *Climate Change*, 20–21; Weart, *Discovery of Global Warming*, 53–58, 70–78, 126–137.

16 Bolin, *A History*, 20–34; Weart, *Discovery of Global Warming*, chaps. 4 and 5.

17 William C. Clark et al., "Acid Rain, Ozone Depletion, and Climate Change: An Historical Overview," in *Learning to Manage Global Environmental Risks*, vol. 1, *A Comparative History of Social Responses to Climate Change, Ozone Depletion and Acid Rain*, ed. The Social Learning Group (Cambridge, MA: MIT Press, 2007), 21–39; Cass R. Sunstein, "Of Montreal and Kyoto: A Tale of Two Protocols," *Harvard Environmental Law Review* 31, no. 1 (2007): 10–22; Intergovernmental Panel on Climate Change, *Climate Change 2007: Synthesis Report; Contribution of Working Groups I, II and III to the Fourth Assessment Report of the Intergovernmental Panel on Climate Change* (Geneva: Intergovernmental Panel on Climate Change, 2007), 2–22; Bolin, *A History*, 44–49; Dessler and Parson, *Global Climate Change*, 12–16. A fascinating interpretation of the scientific community's role in the ozone and climate politics during the 1980s and 1990s is provided in Reiner Grundmann, "Ozone and Climate: Scientific Consensus and Leadership," *Science, Technology, & Human Values* 31, no. 1 (January 2006): 73–101.

18 International Energy Association Special Report, *Energy and Climate Change* (June, 2015), p. 25. According to this document, CO_2 emissions 1988–2014 equaled those prior to 1988.

19 IMF Working Paper 15/105, "How Large Are Global Energy Subsidies?," www.imf.org/external/pubs/ft/wp/2015/wp15105.pdf; *The Economist*, January 17, 2015, 70.

20 E. O. Wilson, "Editor's Foreword," in *Biodiversity*, ed. E. O. Wilson with Frances M. Peter (Washington, DC: National Academy Press, 1988), v; Williams, *Deforesting the Earth*, 437–446.

21 Gordon H. Orians and Martha J. Groom, "Global Biodiversity: Patterns and Processes," in *Principles of Conservation Biology*, ed. Martha J. Groom, Gary K. Meffe, and C. Ronald Carroll (Sunderland, MA: Sinauer Associates, 2006), 30–31; Catherine Badgley, "The Multiple Scales of Biodiversity," *Paleobiology* 29, no. 1 (Winter 2003): 11–13; Martin Jenkins, "Prospects for Biodiversity," *Science* 302, no. 5648 (November 14, 2003): 1175. For dissenting views, see, e.g., Geerat J. Vermeij and Lindsey R. Leighton, "Does Global Diversity Mean Anything?," *Paleobiology* 29, no. 1 (Winter 2003): 3–7; D. M. J. S. Bowman,

"Death of Biodiversity: The Urgent Need for Global Ecology," *Global Ecology and Biogeography Letters* 7, no. 4 (July 1998): 237–240.

22 Craig Hilton-Taylor et al., "State of the World's Species," in *Wildlife in a Changing World: An Analysis of the 2008 IUCN Red List of Threatened Species,* ed. Jean-Christophe Vié, Craig Hilton-Taylor, and Simon N. Stuart (Gland, Switzerland: International Union for Conservation of Nature and Natural Resources, 2009), 15–17; James P. Collins and Martha L. Crump, *Extinction in Our Times: Global Amphibian Decline* (New York: Oxford University Press, 2009), 1–2; Orians and Groom, "Global Biodiversity," 33–34.

23 Jens Mutke et al., "Terrestrial Plant Diversity," in *Plant Conservation: A Natural History Approach,* ed. Gary A. Krupnick and W. John Kress (Chicago: University of Chicago Press, 2005), 15–25; Simon L. Lewis, "Tropical Forests and the Changing Earth System," *Philosophical Transactions: Biological Sciences* 361, no. 1465, Reviews (January 29, 2006): 195–196.

24 Michael L. McKinney, "Is Marine Biodiversity at Less Risk? Evidence and Implications," *Diversity and Distributions* 4, no. 1 (January 1998): 3–8; Beth A. Polidoro et al., "Status of the World's Marine Species," in Vié, Hilton-Taylor, and Stuart, *Wildlife,* 55.

25 Paul K. Dayton, "The Importance of the Natural Sciences to Conservation," *American Naturalist* 162, no. 1 (July 2003): 2; Polidoro et al., "Status," 57–58.

26 E. O. Wilson, "The Current State of Biological Diversity," in Wilson and Peter, *Biodiversity,* 12–13; David S. Woodruff, "Declines of Biomes and Biotas and the Future of Evolution," *Proceedings of the National Academy of Sciences of the United States of America* 98, no. 10 (May 8, 2001): 5471–5476. On the difficulties of estimating species extinction numbers as well as factors, see, e.g., Richard G. Davies et al., "Human Impacts and the Global Distribution of Extinction Risk," *Proceedings: Biological Sciences* 273, no. 1598 (September 7, 2006): 2127–2133; Bruce A. Stein and Warren L. Wagner, "Current Plant Extinctions: Chiaroscuro in Shades of Green," in Krupnick and Kress, *Plant Conservation,* 59–60; A. D. Barnosky et al., "Has the Earth's Sixth Mass Extinction Already Arrived?," *Nature* 471 (March 3, 2011): 51–57.

27 William Adams, *Against Extinction: The Story of Conservation* (London: Earthscan, 2004), 47–50; J. Donald Hughes, "Biodiversity in World History," in *The Face of the Earth: Environment and World History,* ed. J. Donald Hughes (Armonk, NY: M. E. Sharpe, 2000), 35; Jean-Christophe Vié et al., "The IUCN Red List: A Key Conservation Tool," in Vié, Hilton-Taylor, and Stuart, *Wildlife,* 1–13; Hilton-Taylor et al., "State of the World's Species," 15–42; the 2012 Red List is at: http://www.iucnredlist.org/.

28 Martha J. Groom, "Threats to Biodiversity," in Groom, Meffe, and Carroll, *Principles of Conservation Biology,* 64–65. For land use statistics, see McNeill, *Something New,* table 7.1. Bird density data can be found in Kevin J. Gaston, Tim M. Blackburn, and Kees Klein Goldewijk, "Habitat Conversion and Global Avian Biodiversity Loss," *Proceedings: Biological Sciences* 270, no. 1521 (June 22, 2003): table 1.

29 Williams, *Deforesting the Earth,* 386–421. See also Lewis, "Tropical Forests," 197–199.

30 Williams, *Deforesting the Earth,* 420–481.

31 Gary J. Wiles et al., "Impacts of the Brown Tree Snake: Patterns of Decline and Species Persistence in Guam's Avifauna," *Conservation Biology* 17, no. 5 (October 2003): 1350–1360; Dieter C. Wasshausen and Werner Rauh, "Habitat Loss: The Extreme Case of Madagascar," in Krupnick and Kress, *Plant Conservation,* 151–155; Mutke et al., "Terrestrial Plant Diversity," 18; Williams, *Deforesting the Earth,* 343.

32 Michel Meybeck, "Global Analysis of River Systems: From Earth System Controls to Anthropocene Syndromes," *Philosophical Transactions: Biological Sciences* 358, no. 1440 (December 29, 2003): 1935–1955.

33 Controversy still surrounds the first introduction of the Nile Perch into Lake Victoria. Some claim that colonial administrators deliberately introduced the fish in order to improve the lake's commercial fisheries; others claim it was an accidental introduction. See Robert M. Pringle, "The Nile Perch in Lake Victoria: Local Responses and Adaptations," *Africa: Journal of the International African Institute* 75, no. 4 (2005): 510–538.

34 See Dayton, "Importance of the Natural Sciences."

35 Callum Roberts, *The Unnatural History of the Sea* (Washington, DC: Island Press, 2007), chaps. 12, 20–22.

36 Carmel Finley, "A Political History of Maximum Sustained Yield, 1945–1955," in *Oceans Past: Management Insights from the History of Marine Animal Populations,* ed. David J. Starkey, Poul Holm, and Michaele Barnard (London: Earthscan, 2008), 189–206; Roberts, *Unnatural History of the Sea,* 321–323.

37 Roberts, *Unnatural History of the Sea,* 288–302, 314–326. On aquaculture, see James Muir, "Managing to Harvest? Perspectives on the Potential of Aquaculture," *Philosophical Transactions: Biological Sciences* 360, no. 1453 (January 29, 2005): 191–218.

38 Randall Reeves and Tim Smith, "A Taxonomy of World Whaling Operations and Eras," in *Whales, Whaling, and Ocean Ecosystems,* ed. James Estes et al. (Berkeley: University of California Press, 2006), 82–101; John A. Knauss, "The

International Whaling Commission: Its Past and Possible Future," *Ocean Development & International Law* 28, no. 1 (1997): 79–87; "Japan Says It Will Hunt Whales Despite Science Panel's Opposition," *Science*, April 16, 2015, http://news.sciencemag.org/asiapacific/2015/04/japan-says-it-will-hunt-whales-despite-science-panel-s-opposition.

39 Clive Wilkinson, "Status of Coral Reefs of the World: Summary of Threats and Remedial Action," in *Coral Reef Conservation,* ed. Isabelle M. Cote and John D. Reynolds (Cambridge: Cambridge University Press, 2006), 3–21; Zvy Dubinsky and Noga Stambler, eds., *Coral Reefs: An Ecosystem in Transition* (Dordrecht: Springer, 2011).

40 Adams, *Against Extinction,* 176–201; Hughes, "Biodiversity in World History," 35–40. On the ESA and wolves, see, e.g., John Erb and Michael W. DonCarlos, "An Overview of the Legal History and Population Status of Wolves in Minnesota," in *Recovery of Gray Wolves in the Great Lakes Region of the United States: An Endangered Species Success Story,* ed. Adrian P. Wydeven, Timothy R. Van Deelen, and Edward J. Heske (New York: Springer, 2009), 49–85. On Project Tiger and wildlife protection in India, see Mahesh Rangarajan, "The Politics of Ecology: The Debate on Wildlife and People in India, 1970–95," in *Battles over Nature: Science and the Politics of Conservation,* ed. Vasant K. Saberwal and Mahesh Rangarajan (Delhi: Orient Blackswan, 2003), 189–230.

41 Adams, *Against Extinction,* 25–53, 67–96. For a harsh view of European conservationists in African history, see Jonathan S. Adams and Thomas O. McShane, *The Myth of Wild Africa: Conservation without Illusion* (Berkeley: University of California Press, 1996). On Gabon, see Lydia Polgreen, "Pristine African Park Faces Development," *New York Times*, February 22, 2009, A6.

42 Roberts, *Unnatural History of the Sea,* preface, chaps. 1, 25; Louisa Wood et al., "Assessing Progress towards Global Marine Protection Targets: Shortfalls in Information and Action," *Oryx* 42 (2008): 340–351; Juliet Eilperin, "'Biological Gem' Becomes Largest Marine Reserve; Coral, Tuna, Sharks Expected to Thrive in Chagos Islands," *Washington Post*, April 2, 2010, A10; John M. Broder, "Bush to Protect Vast New Pacific Tracts," *New York Times*, January 6, 2009, A13.

43 On whaling disputes, see Stephen Palumbi and Joe Roman, "The History of Whales Read from DNA," and J. A. Estes et al., "Retrospection and Review," both in Estes et al., *Whales, Whaling, and Ocean Ecosystems,* 102–115, 388–393; Juliet Eilperin, "A Crossroads for Whales: With Some Species Rebounding, Commission Weighs Loosening of Hunting Ban," *Washington Post*, March 29, 2010, A01.

44 On tiger conservation, see Virginia Morell, "Can the Wild Tiger Survive?," *Science* 317, no. 5843 (September 7, 2007): 1312–1314.

45 Camille Parmesan and John Matthews, "Biological Impacts of Climate Change," in Groom, Meffe, and Carroll, *Principles of Conservation Biology,* 352; Wilkinson, "Status of Coral Reefs," 19–21.

3. CITIES AND THE ECONOMY

1 Celia Dugger, "U.N. Predicts Urban Population Explosion," *New York Times,* June 28, 2007, 6. Global urban data is from Thomas Brinkhoff, "The Principal Agglomerations of the World," www.citypopulation.de; an "agglomeration" is defined as "a central city and neighboring communities linked to it (e.g.) by continuous built-up areas or commuters," hence Tokyo includes Yokohama, Kawasaki, and Saitama.

2 On New York's ocean dumping, see Martin Melosi, *The Sanitary City: Urban Infrastructure in America from Colonial Times to the Present* (Baltimore: Johns Hopkins University Press, 2000), 180–182, 260. On the urban contribution to greenhouse gas emissions, see Grimm et al., "Global Change and the Ecology of Cities," *Science* 319 (February 6, 2008): 756–760.

3 The quotation is from Martin Melosi, "The Place of the City in Environmental History," *Environmental History Review* 17 (Spring 1993): 7. Nuremberg suffered from the fact that it did not sit along a major navigable river, which meant it could not purchase timber from remote upstream forests. Hence, the city needed to control local sources. See Joachim Radkau, *Nature and Power: A Global History of the Environment* (New York: Cambridge University Press, 2008), 146–147.

4 Verena Winiwarter and Martin Knoll, *Umweltgeschichte: Eine Einführung* (Cologne: Böhlau, 2007), 181–182, 199; Christopher G. Boone and Ali Modarres, *City and Environment* (Philadelphia: Temple University Press, 2006), 77–78, 101–102; Grimm et al., "Global Change," 756–760.

5 Melosi, "Place of the City," 7; Grimm et al., "Global Change," 756. On the complexities of women's fertility in cities, see, e.g., Oğuz Işik and M. Melih Pinarcioğlu, "Geographies of a Silent Transition: A Geographically Weighted Regression Approach to Regional Fertility Differences in Turkey," *European Journal of Population / Revue Européenne de Démographie* 22, no. 4 (December 2006): 399–421; Eric R. Jensen and Dennis A. Ahlburg, "Why Does Migration Decrease Fertility? Evidence from the Philippines," *Population Studies* 58, no. 2 (July 2004): 219–231; Amson Sibanda et al., "The Proximate Determinants of the Decline to Below-Replacement Fertility in Addis Ababa, Ethiopia," *Studies*

in Family Planning 34, no. 1 (March 2003): 1–7; Patrick R. Galloway, Ronald D. Lee, and Eugene A. Hammel, "Urban versus Rural: Fertility Decline in the Cities and Rural Districts of Prussia, 1875 to 1910," *European Journal of Population / Revue Européenne de Démographie* 14, no. 3 (September 1998): 209–264.

6 Kenneth T. Jackson, "Cities," in *The Columbia History of the 20th Century,* ed. Richard W. Bulliet (New York, 1998), 529–530; John Reader, *Cities* (New York: Atlantic Monthly Press, 2004), 122–124. The classic statistical compilation of urban population history is provided by Tertius Chandler and Gerald Fox, *3000 Years of Urban Growth* (New York: Academic Press, 1974); see esp. 300–326.

7 On timber transport, see Radkau, *Nature and Power,* 146. On the limits to cities generally, see the incisive remarks of H. G. Wells, *Anticipations of the Reaction of Mechanical and Scientific Progress upon Human Life and Thought* (New York: Harper Bros., 1902), 44–54, 70–71.

8 On the plague, cholera, and quarantine in Europe, see Gerry Kearns, "Zivilis or Hygaeia: Urban Public Health and the Epidemiologic Transition," in *The Rise and Fall of Great Cities: Aspects of Urbanization in the Western World,* ed. Richard Lawton (New York: Belhaven, 1989), 98–99, 107–111. On Japan, see Susan B. Hanley, "Urban Sanitation in Preindustrial Japan," *Journal of Interdisciplinary History* 18, no. 1 (Summer 1987): 1–26.

9 Wells, *Anticipations,* 54.

10 Jackson, "Cities," 530–532. For a discussion of how London provisioned itself during the nineteenth century, see Reader, *Cities,* 127–132.

11 See generally the United Nations Department for Economic and Social Information and Policy Analysis, Population Division, *The Challenge of Urbanization: The World's Largest Cities* (New York: Author, 1995). On Australia, see Clive Forster, *Australian Cities: Continuity and Change* (Melbourne: Oxford University Press, 1995), chap. 1.

12 P. P. Karan, "The City in Japan," in *The Japanese City,* ed. P. P. Karan and Kristin Stapleton (Lexington: University Press of Kentucky, 1997), 12–21; Forster, *Australian Cities,* 6–12.

13 Wells, *Anticipations,* 54.

14 This reading of Chicago's history is from William Cronon, *Nature's Metropolis: Chicago and the Great West* (New York: Norton, 1991).

15 Martin Melosi, *Effluent America: Cities, Industry, Energy, and the Environment* (Pittsburgh: University of Pittsburgh Press, 2001), 54–56, 178–179; Peter Hall, *Cities of Tomorrow: An Intellectual History of Urban Planning and Design in the Twentieth Century* (Oxford: Blackwell, 1996), 31–33; Leonardo Benevolo,

The Origins of Modern Town Planning (Cambridge, MA: MIT Press, 1967), 20–23; Reader, *Cities,* 147–148.

16 Melosi, *The Sanitary City,* chaps. 2–9. On Haussmann and Paris, see Howard Saalman, *Haussmann: Paris Transformed* (New York: Braziller, 1971), 19–20; Reader, *Cities,* 211–214.

17 André Raymond, *Cairo,* trans. Willard Wood (Cambridge, MA: Harvard University Press, 2000), 309–321; James B. Pick and Edgar W. Butler, *Mexico Megacity* (Boulder, CO: Westview, 2000), 30–37 (data from table 3.2, p. 37). On American transportation history before 1939, see Owen D. Gutfreund, *Twentieth-Century Sprawl: Highways and the Reshaping of the American Landscape* (New York: Oxford University Press, 2004), chap. 1; Clay McShane, *Down the Asphalt Path: The Automobile and the American City* (New York: Columbia University Press, 1994), 103–122; John Jakle, "Landscapes Redesigned for the Automobile," in *The Making of the American Landscape,* ed. Michael P. Conzen (Boston: Unwin Hyman, 1990), 293–299.

18 United Nations Department for Economic and Social Information and Policy Analysis, Population Division, *World Urbanization Prospects: The 2003 Revision* (New York: UN Population Division, 2004), tables 1.1, 1.7 (pp. 3, 11). The number of megacities depends partly on how a city's boundaries are defined.

19 United Nations, Department for Economic and Social Information and Policy Analysis, *World Urbanization Prospects,* tables 1.1, 1.3 (pp. 3–5). Figures are rounded.

20 United Nations Human Settlements Programme (UN-Habitat), *The Challenge of Slums: Global Report on Human Settlements 2003* (London: Earthscan, 2003), 25–27.

21 On the Persian Gulf, see Yasser Elsheshtawy, "Cities of Sand and Fog: Abu Dhabi's Global Ambitions," in *The Evolving Arab City: Tradition, Modernity and Urban Development,* ed. Yasser Elsheshtawy (New York: Routledge, 2008), 258–304; Janet Abu-Lughod, "Urbanization in the Arab World and the International System," in *The Urban Transformation of the Developing World,* ed. Josef Gugler (Oxford: Oxford University Press, 1996), 185–210. On Karachi, see Arif Hasan, "The Growth of a Metropolis," in *Karachi: Megacity of Our Times,* ed. Hamida Khuhro and Anwer Mooraj (Karachi: Oxford University Press, 1997), 174. On China, see Anthony M. Orum and Xiangming Chen, *The World of Cities: Places in Comparative and Historical Perspective* (Malden, MA: Blackwell, 2003), table 4.1 (pp. 101–103).

22 James Heitzman, *The City in South Asia* (London: Routledge, 2008), 179, 187; David Satterthwaite, "In Pursuit of a Healthy Urban Environment in Low- and

Middle-Income Nations," in *Scaling Urban Environmental Challenges: From Local to Global and Back,* ed. Peter J. Marcotullio and Gordon McGranahan (London: Earthscan, 2007), 79; Alan Gilbert, "Land, Housing, and Infrastructure in Latin America's Major Cities," in *The Mega-city in Latin America,* ed. Alan Gilbert (New York: United Nations University Press, 1996), table 4.1 (pp. 74–75); Hasan, "Growth of a Metropolis," 188–189.

23 Satterthwaite, "In Pursuit," 69–71; United Nations Centre for Human Settlements (Habitat), *Cities in a Globalizing World: Global Report on Human Settlements, 2001* (London: Earthscan, 2001), 105–110. On water supply and demand in Indian cities, see Rajendra Sagane, "Water Management in Mega-cities in India: Mumbai, Delhi, Calcutta, and Chennai," in *Water for Urban Areas: Challenges and Perspectives,* ed. Juha I. Uitto and Asit K. Biswas (New York: United Nations University Press, 2000), 84–111.

24 United Nations Human Settlements Programme (UN-Habitat), *The Challenge of Slums,* table 6.8 (p. 113); Gilbert, "Land, Housing," 78–80.

25 Grimm et al., "Global Change," 757; Mario J. Molina and Luisa T. Molina, "Megacities and Atmospheric Pollution," *Journal of the Air and Waste Management Association* 54 (June 2004): 644–680; World Health Organization and United Nations Environment Programme, *Urban Air Pollution in Megacities of the World* (Cambridge, MA: Blackwell Reference, 1992), 56–65, 203–210.

26 United Nations Human Settlements Programme (UN-Habitat), *The Challenge of Slums,* 211–212; World Health Organization and United Nations Environment Programme, *Urban Air Pollution,* 107–113; Robert Cribb, "The Politics of Pollution Control in Indonesia," *Asian Survey* 30, no. 12 (December 1990): 1123–1235; Susan Abeyasekere, *Jakarta: A History* (Singapore: Oxford University Press, 1989), 167–245.

27 United Nations Department for Economic and Social Information and Policy Analysis, *World Urbanization Prospects,* table 1.1 (p. 3).

28 Frank Uekoetter, *The Age of Smoke: Environmental Policy in Germany and the United States, 1880–1970* (Pittsburgh: University of Pittsburgh Press, 2009), 113–195, 209–258; Joel Tarr, "The Metabolism of the Industrial City: The Case of Pittsburgh," *Journal of American History* 28, no. 5 (July 2002): 523–528.

29 World Health Organization and United Nations Environment Programme, *Urban Air Pollution,* 124–134, 172–177, 211–218.

30 Uekoetter, *The Age of Smoke,* 198–207; Molina and Molina, "Megacities and Atmospheric Pollution," 644–661. On Addis, see V. Etyemezian et al., "Results from a Pilot-Scale Air Quality Study in Addis Ababa, Ethiopia," *Atmospheric Environment* 39 (2005): 7849–7860.

31 McShane, *Down the Asphalt Path*, 1–56, 103–122, 203–223; Barbara Schmucki, *Der Traum vom Verkehrsfluss: Städtische Verkehrsplanung seit 1945 im deutsch-deutschen Vergleich* (Frankfurt: Campus, 2001), 100–103, 126, 401; Peter Newman and Jeffrey Kenworthy, *Sustainability and Cities: Overcoming Automobile Dependence* (Washington, DC: Island Press, 1999), table 3.8 (p. 80); Forster, *Australian Cities*, 18; Jakle, "Landscapes Redesigned," 299–300.

32 Jeffrey Kenworthy and Felix Laube, *An International Sourcebook of Automobile Dependence in Cities, 1960–1990* (Niwot, CO: University Press of Colorado, 1999), 361; Newman and Kenworthy, *Sustainability and Cities,* table 3.12; Karan, "The City in Japan," 33; Forster, *Australian Cities*, 15–20.

33 Newman and Kenworthy, *Sustainability and Cities,* tables 3.4, 3.8, 3.9, 3.14; see also Matthew E. Kahn, "The Environmental Impact of Suburbanization," *Journal of Policy Analysis and Management* 19, no. 4 (Autumn 2000): 569–586. On American gasoline prices and automobile size, see Rudi Volti, "A Century of Automobility," *Technology and Culture* 37, no. 4 (October 1996): 663–685.

34 Melosi, *The Sanitary City,* 297–298, 338–341, 373–374, 395–422. On postwar urbanization and land use in Great Britain, see, e.g., Peter Hall, "The Containment of Urban England," *Geographical Journal* 140, no. 3 (October 1974): 386–408.

35 Grimm et al., "Global Change," 756, 758.

36 William E. Rees, "Ecological Footprints and Appropriated Carrying Capacity: What Urban Economics Leaves Out," *Environment and Urbanization* 4, no. 2 (October 1992): 121–130 (quotation at 125). For a summary of criticism of the idea, see Winiwarter and Knoll, *Umweltgeschichte,* 182–185.

37 Charles J. Kibert, "Green Buildings: An Overview of Progress," *Journal of Land Use & Environmental Law* 19 (2004): 491–502; R. R. White, "Editorial: Convergent Trends in Architecture and Urban Environmental Planning," *Environment and Planning D: Society and Space* 11, no. 4 (August 1993): 375–378.

38 Timothy Beatley, "Green Urbanism in European Cities," in *The Humane Metropolis: People and Nature in the 21st-Century City,* ed. Rutherford H. Platt (Amherst: University of Massachusetts Press, 2006), 297–314; Timothy Beatley, *Green Urbanism: Learning from European Cities* (Washington, DC: Island Press, 2000).

39 Anna Lehmann and Ulrich Schulte, "Brüder, zur Sonne, nach Freiburg! . . . ," *TAZ, Die Tageszeitung* (July 31, 2007), Berlin Metro Section, 21; Thomas Schroepfer and Limin Hee, "Emerging Forms of Sustainable Urbanism: Case Studies of Vauban Freiburg and solarCity Linz," *Journal of Green Building* 3, no. 2 (Spring 2008): 67–76. For an example of Freiburg's promotional literature, see

City of Freiburg im Breisgau, *Freiburg Green City* (October 2008), available at www.freiburg.de/greencity.

40 John Pucher and Ralph Buehler, "Making Cycling Irresistible: Lessons from the Netherlands, Denmark, and Germany," *Transport Reviews* 28, no. 4 (July 2008): 495–528; Newman and Kenworthy, *Sustainability and Cities,* 201–208; John Pucher, "Bicycling Boom in Germany: A Revival Engineered by Public Policy," *Transportation Quarterly* 51, no. 4 (Fall 1997): 31–45.

41 This summary of Curitiba is based on Bill McKibben, *Hope, Human and Wild: True Stories of Living Lightly on the Earth* (Minneapolis: Milkweed, 2007), 59–111; Hugh Schwartz, *Urban Renewal, Municipal Revitalization: The Case of Curitiba, Brazil* (Alexandria, VA: Hugh Schwartz, 2004), chap. 1; Donnella Meadows, "The City of First Priorities," *Whole Earth Review* 85 (Spring 1995): 58–59; Jonas Rabinovitch, "Curitiba: Towards Sustainable Urban Development," *Environment and Urbanization* 4, no. 2 (October 1992): 62–73.

42 The discussion of Havana is based on Shawn Miller, *Environmental History of Latin America,* 230–235; Adriana Premat, "Moving between the Plan and the Ground: Shifting Perspectives on Urban Agriculture in Havana, Cuba," in *Agropolis: The Social, Political, and Environmental Dimensions of Urban Agriculture,* ed. Luc J. A. Mougeot (London: Earthscan, 2005), 153–185; Reader, *Cities,* 168–171.

43 Luc J. A. Mougeot, introduction to Mougeot, *Agropolis,* 1–4 and table 17.

44 For a critical take on Barcelona's efforts at greening itself, see Juan Martinez-Alier, *The Environmentalism of the Poor: A Study of Ecological Conflicts and Valuation* (New Delhi: Oxford University Press, 2004), 161–167. On global cars, see United Nations Centre for Human Settlements (Habitat), *Cities in a Globalizing World,* table 11.1. On China and cars, see Yok-shiu F. Lee, "Motorization in Rapidly Developing Cities," in *Scaling Urban Environmental Challenges: From Local to Global and Back,* ed. Peter J. Marcotullio and Gordon McGranahan (London: Earthscan, 2007), 179–205.

45 Angus Maddison, *The World Economy,* vol. 1, *A Millennial Perspective* (Paris: OECD, 2006), 125–126.

46 Jürgen Osterhammel and Niels P. Petersson, *Globalization: A Short History* (Princeton, NJ: Princeton University Press, 2005), 94–103; J. R. McNeill, "Social, Economic, and Political Forces in Environmental Change, Decadal Scale (1900 to 2000)," in *Sustainability or Collapse? An Integrated History and Future of People on Earth,* ed. Robert Costanza, Lisa J. Graumlich, and Will Steffen (Cambridge, MA: MIT Press, 2007), 307–308; Jeffry Frieden, *Global Capitalism: Its Fall and Rise in the 20th Century* (New York: Norton, 2006).

47 Ivan Berend, *Central and Eastern Europe, 1944–1993: Detour from the Periphery to the Periphery* (Cambridge: Cambridge University Press, 1996).

48 Stephen Kotkin, *Armageddon Averted: The Soviet Collapse, 1970–2000* (Oxford: Oxford University Press, 2008), 17–25, 32–34; Maddison, *The World Economy,* vol. 1, table 3-5; Robert C. Allen, *From Farm to Factory: A Reinterpretation of the Soviet Industrial Revolution* (Princeton, NJ: Princeton University Press, 2003).

49 Biomass is not included in these figures despite its continuing importance to millions of families in poor regions of the world. Biomass tends to be collected and used outside of the commercial economy, hence most often unreported. See Vaclav Smil, *Energy in Nature and Society: General Energetics of Complex Systems* (Cambridge, MA: MIT Press, 2008), chap. 9 (see esp. fig. 9.1).

50 Ibid., 241–243, 257–259.

51 Vaclav Smil, *Energy at the Crossroads: Global Perspectives and Uncertainties* (Cambridge, MA: MIT Press, 2005), 65–105.

52 Massimo Livi-Bacci, *A Concise History of World Population* (Cambridge, MA: Blackwell, 1992), table 4.3; Maddison, *The World Economy,* vol. 2, *Historical Statistics* (Paris: OECD Development Centre, 2006), table 5a.

53 Vaclav Smil, *Transforming the Twentieth Century: Technical Innovations and Their Consequences* (New York: Oxford University Press, 2006), 221–224.

54 John McCormick, *Reclaiming Paradise: The Global Environmental Movement* (Bloomington: Indiana University Press, 1989), 55–56, 69–71.

55 Smil, *Transforming the Twentieth Century,* 123–130; Peter Clark, "Versatile Plastics for Future," *Science News-Letter* 76, no. 24 (December 12, 1959): 402–403.

56 John B. Colton Jr., Frederick D. Knapp, and Bruce R. Burns, "Plastic Particles in Surface Waters of the Northwestern Atlantic," *Science* 185, no. 4150 (August 9, 1974): 491–497; "Oily Seas and Plastic Waters of the Atlantic," *Science News* 103, no. 8 (February 24, 1973): 119; Thor Heyerdahl, *The Ra Expeditions* (New York: Doubleday, 1971), 209–210, 235, 312 (quotation at 209).

57 Smil, *Transforming the Twentieth Century,* 123.

58 P. G. Ryan, C. J. Moore, J. A. van Franeker, and C. L. Moloney, "Monitoring the Abundance of Plastic Debris in the Marine Environment," *Philosophical Transactions of the Royal Society (Biology)* 364 (2009): 1999–2012; D. K. A. Barnes, F. Galgani, R. C. Thompson, and M. Barlaz, "Accumulation and Fragmentation of Plastic Debris in Global Environments," *Philosophical Transactions of the Royal Society (Biology)* 364 (2009): 1985–1998; Lindsey Hoshaw, "Afloat in the Ocean, Expanding Islands of Trash," *New York Times,* November 10, 2009, D2; Richard C. Thompson et al., "Lost at Sea: Where Is All the Plastic?," *Science* 304, no. 5672 (May 7, 2004): 838. See also the more popular

treatment, Curtis Ebbesmeyer and Eric Scigliano, *Flotsametrics and the Floating World* (New York: HarperCollins, 2009), 186–221.

59 Peter Dauvergne, *The Shadows of Consumption: Consequences for the Global Environment* (Cambridge, MA: MIT Press, 2008), 99–131; Smil, *Transforming the Twentieth Century,* 41; Catherine Wolfram, Orie Shelef, and Paul J. Gertler, "How Will Energy Demand Develop in the Developing World?," National Bureau of Economic Research Working Paper No. 17747 (2012), at www.nber.org /papers/w17747.

60 Maddison, *The World Economy,* 1:131–134; Rondo Cameron and Larry Neal, *A Concise Economic History of the World from Paleolithic Times to the Present* (New York: Oxford University Press, 2003), 367–370. On the effects of cheap oil in postwar Europe, see Christian Pfister, "The Syndrome of the 1950s," in *Getting and Spending: European and American Consumer Societies in the Twentieth Century,* ed. Susan Strasser, Charles McGovern, and Matthias Judt (Cambridge: Cambridge University Press, 1998), 359–377.

61 Maddison, *The World Economy,* 1:139–141; Yasukichi Yasuba, "Japan's Post-war Growth in Historical Perspective," in *The Economic Development of Modern Japan, 1945–1995,* vol. 1, *From Occupation to the Bubble Economy,* ed. Steven Tolliday (Northampton, MA: Edward Elgar, 2001), 3–16.

62 On Americanization in theory, see Richard Kuisel, "Commentary: Americanization for Historians," *Diplomatic History* 24, no. 3 (Summer 2000): 509–515. There is a massive literature on the Americanization of Europe. See, e.g., Emanuella Scarpellini, "Shopping American Style: The Arrival of the Supermarket in Postwar Italy," *Enterprise and Society* 5, no. 4 (2004): 625–668; Detlef Junker, "The Continuity of Ambivalence: German Views of America, 1933–1945," in *Transatlantic Images and Perceptions: Germany and America since 1776,* ed. David Barkley and Elisabeth Glaser-Schmidt (New York: Cambridge University Press and German Historical Institute, 1997), 243–263; Richard Kuisel, *Seducing the French: The Dilemma of Americanization* (Berkeley: University of California Press, 1993); Frank Costigliola, *Awkward Dominion: American Political, Economic and Cultural Relations with Europe, 1919–33* (Ithaca, NY: Cornell University Press, 1984). On American cultural influence on Japanese consumerism, see Penelope Francks, *The Japanese Consumer: An Alternative Economic History of Modern Japan* (Cambridge: Cambridge University Press, 2009), 151–162; Yasuba, "Japan's Post-war Growth," 13–14. On America and East Asian consumerism generally, see James L. Watson, *Golden Arches East: McDonald's in East Asia* (Stanford, CA: Stanford University Press, 2006).

63 Maddison, *The World Economy,* vol. 2, tables 5a, 5b, 5c (pp. 542–543, 552–553, 562–563).

64 Kotkin, *Armageddon Averted,* chap. 1; Cameron and Neal, *Concise Economic History,* 372–373. For discussion of the effects of collectivization on nature in, and the peoples of, Eastern Europe, see Katrina Z. S. Schwartz, *Nature and National Identity after Communism: Globalizing the Ethnoscape* (Pittsburgh: University of Pittsburgh Press, 2006); Arvid Nelson, *Cold War Ecology: Forests, Farms, and People in the East German Landscape, 1945–1989* (New Haven, CT: Yale University Press, 2005).

65 Kotkin, *Armageddon Averted,* 10–17, 48–53.

66 Ibid., chap. 3.

67 Ibid., chap. 5; Maddison, *The World Economy,* 1:155–161.

68 Ho-fung Hung, "Introduction: The Three Transformations of Global Capitalism," in *China and the Transformation of Global Capitalism,* ed. Ho-fung Hung (Baltimore: Johns Hopkins University Press, 2009), 10–11; Osterhammel and Petersson, *Globalization,* 115–116.

69 Giovanni Arrighi, "China's Market Economy in the Long Run," 1–21; Ho-fung Hung, "Introduction," 6–13; John Minns, "World Economies: Southeast Asia since the 1950s," in *The Southeast Asia Handbook,* ed. Patrick Heenan and Monique Lamontagne (London: Fitzroy Dearborn, 2001), 24–37.

70 On the banana trade, see Marcelo Bucheli and Ian Read, "Banana Boats and Baby Food: The Banana in U.S. History," in *From Silver to Cocaine: Latin American Commodity Chains and the Building of the World Economy, 1500–2000,* ed. Steven Topik, Carlos Marichal, and Zephyr Frank (Durham, NC: Duke University Press, 2006), 204–227.

71 Osterhammel and Petersson, *Globalization,* 128–130; Minns, "World Economies."

72 Maddison, *The World Economy,* 1:151–155 and table 3-5.

73 Martinez-Alier, *Environmentalism of the Poor,* chap. 2; Ramachandra Guha and Juan Martinez-Alier, *Varieties of Environmentalism: Essays North and South* (Delhi: Oxford University Press, 1998), chap. 9; Herman E. Daly, "Steady-State Economics versus Growthmania: A Critique of the Orthodox Conceptions of Growth, Wants, Scarcity, and Efficiency," *Policy Sciences* 5, no. 2 (June 1974): 149–167.

74 Robert Costanza et al., "The Value of the World's Ecosystem Services and Natural Capital," *Nature* 387 (May 15, 1997): 253–260; Robert Costanza, "Ecological Economics: Reintegrating the Study of Humans and Nature," *Ecological Applications* 6, no. 4 (November 1996): 978–990; Kenneth Arrow et al., "Eco-

nomic Growth, Carrying Capacity, and the Environment," *Ecological Applications* 6, no. 1 (February 1996): 13–15; Herman E. Daly, "On Economics as a Life Science," *Journal of Political Economy* 76, no. 3 (May–June 1968): 392–406; Kenneth E. Boulding, "Economics and Ecology," in *Future Environments of North America: Being the Record of a Conference Convened by the Conservation Foundation in April, 1965, at Airlie House, Warrenton, Virginia,* ed. F. Fraser Darling and John P. Milton (Garden City, NY: Natural History Press, 1966), 225–234.

75　David Satterthwaite, *Barbara Ward and the Origins of Sustainable Development* (London: International Institute for Environment and Development, 2006); Susan Baker, *Sustainable Development* (New York: International Institute for Environment and Development, 2006); Lorraine Elliott, *The Global Politics of the Environment* (New York: New York University Press, 2004); Robert Paehlke, "Environmental Politics, Sustainability and Social Science," *Environmental Politics* 10, no. 4 (Winter 2001): 1–22; United Nations Environment Programme, *In Defence of the Earth: The Basic Texts on Environment: Founex—Stockholm—Cocoyoc* (Nairobi: United Nations Environment Programme, 1981).

76　For an outstanding take on this question, see Ramachandra Guha, *How Much Should a Person Consume? Environmentalism in India and the United States* (Berkeley: University of California Press, 2006), chap. 9.

4. COLD WAR AND ENVIRONMENTAL CULTURE

1　Vaclav Smil, *Energy in World History* (Boulder, CO: Westview, 1994), 185; on the USSR, see Paul Josephson, "War on Nature as Part of the Cold War: The Strategic and Ideological Roots of Environmental Degradation in the Soviet Union," in *Environmental Histories of the Cold War,* ed. J. R. McNeill and Corinna Unger (New York: Cambridge University Press, 2010), 46. According to Charles Maier, "The World Economy and the Cold War in the Middle of the Twentieth Century," in *The Cambridge History of the Cold War,* ed. Melvyn Leffler and Arne Westad (Cambridge: Cambridge University Press, 2010), 1:64, the USSR used about 20 percent of its GNP for military spending, whereas the United States, France, and Britain spent 5 to 10 percent of their GNPs for military purposes. The United States devoted about 3 to 4 percent of its oil consumption to the military. A single F-16, a workhorse of the Air Force from 1979 onward, used more fuel in an afternoon than the average American family vehicle did over two years.

2　On the interstate system and its ecological effects, see J. R. McNeill, "The Cold War and the Biosphere," in Leffler and Westad, *Cambridge History of the Cold War,* 3:434–436.

3 Christopher J. Ward, *Brezhnev's Folly: The Building of BAM and Late Soviet Socialism* (Pittsburgh: University of Pittsburgh Press, 2009). This project too had multiple motives, of course.

4 Philip Micklin, "The Aral Sea Disaster," *Annual Review of Earth and Planetary Sciences* 35 (2007): 47–72. One potential problem, linked to the Cold War directly, is that of the former Vozrozhdeniya Island. This was the main testing site of the Soviet biological weapons program, where anthrax, smallpox, and many other pathogens were weaponized. In 2001 the island became part of a peninsula, so rodents and other creatures easily move in and out of the once-isolated testing ground.

5 Yin Shaoting, "Rubber Planting and Eco-Environmental/Socio-cultural Transition in Xishuangbanna," in *Good Earths: Regional and Historical Insights into China's Environment,* ed. Abe Ken-ichi and James E. Nickum (Kyoto: Kyoto University Press, 2009), 136–143; Judith Shapiro, *Mao's War against Nature* (New York: Cambridge University Press, 2001), 172–184; Hongmei Li, T. M. Aide, Youxin Ma, Wenjun Liu, and Min Cao, "Demand for Rubber Is Causing the Loss of High Diversity Rain Forest in SW China," *Biodiversity and Conservation* 16 (2007): 1731–1745; Wenjin Liu, Huabin Hu, Youxin Ma, and Hongmei Li, "Environmental and Socioeconomic Impacts of Increasing Rubber Plantations in Menglun Township, Southwest China," *Mountain Research and Development* 26 (2006): 245–253.

6 On Navajo uranium miners, see B. R. Johnston, S. E. Dawson, and G. Madsen, "Uranium Mining and Milling: Navajo Experiences in the American Southwest," in *Half-Lives and Half-Truths: Confronting the Radioactive Legacies of the Cold War,* ed. Barbara Rose Johnston (Santa Fe, NM: School for Advanced Research Press, 2007), 97–116.

7 Basic data are presented in Arjun Makhijani, Howard Hu, and Katherine Yih, eds., *Nuclear Wastelands: A Global Guide to Nuclear Weapons Production and Its Health and Environmental Effects* (Cambridge MA: MIT Press, 1995).

8 Kate Brown, *Plutopia: Nuclear Families, Atomic Cities, and the Great Soviet and American Plutonium Disasters* (New York: Oxford University Press, 2013); Michele Stenehjem Gerber, *On the Home Front: The Cold War Legacy of the Hanford Nuclear Site* (Lincoln: University of Nebraska Press, 2002); T. E. Marceau et al., *Hanford Site Historic District: History of the Plutonium Production Facilities, 1943–1990* (Columbus, OH: Battelle Press, 2003); John M. Whiteley, "The Hanford Nuclear Reservation: The Old Realities and the New," in *Critical Masses: Citizens, Nuclear Weapons Production, and Environmental Destruction in the United States and Russia,* ed. Russell J. Dalton, Paula Garb, Nicholas

Lovrich, John Pierce, and John Whitely (Cambridge, MA: MIT Press, 1999), 29–58.

9 Ian Stacy, "Roads to Ruin on the Atomic Frontier: Environmental Decision Making at the Hanford Nuclear Reservation, 1942–1952," *Environmental History* 15 (2010): 415–448.

10 Brown, *Plutopia,* 169–170; Gerber, *Home Front,* 90–92; M. A. Robkin, "Experimental Release of 131I: The Green Run," *Health Physics* 62, no. 6 (1992): 487–495.

11 Bengt Danielsson and Marie-Thérèse Danielsson, *Poisoned Reign: French Nuclear Colonialism in the Pacific* (New York: Penguin, 1986); Stewart Firth, *Nuclear Playground* (Honolulu: University of Hawai'i Press, 1986); Mark Merlin and Ricardo Gonzalez, "Environmental Impacts of Nuclear Testing in Remote Oceania, 1946–1996," in McNeill and Unger, *Environmental Histories,* 167–202. On the fate of Marshall Islanders, who unwillingly hosted US nuclear testing for decades, see Barbara Rose Johnston and Holly M. Barker, *Consequential Damages of Nuclear War: The Rongelap Report* (Walnut Creek, CA: Left Coast Press, 2008).

12 Although total radionuclide emissions may have been greater at Tomsk-7, there they were more widely dispersed. Don J. Bradley, *Behind the Nuclear Curtain: Radioactive Waste Management in the Former Soviet Union* (Columbus: Battelle Press, 1997), 451ff. On the Soviet nuclear complex, see Nikolai Egorov, Vladimir Novikov, Frank Parker, and Victor Popov, eds., *The Radiation Legacy of the Soviet Nuclear Complex* (London: Earthscan, 2000); Igor Kudrik, Charles Digges, Alexander Nikitin, Nils Bøhmer, Vladimir Kuznetsov, and Vladislav Larin, *The Russian Nuclear Industry* (Oslo: Bellona Foundation, 2004); John Whiteley, "The Compelling Realities of Mayak," in Dalton et al., *Critical Masses,* 59–96. On human consequences, also see Paula Garb, "Russia's Radiation Victims of Cold War Weapons Production Surviving in a Culture of Secrecy and Denial," and Cynthia Werner and Kathleen Purvis-Roberts, "Unraveling the Secrets of the Past: Contested Visions of Nuclear Testing in the Soviet Republic of Kazakhstan," both in Johnston, *Half-Lives and Half-Truths,* 249–276, 277–298.

13 A Norwegian and Russian research team calculated that accidental and deliberate releases of strontium-90 and cesium-137 between 1948 and 1996 at Mayak amounted to 8,900 petabecquerels. Rob Edwards, "Russia's Toxic Shocker," *New Scientist* 6 (December 1997): 15. One petabecquerel=10^{15} becquerels; 8,900 petabecquerels is about 0.24 billion curies, roughly 1.8 times the official estimate.

14 Bradley, *Behind the Nuclear Curtain,* 399–401; Garb, "Russia's Radiation Victims," 253–260.

15 Zhores Medvedev, *Nuclear Disaster in the Urals* (New York: Norton, 1979).

16 Recent summaries of the Soviet nuclear mess are Paul Josephson, "War on Nature as Part of the Cold War: The Strategic and Ideological Roots of Environmental Degradation in the Soviet Union," in McNeill and Unger, *Environmental Histories*, 43–46; and McNeill, "Cold War and the Biosphere," 437–443 (from which much of this account is drawn). See also Brown, *Plutopia*, 189–212, 231–246.

17 Egorov et al., *Radiation Legacy*, 150–153; Bradley, *Behind the Nuclear Curtain*, 419–420.

18 E.g., Mark Hertsgaard, *Earth Odyssey* (New York: Broadway Books, 1998); Garb, "Russia's Radiation Victims." See also Murray Feshbach, *Ecological Disaster: Cleaning Up the Hidden Legacy of the Soviet Regime* (New York: Twentieth Century Fund, 1995), 48–49; Murray Feshbach and Alfred Friendly Jr., *Ecocide in the USSR* (New York: Basic Books, 1992), 174–179; Brown, *Plutopia*.

19 N. A. Koshikurnikova et al., "Mortality among Personnel Who Worked at the Mayak Complex in the First Years of Its Operation," *Health Physics* 71 (1996): 90–99; M. M. Kossenko, "Cancer Mortality among Techa River Residents and Their Offspring," *Health Physics* 71 (1996): 77–82; N. A. Koshikurnikova et al., "Studies on the Mayak Nuclear Workers: Health Effects," *Radiation and Environmental Biophysics* 41 (2002): 29–31; Mikhail Balonov et al., "Assessment of Current Exposure of the Population Living in the Techa Basin from Radioactive Releases from the Mayak Facility," *Health Physics* 92 (2007): 134–147. Ongoing US Department of Energy studies also suggest serious health problems among former Mayak workers. See http://hss.energy.gov/HealthSafety/IHS/ihp/jccrer/active_projects.html. A good recent summary is W. J. F. Standring, Mark Dowdall, and Per Strand, "Overview of Dose Assessment Developments and the Health of Riverside Residents Close to the 'Mayak' PA Facilities, Russia," *International Journal of Environmental Research and Public Health* 6 (2009): 174–199.

20 Whiteley, "Compelling Realities," 90, citing Paula Garb, "Complex Problems and No Clear Solutions: Difficulties of Defining and Assigning Culpability for Radiation Victimization in the Chelyabinsk Region of Russia," in *Life and Death Matters: Human Rights at the End of the Millennium,* ed. B. R. Johnston (Walnut Creek, CA: AltaMira Press, 1997).

21 The least clear situation is that of China, where data are fewer and even less reliable than for Russia. See Alexandra Brooks and Howard Hu, "China," in Makhijani et al., *Nuclear Wastelands*, 515–518.

22 Bellona Foundation, *Bellona Report No. 8: Sellafield,* at www.bellona.org. See also Jacob Hamblin, *Poison in the Well: Radioactive Waste in the Oceans at the Dawn of the Nuclear Age* (New Brunswick, NJ: Rutgers University Press, 2008).

23 In 2006 a Russian court determined that a Mayak director, Vitaly Sadovnikov, had authorized the dumping of tens of millions of cubic meters of radioactive wastes into the Techa River in 2001–2004, in order to cut costs and pay himself more. See the Bellona post of March 20, 2006, at www.bellona.ru/bellona.org /news/news_2006/Mayak_plant_%20general_director_dismissed_from_his _post.

24 National Geographic News: http://news.nationalgeographic.com/news/2001 /08/0828_wirenukesites.html.

25 Strontium-90 in some biochemical respects mimics calcium and is readily absorbed through food and drink into human teeth, bones, and bone marrow, where it can cause cancers and leukemia.

26 Arhun Makhijani and Stephen I. Schwartz, "Victims of the Bomb," in *Atomic Audit: The Costs and Consequences of U.S. Nuclear Weapons since 1940,* ed. Stephen I. Schwartz (Washington, DC: Brookings Institution Press, 1998), 395, gives a range of 70,000 to 800,000 for global cancer deaths attributable to US atmospheric testing. Estimates for deaths due to other aspects of nuclear weapons programs are still more inexact, especially where China and the USSR are concerned.

27 In the United States, Edward Teller was the leading proponent of what he called "geographical engineering." Teller, a Budapest-born and German-educated vehement anticommunist, matched the most enthusiastic Soviet visionaries when it came to geoengineering uses for nuclear explosions. Teller et al., *The Constructive Uses of Nuclear Explosives* (New York: McGraw-Hill, 1968); Scott Kirsch, *Proving Grounds: Project Plowshare and the Unrealized Dream of Nuclear Earthmoving* (New Brunswick, NJ: Rutgers University Press, 2005).

28 This was one of a few dozen accidents involving aircraft and nuclear weapons, none of which produced full-blown catastrophes. Randall C. Maydew, *America's Lost H-Bomb: Palomares, Spain, 1966* (Manhattan, KS: Sunflower University Press, 1997); a readable journalistic account is Barbara Moran, *The Day We Lost the H-Bomb: Cold War, Hot Nukes, and the Worst Nuclear Weapons Disaster in History* (New York: Presidio Press, 2009).

29 Speech quoted in Frank Dikötter, *Mao's Great Famine: The History of China's Most Devastating Catastrophe, 1958–1962* (New York: Walker and Co., 2010), 174. On the Great Leap Forward itself, see Alfred Chan, *Mao's Crusade: Politics*

and Policy Implementation in China's Great Leap Forward (New York: Oxford University Press, 2001); Dali Yang, *Calamity and Reform in China: State, Rural Society, and Institutional Change since the Great Leap Forward* (Stanford, CA: Stanford University Press, 1998). A well-regarded journalistic overview is Jasper Becker, *Hungry Ghosts: Mao's Secret Famine* (New York: Holt, 1998). A detailed political account is Roderick MacFarquhar, *The Origins of the Cultural Revolution,* vol. 2, *The Great Leap Forward* (New York: Columbia University Press, 1983). The most authoritative treatment is probably Yang Jisheng, *Bu Mei,* now in English as *Tombstone: The Great Chinese Famine, 1958–62* (New York: Farrar, Straus and Giroux, 2012). On the environmental aspects, see Shapiro, *Mao's War against Nature,* 70–93; Elizabeth Economy, *The River Runs Black: The Environmental Challenge to China's Future* (Ithaca, NY: Cornell University Press, 2004), 51–53; and Dikötter, *Mao's Great Famine,* 174–188.

30 Most scholars offer figures around 30 million, and Yang Jisheng, *Tombstone,* gives 38 million. Dikötter says at least 45 million in *Mao's Great Famine.* Unusually, this famine was most deadly among males over age forty, whereas typically famines kill more small children. Susan Cotts Watkins and Jane Menken, "Famines in Historical Perspective," *Population and Development Review* 11 (1985): 647–675.

31 At one point he aimed to surpass US steel production within seven years. Bao Maohong, "The Evolution of Environmental Problems and Environmental Policy in China," in McNeill and Unger, *Environmental Histories,* 317, citing Xie Chuntao, *The Roaring Waves of the Great Leap Forward* (Henan: People Press, 1990), 25 (in Chinese).

32 Roderick MacFarquhar, Timothy Cheek, and Eugene Wu, eds., *The Secret Speeches of Chairman Mao: From the Hundred Flowers to the Great Leap Forward* (Cambridge, MA: Harvard University Press, 1989), 377–517, esp. 409, 511; MacFarquhar, *Origins of the Cultural Revolution,* 2:90.

33 The ninety million figure is Mao's and could well be fanciful, although it is widely repeated by scholars. MacFarquhar, *Origins of the Cultural Revolution,* 2:113–116, 128–130; Bao Maohong, "Evolution of Environmental Problems," 326–327; Economy, *River Runs Black,* 53; Shapiro, *Mao's War against Nature,* 81.

34 Shapiro, *Mao's War against Nature,* 81–83; Dikötter, *Mao's Great Famine,* 176–178. For Sichuan, John Studley, "Forests and Environmental Degradation in SW China," *International Forestry Review* 1 (1999): 260–265. See also S. D. Richardson, *Forests and Forestry in China* (Washington, DC: Island Press, 1990); and for the long view, Mark Elvin, *Retreat of the Elephants* (New Haven, CT: Yale University Press, 2004), 19–85.

35 Data from Bao Maohong, "Evolution of Environmental Problems," 327.

36 McFarquhar et al., *Secret Speeches of Chairman Mao*, 378.

37 Bao Maohong, "Evolution of Environmental Problems," 328.

38 Frantic urgency, and competition with foreigners, pervaded all ranks during the Great Leap Forward: The Chinese Association of Paleontologists vowed to overtake capitalist fossil collectors within seven years. Stanley Karnow, *Mao and China* (New York: Viking Penguin, 1990), 89.

39 Lillian Li, *Fighting Famine in North China: State, Market, and Environmental Decline* (Stanford, CA: Stanford University Press, 2007), 369–370.

40 Karnow, *Mao and China*, 91–92.

41 Dikötter, *Mao's Great Famine*, 188. The best sources on the environmental costs of the Great Leap Forward are Shapiro, *Mao's War against Nature*, and Dikötter, *Mao's Great Famine*, supplemented by Bao Maohong, "Evolution of Environmental Problems." See also Mao's pronouncements in McFarquhar et al., *Secret Speeches of Chairman Mao*, esp. 379, 403, 409, 441, 450.

42 Barry Naughton, "The Third Front: Defence Industrialization in the Chinese Interior," *China Quarterly* 115 (1988): 351–386.

43 On the environmental costs, see Shapiro, *Mao's War against Nature*, 154–156.

44 McFarquhar et al., *Secret Speeches of Chairman Mao*, 384. His wondering aloud came in a speech of January 4, 1958.

45 Qu Geping and Li Jinchang, *Population and the Environment in China* (Boulder, CO: Lynne Rienner, 1994), 180.

46 Bao Maohong, "Evolution of Environmental Problems," 330–339.

47 For the international politics of these wars in Southern Africa, see Chris Saunders and Sue Onslow, "The Cold War and Southern Africa, 1976–1990," in Leffler and Westad, *Cambridge History of the Cold War*, 3:222–243. For the social and environmental effects, see Emmanuel Kreike, "War and Environmental Effects of Displacement in Southern Africa (1970s–1990s)," in *African Environment and Development: Rhetoric, Programs, Realities,* ed. William Moseley and B. Ikubolajeh Logan (Aldershot, UK: Ashgate, 2004), 89–110; Joseph P. Dudley, J. R. Ginsberg, A. J. Plumptre, J. A. Hart, and L. C. Campos, "Effects of War and Civil Strife on Wildlife and Wildlife Habitats," *Conservation Biology* 16, no. 2 (2002): 319–329.

48 Rodolphe de Koninck, *Deforestation in Viet Nam* (Ottawa: International Development Research Centre, 1999), 12. The stories of defoliants and Rome plows are recounted in many texts, and tidily summarized in Greg Bankoff, "A Curtain of Silence: Asia's Fauna in the Cold War," in McNeill and Unger, *Environmental Histories*, 215–216. See also David Biggs, *Quagmire:*

Nation-Building and Nature in the Mekong Delta (Seattle: University of Washington Press, 2012).

49 The foremost authority on ecological effects of war in Vietnam is A. H. Westing. See, e.g., Westing, ed., *Herbicides in War: The Long-Term Ecological and Human Consequences* (London: Taylor and Francis, 1984).

50 Bankoff, "Curtain of Silence."

51 Dudley et al., "Effects of War." See also M. J. Chase and C. R. Griffin, "Elephants Caught in the Middle: Impacts of War, Fences, and People on Elephant Distribution and Abundance in the Caprivi Strip, Namibia," *African Journal of Ecology* 47 (2009): 223–233.

52 Andrew Terry, Karin Ullrich, and Uwe Riecken, *The Green Belt of Europe: From Vision to Reality* (Gland, Switzerland: IUCN, 2006).

53 Lisa Brady, "Life in the DMZ: Turning a Diplomatic Failure into an Environmental Success," *Diplomatic History* 32 (2008): 585–611; Ke Chung Kim, "Preserving Korea's Demilitarized Corridor for Conservation: A Green Approach to Conflict Resolution," in *Peace Parks: Conservation and Conflict Resolution,* ed. Saleem Ali (Cambridge, MA: MIT Press, 2007), 239–260; Hall Healy, "Korean Demilitarized Zone Peace and Nature Park," *International Journal on World Peace* 24 (2007): 61–84.

54 Franz-Josef Strauss, quoted in Ramachandra Guha, *Environmentalism* (New York: Longman, 2000), 97.

55 Guha, *Environmentalism,* 69–79; Miller, *Environmental History of Latin America,* 204–205. On Carson and the reception of *Silent Spring,* see Linda J. Lear, "Rachel Carson's 'Silent Spring,'" *Environmental History Review* 17, no. 2 (Summer 1993): 23–48. On perceptions of DDT before and after *Silent Spring,* see Thomas R. Dunlap, ed., *DDT, Silent Spring, and the Rise of Environmentalism: Classic Texts* (Seattle: University of Washington Press, 2008).

56 William Cronon, for one, has argued against oversimplifying the impact of Carson and *Silent Spring,* while acknowledging the enormous debt that should be paid to both. See his foreword to Dunlap, *DDT, "Silent Spring,"* ix–xii.

57 Uekoetter, *The Age of Smoke,* 113–207.

58 Adam Rome, "'Give Earth a Chance': The Environmental Movement and the Sixties," *Journal of American History* 90, no. 2 (September 2003): 525–554; McCormick, *Reclaiming Paradise,* 52–54. Guha has dubbed the first two decades after World War II the "age of ecological innocence." See Guha, *Environmentalism,* 63–68.

59 Russell J. Dalton, *The Green Rainbow: Environmental Groups in Western Europe* (New Haven, CT: Yale University Press, 1994), 36–37.

60 Jeffrey Broadbent, *Environmental Politics in Japan: Networks of Power and Protest* (Cambridge: Cambridge University Press, 1998), 12–19; Miranda Schreurs, *Environmental Politics in Japan, Germany, and the United States* (Cambridge: Cambridge University Press, 2003), 35–46; Rome, " 'Give Earth a Chance' "; Catherine Knight, "The Nature Conservation Movement in Post-War Japan," *Environment and History* 16 (2010): 349–370; Brett Walker, *Toxic Archipelago: A History of Industrial Disease in Japan* (Seattle: University of Washington Press, 2010).

61 Publications like *The Limits to Growth* stimulated a fierce and intellectually vigorous reaction. The American economist Julian Simon was among the more famous of its critics. See, e.g., Julian Simon, *The Ultimate Resource* (Princeton, NJ: Princeton University Press, 1981).

62 McCormick, *Reclaiming Paradise,* 144–145; Frank Zelko, *Make It a Green Peace: The Rise of Countercultural Environmentalism* (New York: Oxford University Press, 2013).

63 Martinez-Alier, *Environmentalism of the Poor*; Guha and Martinez-Alier, *Varieties of Environmentalism,* 3–5.

64 Ramachandra Guha, "Environmentalist of the Poor," *Economic and Political Weekly* 37, no. 3 (January 19–25, 2002): 204–207. The postmaterialist hypothesis is most closely associated with the American political scientist Ronald Inglehart.

65 Two Indian intellectuals, Anil Agarwal and Ramachandra Guha, were particularly important in igniting a debate between environmentalists in rich and poor countries. Guha has acknowledged an intellectual and emotional debt to Agarwal; see Guha, "Environmentalist of the Poor." On Chipko, see Guha's *The Unquiet Woods: Ecological Change and Peasant Resistance in the Himalayas* (Berkeley: University of California Press, 2000), 152–179, 197–200. On American environmental history and its reception of the Indian critique, see Paul Sutter, "When Environmental Traditions Collide: Ramachandra Guha's *The Unquiet Woods* and U.S. Environmental History," *Environmental History* 14 (July 2009): 543–550. For a summary of the many Chipko interpretations, see Haripriya Rangan, *Of Myths and Movements: Rewriting Chipko into Himalayan History* (London: Verso, 2000), 13–38. One of the more romantic is provided by Vandana Shiva, "The Green Movement in Asia," in *Research in Social Movements, Conflicts and Change: The Green Movement Worldwide,* ed. Matthias Finger (Greenwich, CT: JAI Press, 1992), 195–215 (see esp. 202).

66 On Chico Mendes, see Kathryn Hochstetler and Margaret E. Keck, *Greening Brazil: Environmental Activism in State and Society* (Durham, NC: Duke

University Press, 2007), 111–112. On Narmada, see Madhav Gadgil and Ramachandra Guha, *Ecology and Equity: The Use and Abuse of Nature in Contemporary India* (London: Routledge, 1995), 61–63, 73–76. A short summary of Ken Saro-Wiwa's career is provided in Guha and Martinez-Alier, *Varieties of Environmentalism,* xviii–xix.

67 Martinez-Alier, *Environmentalism of the Poor,* 168–194. A classic text in the American environmental justice literature is Robert D. Bullard, *Dumping in Dixie: Race, Class and Environmental Quality* (Boulder, CO: Westview, 1990).

68 Shapiro, *Mao's War against Nature,* 21–65.

69 Valery J. Cholakov, "Toward Eco-Revival? The Cultural Roots of Russian Environmental Concerns," in Hughes, *Face of the Earth,* 155–157. On interwar conservationism, see Guha, *Environmentalism,* 125–130. On Soviet rivers, see Charles Ziegler, "Political Participation, Nationalism and Environmental Politics in the USSR," in *The Soviet Environment: Problems, Policies, and Politics,* ed. John Massey Stewart (New York: Cambridge University Press, 1992), 32–33. On Cuba, see Sergio Diaz-Briquets and Jorge Perez-Lopez, *Conquering Nature: The Environmental Legacy of Socialism in Cuba* (Pittsburgh: University of Pittsburgh Press, 2000), 13–17.

70 Marshall Goldman, "Environmentalism and Nationalism: An Unlikely Twist in an Unlikely Direction," in Stewart, *The Soviet Environment,* 2–3. See also Stephen Brain, *Song of the Forest: Russian Forestry and Stalin's Environmentalism* (Pittsburgh: University of Pittsburgh Press, 2011).

71 Cholakov, "Toward Eco-Revival?," 157–158; Ziegler, "Political Participation," 30–32.

72 Merrill E. Jones, "Origins of the East German Environmental Movement," *German Studies Review* 16, no. 2 (May 1993): 238–247; William T. Markham, *Environmental Organizations in Modern Germany: Hardy Survivors in the Twentieth Century and Beyond* (New York: Berghahn, 2008), 134–141.

73 Oleg N. Yanitsky, "Russian Environmental Movements," in *Earth, Air, Fire, Water: Humanistic Studies of the Environment,* ed. Jill Ker Conway, Kenneth Keniston, and Leo Marx (Amherst: University of Massachusetts Press, 1999), 184–186; Cholakov, "Toward Eco-Revival?," 161; Ze'ev Wolfson and Vladimir Butenko, "The Green Movement in the USSR and Eastern Europe," in Finger, *Research in Social Movements,* 41–50.

74 Yanfei Sun and Dingxin Zhao, "Environmental Campaigns," in *Popular Protest in China,* ed. Kevin J. O'Brien (Cambridge, MA: Harvard University Press, 2008), 144–162; Robert Weller, *Discovering Nature: Globalization and*

Environmental Culture in China and Taiwan (Cambridge: Cambridge University Press 2006), 115–129.

75 Uekoetter, *The Age of Smoke,* 252–258; Miller, *Environmental History of Latin America,* 206–208; Russell J. Dalton, "The Environmental Movement in Western Europe," in *Environmental Politics in the International Arena: Movements, Parties, Organizations, and Policy,* ed. Sheldon Kamieniecki (Albany: SUNY Press, 1993), 52–53; McCormick, *Reclaiming Paradise,* 125–131. On Nixon, see Ted Steinberg, *Down to Earth: Nature's Role in American History* (New York: Oxford University Press, 2009), 251.

76 Lorraine Elliott, *The Global Politics of the Environment* (New York: New York University Press, 2004), 7–13; Hughes, "Biodiversity in World History," 35–36.

77 McCormick, *Reclaiming Paradise,* 88–105.

78 Samuel P. Hays, *A History of Environmental Politics since 1945* (Pittsburgh: University of Pittsburgh Press, 2000), 95–117; Hays, *Explorations in Environmental History: Essays by Samuel P. Hays* (Pittsburgh: University of Pittsburgh Press, 1998), 223–258.

79 Wangari Maathai, *Unbowed: A Memoir* (New York: Knopf, 2006), 119–138; Maathai, *The Green Belt Movement: Sharing the Approach and Experience* (New York: Lantern Books, 2003).

80 Although Brazil had a long and admirable conservationist tradition, its leaders possessed very little power. See the essays by José Luiz de Andrade Franco and José Augusto Drummond appearing in consecutive issues of *Environmental History* 13 (October 2008): 724–750, and 14 (January 2009): 82–102.

81 Hochstetler and Keck, *Greening Brazil,* 26–33, 70–81, 97–130. For an example of environmentalists' attention to Brazilian–West German nuclear cooperation, see *Das deutsch-brasilianische Atomgeschäft* (Bonn, 1977), self-published by Amnesty International/Brasilienkoordinationsgruppe, Arbeitsgemeinschaft katholischer Studenten- und Hochschulgemeinden, and Bundesverband Bürgerinitiativen Umweltschutz.

82 See the global greens website, www.globalgreens.org/.

83 Massive supertanker accidents would occur several more times by century's end (see above section on coal and oil transport). The most notorious were the *Amoco Cadiz,* off Brittany in 1978, and the *Exxon Valdez,* off Alaska in 1989. Both were about twice the size of the *Torrey Canyon.* See Joanna Burger, *Oil Spills* (New Brunswick, NJ: Rutgers University Press, 1997), 28–61.

84 Christopher Key Chapple, "Toward an Indigenous Indian Environmentalism," in *Purifying the Earthly Body of God: Religion and Ecology in Hindu India,* ed.

Lance E. Nelson (Albany, NY: SUNY Press, 1998), 13–38; Miller, *Environmental History of Latin America*, 209–211; Dalton, "The Environmental Movement," 58. For a discussion of French nuclear politics before and after Chernobyl, see Michael Bess, *The Light-Green Society: Ecology and Technological Modernity in France, 1960–2000* (Chicago: University of Chicago Press, 2003), 92–109.

85 Ironically, Cousteau had a difficult relationship with French environmentalists, who considered him naive. This did not prevent them from extending invitations to Cousteau to head green parties in national elections, which he rebuffed. See Bess, *The Light-Green Society,* 72–73.

86 Not all of this has been driven by profit. Cuba has been running perhaps the world's largest experiment in organic farming. After losing access to Soviet oil in the 1990s, the country turned, out of desperation, to organic methods. Some argue that the Cuban population enjoys a healthier, tastier, and more sustainable diet now than at any time before. See Miller, *Environmental History of Latin America,* 230–235.

Selected Bibliography

Bavington, Dean. *Managed Annihilation: An Unnatural History of the Newfoundland Cod Collapse.* Vancouver: University of British Columbia Press, 2010.

Bess, Michael. *The Light-Green Society: Ecology and Technological Modernity in France, 1960–2000.* Chicago: University of Chicago Press, 2003.

Blackbourn, David. *The Conquest of Nature: Water, Landscape, and the Making of Modern Germany.* New York: Norton, 2007.

Broadbent, Jeffrey. *Environmental Politics in Japan: Networks of Power and Protest.* Cambridge: Cambridge University Press, 1998.

Brown, Kate. *Plutopia: Nuclear Families, Atomic Cities, and the Great Soviet and American Plutonium Disasters.* New York: Oxford University Press, 2013.

Bullard, Robert D. *Dumping in Dixie: Race, Class and Environmental Quality.* Boulder, CO: Westview, 1990.

Burger, Joanna. *Oil Spills.* New Brunswick, NJ: Rutgers University Press, 1997.

Chan, Chak K., and Xiaohong Yao. "Air Pollution in Mega Cities in China." *Atmospheric Environment* 42 (2008): 1–42.

Chase, Michael J., and Curtice R. Griffin. "Elephants Caught in the Middle: Impacts of War, Fences and People on Elephant Distribution and Abundance in the Caprivi Strip, Namibia." *African Journal of Ecology* 47 (2009): 223–233.

Clark, William C., et al. "Acid Rain, Ozone Depletion, and Climate Change: An Historical Overview." In *Learning to Manage Global Environmental Risks,* vol. 1: *A Comparative History of Social Responses to Climate Change, Ozone Depletion, and Acid Rain,* ed. Social Learning Group. Cambridge, MA: MIT Press, 2007.

Cohen, Aaron J., et al. "The Global Burden of Disease Due to Outdoor Air Pollution." *Journal of Toxicology and Environmental Health* 68 (2005): 1301–1307.

Cohen, Joel E. *How Many People Can the Earth Support?* New York: Norton, 1995.

Collins, James P., and Martha L. Crump. *Extinction in Our Times: Global Amphibian Decline.* New York: Oxford University Press, 2009.

Costanza, Robert, et al. "The Value of the World's Ecosystem Services and Natural Capital." *Nature* 387 (May 15, 1997): 253–260.

Costanza, Robert, Lisa J. Graumlich, and Will Steffen, eds. *Sustainability or Collapse? An Integrated History and Future of People on Earth.* Cambridge, MA: MIT Press, 2007.

Cowie, Jonathan. *Climate Change: Biological and Human Aspects*. Cambridge: Cambridge University Press, 2007.

Cribb, Robert. "The Politics of Pollution Control in Indonesia." *Asian Survey* 30, no. 12 (December 1990): 1123–1135.

Crosby, Alfred W. *Children of the Sun: A History of Humanity's Unappeasable Appetite for Energy*. New York: Norton, 2006.

Crutzen, Paul, and Eugene Stoermer. "The Anthropocene." *IGBP Global Change Newsletter* 41 (2000): 17–18.

Cryer, Martin, Bruce Hartill, and Steve O'Shea. "Modification of Marine Benthos by Trawling: Toward a Generalization for the Deep Ocean?" *Ecological Applications* 12 (2002): 1824–1839.

Dalton, Russell J. *The Green Rainbow: Environmental Groups in Western Europe*. New Haven, CT: Yale University Press, 1994.

Dalton, Russell J., et al. *Critical Masses: Citizens, Nuclear Weapons Production, and Environmental Destruction in the United States and Russia*. Cambridge MA: MIT Press, 1999.

Daly, Herman E. "Steady-State Economics versus Growthmania: A Critique of the Orthodox Conceptions of Growth, Wants, Scarcity, and Efficiency." *Policy Sciences* 5, no. 2 (1974): 149–167.

Danielsson, Bengt, and Marie-Thérèse Danielsson. *Poisoned Reign: French Nuclear Colonialism in the Pacific*. Rev. ed. New York: Penguin, 1986.

Dauvergne, Peter. "The Politics of Deforestation in Indonesia." *Pacific Affairs* 66, no. 4 (Winter, 1993–1994): 497–518.

Davies, Richard G., et al. "Human Impacts and the Global Distribution of Extinction Risk." *Proceedings of the Royal Society: Biological Sciences* 273, no. 1598 (September 7, 2006): 2127–2133.

Davis, Devra. *When Smoke Ran Like Water: Tales of Environmental Deception and the Battle against Pollution*. New York: Basic Books, 2002.

DeFries, Ruth. *The Big Ratchet: How Humanity Thrives in the Face of Natural Crisis*. New York: Basic Books, 2014.

Díaz-Briquets, Sergio, and Jorge Pérez-López. *Conquering Nature: The Environmental Legacy of Socialism in Cuba*. Pittsburgh: University of Pittsburgh Press, 2000.

Dikötter, Frank. *Mao's Great Famine: The History of China's Most Devastating Catastrophe, 1958–1962*. New York: Walker, 2010.

Douglas, Ian. *Cities: An Environmental History*. London: I. B. Tauris, 2013.

Dubinsky, Zvy, and Noga Stambler, eds. *Coral Reefs: An Ecosystem in Transition*. New York: Springer, 2011.

Dudley, Joseph P., et al. "Effects of War and Civil Strife on Wildlife and Wildlife Habitats." *Conservation Biology* 16, no. 2 (2002): 319–329.

Dukes, J. S. "Burning Buried Sunshine: Human Consumption of Ancient Solar Energy." *Climatic Change* 61 (2003): 31–44.

Dunlap, Thomas R., ed. *DDT, Silent Spring, and the Rise of Environmentalism: Classic Texts*. Seattle: University of Washington Press, 2008.

Economy, Elizabeth. *The River Runs Black: The Environmental Challenge to China's Future*. Ithaca, NY: Cornell University Press, 2004.

Egorov, Nikolai N., Vladimir M. Novikov, Frank L. Parker, and Victor K. Popov, eds. *The Radiation Legacy of the Soviet Nuclear Complex: An Analytical Overview*. London: Earthscan, 2000.

Elliott, Lorraine. *The Global Politics of the Environment*. New York: New York University Press, 2004.

Elsheshtawy, Yasser, ed. *The Evolving Arab City: Tradition, Modernity and Urban Development*. London: Routledge, 2008.

Fang, Ming, Chak K. Chan, and Xiaohong Yao. "Managing Air Quality in a Rapidly Developing Nation: China." *Atmospheric Environment* 43, no. 1 (2009): 79–86.

Fearnside, Philip M. "Deforestation in Brazilian Amazonia: History, Rates, and Consequences." *Conservation Biology* 19, no. 3 (2005): 680–688.

Fenger, Jes. "Air Pollution in the Last 50 Years: From Local to Global." *Atmospheric Environment* 43 (2009): 13–22.

Feshbach, Murray. *Ecological Disaster: Cleaning Up the Hidden Legacy of the Soviet Regime*. New York: Twentieth Century Fund, 1995.

Feshbach, Murray, and Alfred Friendly Jr. *Ecocide in the USSR: Health and Nature under Siege*. New York: Basic Books, 1992.

Fiege, Mark. *The Republic of Nature: An Environmental History of the United States*. Seattle: University of Washington Press, 2013.

Finley, Carmel. "A Political History of Maximum Sustained Yield, 1945–1955." In *Oceans Past: Management Insights from the History of Marine Animal Populations*, ed. David J. Starkey, Poul Holm, and Michaela Barnard. London: Earthscan, 2008.

Firth, Stewart. *Nuclear Playground*. Honolulu: University of Hawai'i Press, 1986.

Fischer-Kowalski, Marina, et al. "A Socio-metabolic Reading of the Anthropocene: Modes of Subsistence, Population Size, and Human Impact on Earth." *Anthropocene Review* 1 (2014): 8–33.

Fleming, James Rodger. *Fixing the Sky: The Checkered History of Weather and Climate Control*. New York: Columbia University Press, 2010.

Forster, Clive. *Australian Cities: Continuity and Change*. Melbourne: Oxford University Press, 1995.

Franklin, H. Bruce. *The Most Important Fish in the Sea: Menhaden and America*. Washington, DC: Island Press, 2007.

Freese, Barbara. *Coal: A Human History*. Cambridge, MA: Perseus, 2003.

Gadgil, Madhav, and Ramachandra Guha. *Ecology and Equity: The Use and Abuse of Nature in Contemporary India*. London: Routledge, 1995.

Gaston, Kevin J., Tim M. Blackburn, and Kees Klein Goldewijk. "Habitat Conversion and Global Avian Biodiversity Loss." *Proceedings of the Royal Society of London: Biological Sciences* 270, no. 1521 (June 22, 2003): 1293–1300.

Gerber, Michele Stenehjem. *On the Home Front: The Cold War Legacy of the Hanford Nuclear Site*. 2nd ed. Lincoln: University of Nebraska Press, 2002.

Gerlach, Allen. *Indians, Oil, and Politics: A Recent History of Ecuador*. Wilmington, DE: Scholarly Resources, 2003.

Gilbert, Alan, ed. *The Mega-city in Latin America*. New York: United Nations University Press, 1996.

Gildeeva, Irina. "Environmental Protection during Exploration and Exploitation of Oil and Gas Fields." *Environmental Geosciences* 6 (1999): 153–154.

Gössling, Stefan, Carina Borgström Hansson, Oliver Hörstmeir, and Stefan Saggel. "Ecological Footprint Analysis as a Tool to Assess Tourism Sustainability." *Ecological Economics* 43 (2002): 199–211.

Greenhalgh, Susan. *Cultivating Global Citizens: Population in the Rise of China*. Cambridge, MA: Harvard University Press, 2010.

———. *Just One Child: Science and Policy in Deng's China*. Berkeley: University of California Press, 2008.

Grimm, Nancy B., et al. "Global Change and the Ecology of Cities." *Science* 319 (February 8, 2008): 756–760.

Grundmann, Reiner. "Ozone and Climate: Scientific Consensus and Leadership." *Science, Technology, & Human Values* 31, no. 1 (January 2006): 73–101.

Guha, Ramachandra. *Environmentalism: A Global History*. New York: Longman, 2000.

———. *The Unquiet Woods: Ecological Change and Peasant Resistance in the Himalayas*. Rev. ed. Berkeley: University of California Press, 2000.

Guha, Ramachandra, and Juan Martinez-Alier. *Varieties of Environmentalism: Essays North and South*. Delhi: Oxford University Press, 1998.

Gutfreund, Owen D. *Twentieth-Century Sprawl: Highways and the Reshaping of the American Landscape*. New York: Oxford University Press, 2004.

Hall, Charles, et al. "Hydrocarbons and the Evolution of Human Culture." *Nature* 426 (2003): 318–322.

Hall, Peter. *Cities of Tomorrow: An Intellectual History of Urban Planning and Design in the Twentieth Century.* Rev. ed. Oxford, UK: Blackwell, 1996.

Haller, Tobias, et al., eds. *Fossil Fuels, Oil Companies, and Indigenous Peoples: Strategies of Multinational Oil Companies, States, and Ethnic Minorities; Impact on Environment, Livelihoods, and Cultural Change.* Zurich: Lit, 2007.

Hamblin, Jacob Darwin. *Poison in the Well: Radioactive Waste in the Oceans at the Dawn of the Nuclear Age.* New Brunswick, NJ: Rutgers University Press, 2008.

Hardjono, J. "The Indonesian Transmigration Scheme in Historical Perspective." *International Migration* 26 (1988): 427–438.

Hashimoto, M. "History of Air Pollution Control in Japan." In *How to Conquer Air Pollution: A Japanese Experience*, ed. H. Nishimura. Amsterdam: Elsevier, 1989.

Hays, Samuel P. *Explorations in Environmental History: Essays.* Pittsburgh: University of Pittsburgh Press, 1998.

———. *A History of Environmental Politics since 1945.* Pittsburgh: University of Pittsburgh Press, 2000.

Heitzman, James. *The City in South Asia.* New York: Routledge, 2008.

Hochstetler, Kathryn, and Margaret E. Keck. *Greening Brazil: Environmental Activism in State and Society.* Durham, NC: Duke University Press, 2007.

Hughes, J. Donald, ed. *The Face of the Earth: Environment and World History.* Armonk, NY: M. E. Sharpe, 2000.

Isenberg, Andrew, ed. *The Oxford Handbook of Environmental History.* New York: Oxford University Press, 2014.

Jacobs, Nancy. *Environment, Power and Injustice: A South African History.* New York: Cambridge University Press, 2003.

Jenkins, Martin. "Prospects for Biodiversity." *Science* 302, no. 5648 (November 14, 2003): 1175–1177.

Johnston, Barbara Rose, ed. *Half-Lives and Half-Truths: Confronting the Radioactive Legacies of the Cold War.* Santa Fe, NM: School for Advanced Research Press, 2007.

Johnston, Barbara Rose, and Holly M. Barker. *Consequential Damages of Nuclear War: The Rongelap Report.* Walnut Creek, CA: Left Coast, 2008.

Jones, Merrill E. "Origins of the East German Environmental Movement." *German Studies Review* 16, no. 2 (1993): 235–264.

Josephson, Paul, et al. *An Environmental History of Russia.* New York: Cambridge University Press, 2013.

Kahn, Matthew E. "The Environmental Impact of Suburbanization." *Journal of Policy Analysis and Management* 19, no. 4 (2000): 569–586.

Karan, P. P., and Kristin Stapleton, eds. *The Japanese City*. Lexington: University Press of Kentucky, 1997.

Kashi, Ed. *The Curse of the Black Gold: 50 Years of Oil in the Niger Delta*. Edited by Michael Watts. Brooklyn: PowerHouse, 2009.

Ken-ichi, Abe, and James E. Nickum, eds. *Good Earths: Regional and Historical Insights into China's Environment*. Kyoto: Kyoto University Press, 2009.

Khuhro, Hamida, and Anwer Mooraj, eds. *Karachi: Megacity of Our Times*. Karachi: Oxford University Press, 1997.

Kimmerling, Judith. "Oil Development in Ecuador and Peru: Law, Politics, and the Environment." In *Amazonia at the Crossroads: The Challenge of Sustainable Development*, ed. Anthony Hall. London: Institute of Latin American Studies, 2000.

Knight, Catherine. "The Nature Conservation Movement in Post-war Japan." *Environment and History* 16 (2010): 349–370.

Koninck, Rodolphe de. *Deforestation in Viet Nam*. Ottawa: International Development Research Centre, 1999.

Kreike, Emmanuel. "War and Environmental Effects of Displacement in Southern Africa (1970s–1990s)." In *African Environment and Development: Rhetoric, Programs, Realities*, ed. William G. Moseley and B. Ikubolajeh Logan. Burlington, VT: Ashgate, 2003.

Kudrik, Igor, et al. *The Russian Nuclear Industry*. Oslo: Bellona Foundation, 2004.

Langston, Nancy. *Toxic Bodies*. New Haven: Yale University Press, 2010.

Lawton, Richard, ed. *The Rise and Fall of Great Cities: Aspects of Urbanization in the Western World*. New York: Belhaven, 1989.

Lewis, Simon L. "Tropical Forests and the Changing Earth System." *Philosophical Transactions: Biological Sciences* 361, no. 1465 (January 29, 2006): 195–196.

Li, Hongmei, et al. "Demand for Rubber Is Causing the Loss of High Diversity Rain Forest in SW China." *Biodiversity and Conservation* 16 (2007): 1731–1745.

Li, Lillian M. *Fighting Famine in North China: State, Market, and Environmental Decline, 1690s–1990s*. Stanford, CA: Stanford University Press, 2007.

Liu, Wenjun, Huabin Hu, Youxin Ma, and Hongmei Li. "Environmental and Socioeconomic Impacts of Increasing Rubber Plantations in Menglun Township, Southwest China." *Mountain Research and Development* 26 (2006): 245–253.

Lu, Z., et al. "Sulfur Dioxide Emissions in China and Sulfur Trends in East Asia since 2000." *Atmospheric Chemistry and Physics Discussion* 10 (2010): 8657–8715.

Ma, Yonghuan, and Fan Shengyue. "The Protection Policy of Eco-environment in Desertification Areas of Northern China: Contradiction and Countermeasures." *Ambio* 35 (2006): 133–134.

Maathai, Wangari. *Unbowed: A Memoir.* New York: Knopf, 2006.

MacDowell, Laurel Sefton. *An Environmental History of Canada.* Vancouver: University of British Columbia Press, 2012.

Makhijani, Arjun, Howard Hu, and Katherine Yih, eds. *Nuclear Wastelands: A Global Guide to Nuclear Weapons Production and Its Health and Environmental Effects.* Cambridge, MA: MIT Press, 1995.

Markham, William T. *Environmental Organizations in Modern Germany: Hardy Survivors in the Twentieth Century and Beyond.* New York: Berghahn, 2008.

Marks, Robert. *China: Its Environment and History.* Lanham, MD: Rowman and Littlefield, 2013.

Martinez-Alier, Juan. *The Environmentalism of the Poor: A Study of Ecological Conflicts and Valuation.* New Delhi: Oxford University Press, 2004.

McCormick, John. *Reclaiming Paradise: The Global Environmental Movement.* Bloomington: Indiana University Press, 1989.

McKibben, Bill. *Hope, Human and Wild: True Stories of Living Lightly on the Earth.* Minneapolis: Milkweed, 2007.

McNeill, J. R. "The Cold War and the Biosphere." In *The Cambridge History of the Cold War,* vol. 3: *Endings,* ed. Melvyn P. Leffler and Odd Arne Westad. Cambridge: Cambridge University Press, 2010.

———. *The Mountains of the Mediterranean World: An Environmental History.* Cambridge: Cambridge University Press, 1992.

———. *Something New under the Sun: An Environmental History of the Twentieth-Century World.* New York: Norton, 2000.

McNeill, J. R., and Corinna Unger, eds. *Environmental Histories of the Cold War.* New York: Cambridge University Press, 2010.

McNeill, William H. *Plagues and Peoples.* Garden City, NY: Anchor/Doubleday, 1976.

McShane, Clay. *Down the Asphalt Path: The Automobile and the American City.* New York: Columbia University Press, 1994.

Medvedev, Zhores A. *Nuclear Disaster in the Urals.* New York: Norton, 1979.

Melosi, Martin V. *Effluent America: Cities, Industry, Energy, and the Environment.* Pittsburgh: University of Pittsburgh Press, 2001.

———. "The Place of the City in Environmental History." *Environmental History Review* 17 (1993): 1–23.

———. *The Sanitary City: Urban Infrastructure in America from Colonial Times to the Present.* Baltimore: Johns Hopkins University Press, 2000.

Micklin, Philip. "The Aral Sea Disaster." *Annual Review of Earth and Planetary Sciences* 35 (2007): 47–72.

Mikhail, Alan, ed. *Water on Sand: Environmental Histories of the Middle East and North Africa.* New York: Oxford University Press, 2013.

Miles, Edward L. "On the Increasing Vulnerability of the World Ocean to Multiple Stresses." *Annual Review of Environment and Resources* 34 (2009): 18–26.

Miller, Char, ed. *On the Border: An Environmental History of San Antonio.* Pittsburgh: University of Pittsburgh Press, 2001.

Miller, Ian J., Julia A. Thomas, and Brett Walker, eds. *Japan at Nature's Edge: The Environmental Context of a Global Power.* Honolulu: University of Hawai'i Press, 2013.

Miller, Shawn William. *An Environmental History of Latin America.* New York: Cambridge University Press, 2007.

Mirza, M. Monirul Qader. "Climate Change, Flooding and Implications in South Asia." *Regional Environmental Change* 11, supp. 1 (2011): 95–107.

Molina, Mario J., and Luisa T. Molina. "Megacities and Atmospheric Pollution." *Journal of the Air and Waste Management Association* 54 (2004): 644–680.

Montrie, Chad. *To Save the Land and People: A History of Opposition to Surface Mining in Appalachia.* Chapel Hill: University of North Carolina Press, 2003.

Mudd, G. M. "Gold Mining in Australia: Linking Historical Trends and Environmental and Resource Sustainability." *Environmental Science and Policy* 10 (2007): 629–644.

Mukherjee, Suroopa. *Surviving Bhopal: Dancing Bodies, Written Texts, and Oral Testimonials of Women in the Wake of an Industrial Disaster.* New York: Palgrave Macmillan, 2010.

Muscolino, Micah. *The Ecology of War in China: Henan Province, the Yellow River, and Beyond.* New York: Cambridge University Press, 2014.

Nelson, Arvid. *Cold War Ecology: Forests, Farms, and People in the East German Landscape, 1945–1989.* New Haven, CT: Yale University Press, 2005.

Nelson, Lane E., ed. *Purifying the Earthly Body of God: Religion and Ecology in Hindu India.* Albany: State University of New York Press, 1998.

Nesterenko, Alexey B., Vassily B. Nesterenko, and Alexey V. Yablokov. "Consequences of the Chernobyl Catastrophe for Public Health." *Annals of the New York Academy of Sciences* 1181 (2009): 31–220.

Newman, Peter, and Jeffrey Kenworthy. *Sustainability and Cities: Overcoming Automobile Dependence.* Washington, DC: Island Press, 1999.

Niele, Frank. *Energy: Engine of Evolution.* Amsterdam: Elsevier, 2005.

Nilsen, Alf Gunvald. *Dispossession and Resistance in India: The River and the Rage.* London: Routledge, 2010.

Olajide, P. A., et al. "Fish Kills and Physiochemical Qualities of a Crude Oil Polluted River in Nigeria." *Research Journal of Fisheries and Hydrobiology* 4 (2009): 55–64.

Omotola, J. Shola "'Liberation Movements' and Rising Violence in the Niger Delta: The New Contentious Site of Oil and Environmental Politics." *Studies in Conflict and Terrorism* 33 (2010): 36–54.

O'Rourke, Dara, and Sarah Connolly. "Just Oil? The Distribution of Environmental and Social Impacts of Oil Production and Consumption." *Annual Review of Environment and Resources* 28 (2003): 587–617.

Orum, Anthony M., and Xiangming Chen, *The World of Cities: Places in Comparative and Historical Perspective*. Malden, MA: Blackwell, 2003.

Pfister, Christian. "The 'Syndrome of the 1950s' in Switzerland: Cheap Energy, Mass Consumption, and the Environment." In *Getting and Spending: European and American Consumer Societies in the Twentieth Century*, ed. Susan Strasser, Charles McGovern, and Matthias Judt. Cambridge: Cambridge University Press, 1998.

Pick, James B., and Edgar W. Butler. *Mexico Megacity*. Boulder, CO: Westview, 2000.

Premat, Adriana. "Moving between the Plan and the Ground: Shifting Perspectives on Urban Agriculture in Havana, Cuba." In *Agropolis: The Social, Political, and Environmental Dimensions of Urban Agriculture*, ed. Luc J. A. Mougeot. London: Earthscan, 2005.

Purvis, Nigel, and Andrew Stevenson. *Rethinking Climate Diplomacy: New Ideas for Transatlantic Cooperation Post-Copenhagen*. Washington, DC: German Marshall Fund of the United States, 2010. http://www.gmfus.org/archives /rethinking-climate-diplomacy-new-ideas-for-transatlantic-cooperation-post -copenhagen.

Qu, Geping, and Li Jinchang. *Population and the Environment in China*. Edited by Robert B. Boardman. Translated by Jiang Baozhong and Gu Ran. Boulder, CO: Lynne Rienner, 1994.

Radkau, Joachim. *The Age of Ecology*. London: Polity, 2014.

———. *Nature and Power: A Global History of the Environment*. Translated by Thomas Dunlap. Cambridge: Cambridge University Press, 2008.

Rangarajan, Mahesh. "The Politics of Ecology: The Debate on Wildlife and People in India, 1970–95." In *Battles over Nature: Science and the Politics of Conservation*, ed. Vasant K. Saberwal and Mahesh Rangarajan. Delhi: Orient Blackswan, 2003.

Reader, John. *Cities*. New York: Atlantic Monthly, 2004.

Rees, William E. "Ecological Footprints and Appropriated Carrying Capacity: What Urban Economics Leaves Out." *Environment and Urbanization* 4, no. 2 (1992): 121–130.

Roberts, Callum. *The Unnatural History of the Sea*. Washington, DC: Island Press, 2007.

Rome, Adam. *The Genius of Earth Day*. New York: Hill and Wang, 2014.

———."'Give Earth a Chance': The Environmental Movement and the Sixties." *Journal of American History* 90, no. 2 (September 2003): 525–554.

Ruddiman, William H. *Plows, Plagues and Petroleum: How Humans Took Control of Climate*. Princeton, NJ: Princeton University Press, 2005.

Sagane, Rajendra. "Water Management in Mega-cities in India: Mumbai, Delhi, Calcutta, and Chennai." In *Water for Urban Areas: Challenges and Perspectives*, ed. Juha I. Uitto and Asit K. Biswas. New York: United Nations University Press, 2000.

San Sebastián, Miguel, and Anna-Karin Hurtig. "Oil Exploitation in the Amazon Basin of Ecuador: A Public Health Emergency." *Revista panamericana de salud pública* 15 (2004): 205–211.

Satterthwaite, David. *Barbara Ward and the Origins of Sustainable Development*. London: International Institute for Environment and Development, 2006.

Scharping, Thomas. *Birth Control in China, 1949–2000: Population Policy and Demographic Development*. London: RoutledgeCurzon, 2003.

Schmucki, Barbara. *Der Traum vom Verkehrsfluss: Städtische Verkehrsplanung seit 1945 im deutsch-deutschen Vergleich*. Frankfurt: Campus, 2001.

Schreurs, Miranda A. *Environmental Politics in Japan, Germany, and the United States*. Cambridge: Cambridge University Press, 2002.

Schwartz, Stephen I., ed., *Atomic Audit: The Costs and Consequences of U.S. Nuclear Weapons since 1940*. Washington, DC: Brookings Institution, 1998.

Sewell, John. *The Shape of the Suburbs: Understanding Toronto's Sprawl*. Toronto: University of Toronto Press, 2009.

Shapiro, Judith. *Mao's War against Nature: Politics and the Environment in Revolutionary China*. Cambridge: Cambridge University Press, 2001.

Sharan, Awadhendra. *In the City, out of Place: Nuisance, Pollution, and Dwelling in Delhi, c. 1850–2000*. New Delhi: Oxford University Press, 2014.

Shi, Anqing. "The Impact of Population Pressure on Global Carbon Emissions, 1975–1996: Evidence from Pooled Cross-Country Data." *Ecological Economics* 44 (2003): 29–42.

Singh, Satyajit. *Taming the Waters: The Political Economy of Large Dams in India*. Delhi: Oxford University Press, 1997.

Smil, Vaclav. *Energy at the Crossroads: Global Perspectives and Uncertainties*. Cambridge, MA: MIT Press, 2003.

———. *Energy in Nature and Society: General Energetics of Complex Systems.* Cambridge, MA: MIT Press, 2008.

———. *Energy in World History.* Boulder, CO: Westview, 1994.

———. *Transforming the Twentieth Century: Technical Innovations and Their Consequences.* New York: Oxford University Press, 2006.

Smith, Jim T., and Nicholas A. Beresford. *Chernobyl: Catastrophe and Consequences.* Berlin: Springer, 2005.

Solomon, Lawrence. *Toronto Sprawls: A History.* Toronto: University of Toronto Press, 2007.

Sovacool, Benjamin K. "The Costs of Failure: A Preliminary Assessment of Major Energy Accidents, 1907–2007." *Energy Policy* 36 (2008): 1802–1820.

Stacy, Ian. "Roads to Ruin on the Atomic Frontier: Environmental Decision Making at the Hanford Nuclear Reservation, 1942–1952." *Environmental History* 15 (2010): 415–448.

Steffen, Will, Paul J. Crutzen, and J. R. McNeill. "The Anthropocene: Are Humans Now Overwhelming the Great Forces of Nature?" *Ambio* 36 (2007): 614–621.

Steffen, Will, et al. "The Trajectory of the Anthropocene: The Great Acceleration." *Anthropocene Review* 2 (2015): 81–98.

Steinberg, Ted. *Down to Earth: Nature's Role in American History.* 2nd ed. New York: Oxford University Press, 2009.

Stern, David I. "Global Sulfur Emissions from 1850 to 2000." *Chemosphere* 58 (2005): 163–175.

Sternberg, R. "Hydropower: Dimensions of Social and Environmental Coexistence." *Renewable and Sustainable Energy Reviews* 12 (2008): 1588–1621.

Stoll, Mark. *Inherit the Holy Mountain: Religion and the Rise of American Environmentalism.* New York: Oxford University Press, 2015.

Terry, Andrew, Karin Ullrich, and Uwe Riecken. *The Green Belt of Europe: From Vision to Reality.* Gland, Switzerland: International Union for Conservation of Nature, 2006.

Thukral, Enakshi Ganguly, ed. *Big Dams, Displaced People: Rivers of Sorrow, Rivers of Change.* New Delhi: Sage, 1992.

Tiffen, Mary, Michael Mortimore, and Francis Gichuki. *More People, Less Erosion: Environmental Recovery in Kenya.* Chichester, UK: Wiley, 1994.

Uekoetter, Frank. *The Age of Smoke: Environmental Policy in Germany and the United States, 1880–1970.* Pittsburgh: University of Pittsburgh Press, 2009.

Unger, Nancy. *Beyond Nature's Housekeepers: American Women in Environmental History.* New York: Oxford University Press, 2012.

Vermeij, Geerat J., and Lindsey R. Leighton. "Does Global Diversity Mean Anything?" *Paleobiology* 29, no. 1 (2003): 3–7.

Vilchek, G. E., and A. A. Tishkov. "Usinsk Oil Spill." In *Disturbance and Recovery in Arctic Lands: An Ecological Perspective*, ed. R. M. M. Crawford. Dordrecht, Netherlands: Kluwer Academic, 1997.

Volti, Rudi. "A Century of Automobility." *Technology and Culture* 37, no. 4 (1996): 663–685.

Walker, Brett L. *Toxic Archipelago: A History of Industrial Disease in Japan*. Seattle: University of Washington Press, 2010.

Walker, J. Samuel. *Three Mile Island: A Nuclear Crisis in Historical Perspective*. Berkeley: University of California Press, 2004.

Watt, John, Johan Tidblad, Vladimir Kucera, and Ron Hamilton, eds. *The Effects of Air Pollution on Cultural Heritage*. Berlin: Springer, 2009.

Weart, Spencer R. *The Discovery of Global Warming*. Rev. ed. Cambridge, MA: Harvard University Press, 2008.

Webb, James L. A., Jr. *Humanity's Burden: A Global History of Malaria*. Cambridge: Cambridge University Press, 2009.

Weller, Robert P. *Discovering Nature: Globalization and Environmental Culture in China and Taiwan*. Cambridge: Cambridge University Press, 2006.

Westing, Arthur H., ed. *Herbicides in War: The Long-Term Ecological and Human Consequences*. London: Taylor and Francis, 1984.

White, Richard. *The Organic Machine: The Remaking of the Columbia River*. New York: Hill and Wang, 1995.

White, Tyrene. *China's Longest Campaign: Birth Planning in the People's Republic, 1949–2005*. Ithaca, NY: Cornell University Press, 2006.

Williams, Michael. *Deforesting the Earth: From Prehistory to Global Crisis*. Chicago: University of Chicago Press, 2003.

Wilson, E. O., with Frances M. Peter, eds. *Biodiversity*. Washington, DC: National Academy Press, 1986.

Winiwarter, Verena, and Martin Knoll. *Umweltgeschichte: Eine Einführung*. Cologne: Böhlau, 2007.

Wood, John R. *The Politics of Water Resource Development in India: The Narmada Dams Controversy*. Los Angeles: Sage, 2007.

Worster, Donald. *Dust Bowl: The Southern Plains in the 1930s*. New York: Oxford University Press, 1978.

———. *Rivers of Empire: Water, Aridity, and the Growth of the American West*. New York: Oxford University Press, 1992.

Yablokov, Alexey V., Vassily B. Nesterenko, and Alexey V. Nesterenko. "Consequences of the Chernobyl Catastrophe for the Environment." *Annals of the New York Academy of Sciences* 1181 (2009): 221–286.

Zelko, Frank. *Make It a Green Peace: The Rise of Countercultural Environmentalism.* New York: Oxford University Press, 2013.

Acknowledgments

We extend our gratitude to the following Georgetown colleagues, a category that includes graduate students, who have read all or parts of this book and provided useful feedback: Clark Alejandrino, Carol Benedict, Meredith Denning, Toshi Higuchi, Faisal Husain, Adrienne Kates, Lindsay Levine, Robynne Mellor, Michelle Melton, Robert Mevissen, Graham Pitts, Colleen Riley, Alan Roe, and Yubin Shen. Beyond the Hilltop, helpful information or comments also came from Akira Iriye, Stephen Macekura, Marie Sylvia O'Neill, Jürgen Osterhammel, and Jan Zalaciewicz, to whom we are also grateful.

Index